Study Guide

Practical Financial Management
FOURTH EDITION

Study Guide

Practical Financial Management
FOURTH EDITION

William R. Lasher
Nichols College

Prepared by

John A. McDougald
Northern Illinois University

THOMSON

SOUTH-WESTERN

Australia · Canada · Mexico · Singapore · Spain · United Kingdom · United States

Study Guide for

Practical Financial Management, Fourth Edition

William R. Lasher

VP/Editorial Director:
Jack W. Calhoun

VP/Editor-in-Chief:
Mike Roche

Executive Editor:
Mike Reynolds

Senior Developmental Editor:
Susanna C. Smart

Marketing Manager:
Heather MacMaster

Production Editor:
Cliff Kallemeyn

Media Technology Editor:
Vicky True

Media Developmental Editor:
John Barans

Media Production Editor:
Mark Sears

Design Project Manager:
Bethany Casey

Manufacturing Coordinator:
Doug Wilke

Printer:
Von Hoffmann Graphics
Frederick, MD

COPYRIGHT © 2005
by South-Western, part of the Thomson Corporation. South-Western, Thomson, and the Thomson logo are trademarks used herein under license.

Printed in the United States of America
 2 3 4 5   07 06 05

ISBN: 0-324-28259-1

ALL RIGHTS RESERVED.

No part of this work covered by the copyright hereon may be reproduced or used in any form or by any means—graphic, electronic, or mechanical, including photocopying, recording, taping, Web distribution or information storage and retrieval systems—without the written permission of the publisher.

For permission to use material from this text or product, contact us by
Tel (800) 730-2214
Fax (800) 730-2215
http://www.thomsonrights.com

For more information
contact South-Western,
5191 Natorp Boulevard,
Mason, Ohio 45040.
Or you can visit our Internet site at:
http://www.swlearning.com

TO THE STUDENT

We have provided the *Study Guide for Practical Financial Management, 4th Edition*, to help you learn through active practice the basic concepts, vocabulary, and tools of financial management presented in your text.

The *Study Guide* contains the following elements to help you grasp the concepts presented in the textbook:
- Learning Objectives
- Chapter Summary
- Chapter Review with key equations highlighted
- True/False, Multiple Choice, and Fill-In questions
- Problems
- Answers to all questions and problems at the end of each chapter.

Using the *Study Guide* will help you prepare for exams and see what topics may need your further study. As you work through each chapter, write your answers on the lines and spaces provided; the combination of reading, testing, and writing is a useful learning method for many students.

Take advantage of any other resources for study provided with your text and the many features provided on the text Web site at http://lasher.swlearning.com. Enjoy the course!

John A. McDougald
and
South-Western/Thomson Learning

Contents

Chapter 1: Foundations..1

Chapter 2: Financial Background: A Review of Accounting, Financial Statements, and Taxes............11

Chapter 3: Cash Flows and Financial Analysis...25

Chapter 4: The Financial System and Interest...41

Chapter 5: The Time Value of Money...53

Chapter 6: The Valuation and Characteristics of Bonds..67

Chapter 7: The Valuation and Characteristics of Stock..81

Chapter 8: Risk and Return..97

Chapter 9: Capital Budgeting..111

Chapter 10: Cash Flow Estimation...125

Chapter 11: Risk Topics and Real Options in Capital Budgeting......................................137

Chapter 12: Cost of Capital..149

Chapter 13: Capital Structure and Leverage..161

Chapter 14: Dividends...177

Chapter 15: The Management of Working Capital..191

Chapter 16: Financial Planning..209

Chapter 17: Corporate Restructuring..223

Chapter 18: International Finance..237

CHAPTER ONE

FOUNDATIONS

LEARNING OBJECTIVES

After studying this chapter you should understand the following terms and concepts:

1. the definition of the discipline of finance;
2. the difference between real assets and financial assets;
3. how financial markets facilitate businesses and investors;
4. the historic and the current focus of financial management;
5. the relationship between finance and accounting;
6. comparing and contrasting the primary forms of business organizations;
7. why maximizing shareholder wealth should be the goal of management;
8. identifying various business stakeholders and how conflicts can occur between them.

CHAPTER SUMMARY

This chapter provides a foundation on which the study of finance is built. Two primary areas of finance are identified: (1) investments and financial markets, and (2) the financial management of companies. The relationship between companies and their investors is established, along with the definition of financial assets and financial markets which are used to facilitate this relationship. The disciplines of finance and accounting are explored, and the importance of cash flow is identified as a primary conceptual difference between them. The corporate form of business is compared to other less complex forms, and the differences in taxes, liability and the ability to raise capital are discussed. The primary goal of management is defined as maximizing shareholder wealth, and potential conflicts of interest between management and other stakeholders are identified, along with possible solutions.

CHAPTER REVIEW

AN OVERVIEW OF FINANCE

1. **Finance** is the art and science of handling money and includes (1) investments and financial markets and (2) the financial management of companies. **Financial assets,** such as stocks and bonds (also called **securities**), are pieces of paper whose value comes from their owners'

expectations of claims to future cash flows. **Stocks** represent an ownership interest in a business and the expected future cash flows are (1) dividends and (2) proceeds from the sale of the stock. **Bonds** represent a debt relationship and the expected future cash flows are (1) interest payments and (2) the return of principal.

2. **Financial markets** are frameworks of brokers and exchanges through which people can buy and sell securities. These markets serve as intermediaries in the process of buying and selling securities and moving cash between investors (who have excess cash) and companies (who require cash to grow).

3. The term **"to finance"** most commonly means to raise money for the acquisition of assets. Companies can finance asset acquisition by borrowing money, selling stock, using earned money, or by leasing assets. **Debt financing** is defined as using "borrowed" funds for financing, typically through the issuance of bonds. **Equity financing** is defined as acquiring funds through the sale of stock.

4. Finance has evolved and expanded into a field that not only concerns itself with raising money, but also with the goals and activities of the investor, and the management and control of money and money-related operations within an organization.

FINANCE AND ACCOUNTING

5. Accounting and finance are linked, but they have important differences. The accounting function records business activities on a transactional basis so that a firm's operations can be reported to the outside world in an objective manner. The treasury function is normally responsible for raising money and handling relationships with banks, shareholders and the investment community. Accounting and treasury are often part of the same organization within a business headed by the Chief Financial Officer (CFO). The treasury functions are usually identified as "finance," and these activities are much more concerned with **cash flow** than the accounting functions.

FINANCIAL THEORY – THE RELATIONSHIP WITH ECONOMICS

6. Modern financial theory began as a branch of economics in the 1950s. Its techniques are very similar to those of advanced economics.

FORMS OF BUSINESS ORGANIZATION AND THEIR FINANCIAL IMPACT

7. A business can legally be organized as a sole proprietorship, a partnership, or as a corporation. The type of organization will affect taxes, the financial liability of its owners, and the raising of funds. For our purposes, **sole proprietorships and partnerships** have essentially the same characteristics except that a partnership has more than one owner. Proprietorships and partnerships are easy to set up, their profits are taxed once at a personal tax rate, and the owners and their businesses are indistinguishable. Thus, owners have unlimited financial liability for the debts of the business, and financing is available only in the form of loans that can be very difficult to obtain without collateral.

Corporations are more expensive to start, with legal assistance normally required. Profits are doubly taxed, once at corporate rates and again when profits are distributed as dividends to owners at personal tax rates. The owners of the business are not financially liable for the debts of the business (see the discussion about limited liability on page 14 of the text), and funds can be obtained through debt or equity financing. The potential for equity investors to share in the growth and profit of the company is attractive to investors and allows corporations to raise funds more easily than other forms of business.

S-type corporations allow small businesses to incorporate without the disadvantage of double-taxation. Earnings are taxed at a personal income tax rate, yet the sale of stock for financing is allowed, and some limited liability is available. The **Limited Liability Company (LLC)** is a business form that is rapidly replacing the S-type corporation as the preferred form for medium and, in some cases, large businesses. As the name implies, it provides more effective limited liability and is more flexible in several other areas than the S-type corporation.

THE GOALS OF MANAGEMENT

8. The **goal of management** is not to maximize profits, which can lead to short-term gains at the expense of long-term success, but instead the goal is to **maximize shareholder wealth** as measured by the price of the company's stock. This goal allows management to balance short-term and long-term financial objectives.

9. **Stakeholders** are groups of people who have a special interest in how a company is operated. Stockholders, management, employees, creditors, customers, suppliers and even the local community are all stakeholders in a company. The interests of these groups vary and often conflict with each other. Management is responsible for addressing these conflicts and resolving them in favor of their goal of maximizing shareholder wealth.

MANAGEMENT – A PRIVILEGED STAKEHOLDER GROUP

10. Managers are a special group of stakeholders because of their agency relationship with the firm's stockholders. Management serves as the agent of the stockholders because they are hired to make the decisions on how to run to company. Management can abuse the agency relationship by receiving excessive compensation from funds that would normally go to the stockholders. The stockholders can use the following techniques to address these potential agency problems: monitoring management to review their activities; tying top management's compensation to company performance.

CREDITORS VERSUS STOCKHOLDERS – A FINANCIALLY IMPORTANT CONFLICT OF INTEREST

15. Creditors and stockholders take on similar risks with respect to business losses. If a business fails, both will lose their entire investment. However, if a business succeeds, virtually all of the profits accrue to the stockholders. This disparity in treatment of creditors and stockholders is especially acute if businesses take on riskier projects **after** borrowing money from creditors.

TESTING YOUR UNDERSTANDING

TRUE-FALSE QUESTIONS

_____ 1. Finance is the language of accounting.

_____ 2. An advantage of a sole proprietorship is limited liability for owners.

____3. Maximizing shareholder wealth is the equivalent of maximizing the value of the company's stock.

____4. Executive compensation is always tied to the performance of the organization.

____5. The price that investors are willing to pay for securities is influenced only by how well or poorly the issuing company is currently performing.

____6. Maximizing profits is a short-term objective that can actually harm the business in the long term.

____7. Stockholders and managers are two groups of stakeholders who often find themselves in conflict.

____8. Efforts to control the agency problem have been only partially successful.

____9. Accounting is more concerned with cash flow than is finance.

____10. It is important for persons in finance to have a thorough understanding of Accounting.

____11. There is nothing lenders can do to prevent companies from taking on riskier ventures after borrowing than the companies took on before borrowing.

____12. The effect of government efforts to limit the corporate tax deductibility of expensive meals and excessive executive compensation has had a major impact on eliminating the agency problem.

____13. Eliminating the R & D department can contribute to the short-term goal of maximizing profit.

____14. The financial department has an oversight responsibility for the operations of other departments.

____15. Real assets never provide a service but must produce a tangible good.

____16. It is usually easier to get people to buy stock in a corporation than to make an uncollateralized loan.

____17. Financial assets are issued to raise money that in turn is generally used to buy real assets.

MULTIPLE CHOICE QUESTIONS

1. One option to raise money that a corporation has but a sole proprietorship does not have is:
   a. borrowing from banks.
   b. selling stock to investors.
   c. investment by owners.
   d. none of the above.

2. A major disadvantage of a sole proprietorship is:
   a. income is taxed at a personal tax rate.
   b. the owner has unlimited financial liability.
   c. it is easy to set up.
   d. all of the above.

3. Which of the following is **not** an activity performed by the finance department?
   a. paying employees and vendors
   b. purchasing assets
   c. selling stock
   d. hiring personnel

4. The S-type corporation:
   a. has the ability to sell stock.
   b. has income taxed at corporate tax rates.
   c. has owners with unlimited financial liability.
   d. primarily was developed to encourage large business.

5. The goal of management when operating a business in the real world should be:
   a. maximizing shareholder wealth.
   b. maximizing profits.
   c. making sure employees are well-paid.
   d. paying the highest amount of taxes possible.

6. Which of the following is **not** a real asset?
   a. Machinery
   b. Stocks
   c. Bonds
   d. both b and c

7. Which of the following groups are usually stakeholders of a business?
   a. Employees
   b. Customers
   c. Suppliers
   d. all of the above

8. Which of the following is an example of an attempt to control the agency problem?
   a. tying executive bonuses to company profits
   b. auditors
   c. government limitations on tax deductibility of expenses
   d. all of the above

9. With respect to fixed assets, the finance department will be primarily concerned with the:
   a. accumulated depreciation on a balance sheet.
   b. cash outflow and tax savings from the depreciation deduction.
   c. value of assets on an income statement.
   d. none of the above

10. The choice of how to organize a business is important because the form affects:
    a. raising money
    b. financial liability of owners
    c. how income is taxed
    d. all of the above

6   Chapter 1

11. The primary financial disadvantage of a corporation is:
    a. that a corporation can raise money by issuing stock to investors.
    b. the double taxation of corporate earnings.
    c. its existence as a separate legal entity.
    d. the cost of the legal incorporation process.

12. Which of the following is not a financial asset?
    a. common stock
    b. articles of incorporation
    c. mutual funds
    d. bonds

13. All of the following are part of the financial markets except:
    a. the New York Stock Exchange
    b. stockbrokers
    c. corporate treasury departments
    d. all of the above are part of the financial markets

14. Money raised by a company for the purchase of fixed assets through the sale of stock is called:
    a. equity financing
    b. debt financing
    c. lease financing
    d. any of the above terms could be used

15. Which of the following functions is typically not performed in the Treasury Department of a company?
    a. handling relationships with banks
    b. raising money through the sale of stock
    c. maintaining relationships with shareholders
    d. preparing financial statements

16. Which of the following activities associated with the purchase and sale of fixed assets affect the cash flow of a business?
    a. the purchase of an asset for cash
    b. recognizing the annual depreciation on a fixed asset
    c. the sale of an asset for its book value
    d. all of the above affect the cash flow of a business

17. Which of the following best describes the relationship of the study of economics and the study of finance?
    a. the study of economics is an outgrowth of the study of finance
    b. the study of finance is an outgrowth of the study of economics
    c. the study of finance and the study of economics are unrelated
    d. the study of economics and finance are both an outgrowth of the study of accounting

18. If you wanted to start a business and wanted to minimize your tax burden without regard to the liability issue, which form of business would you choose?
    a. a corporation
    b. an S-type corporation
    c. a sole proprietorship
    d. either b. or c. would minimize the tax burden

19. If your primary concern with respect to beginning a new business is the ability to raise large amounts of money, which form of business would you choose?
    a. a corporation
    b. an S-type corporation
    c. a sole proprietorship
    d. a partnership

20. Which of the following best describes the risks of stockholders and bondholders?
    a. stockholders and bondholders share the risk of loss and the potential for gain equally
    b. stockholders and bondholders share the risk of loss equally, but the potential for gain favors the stockholder.
    c. stockholders and bondholders share the risk of loss equally, but the potential for gain favors the bondholder.
    d. stockholders and bondholders share the potential for gain equally, but the risk of loss favors the stockholder.

FILL-IN THE BLANK QUESTIONS

1. A company financed by borrowed money is said to be _____ financed.

2. _____ are groups of people with an interest in the way a company is operated.

3. Another name for a financial asset is a _____.

4. _____ is the language of finance.

5. A bond signifies a _____ relationship.

6. Benefits such as expense account meals, paid country club memberships, and limousines are known as _____.

7. An _____ relationship is created when a person hires another and gives him/her decision making authority over something.

8. The tax system treats S-type corporations as _____.

9. Lenders often bypass the protection that incorporation gives to business owners from having personal assets seized by requiring _____ from small businesses.

10. A regular type of corporation is also known as a _____.

11. Modern financial theory actually began as a branch of _____.

12. The controller and treasurer of a financial department usually report to the _____.

13. The best-known financial market is the _____.

14. When assets are acquired through leasing, they are said to be _____ financed.

15. A person who buys a financial asset such as a stock or a bond is called an _____.

16. _____ corporations may sell stock but have earnings taxed at personal tax rates.

PROBLEMS

1. A person purchases 5% of the stock in a C-type corporation and does not participate in the running of the business itself. The corporation is found to be legally liable for producing and selling defective products and has a legal judgment entered against it for $5,000,000. How much of this judgement will the 5% stockholder be liable for? Explain your answer.

2. Compare the total tax bill under the sole proprietorship form of business organization and the corporate form of organization for a single owner who wants to take all the earnings home and spend them: $256,900 pre-tax earnings. For the sake of this example, assume a flat tax 30% for individuals and 35% for corporations on the entire amount of earnings. Round taxes to nearest dollar.

ANSWERS TO QUESTIONS

TRUE-FALSE ANSWERS

1. f
2. f
3. t
4. f
5. f
6. t
7. t
8. t
9. f
10. t
11. f
12. f
13. t
14. t
15. f
16. t
17. t

FILL IN THE BLANK ANSWERS

1. debt
2. Stakeholders
3. security
4. Accounting
5. debt
6. perquisites
7. agency
8. partnerships
9. Personal guarantees
10. C-type corporation
11. economics
12. Chief Financial Officer
13. stock market
14. lease
15. investor
16. S-type

MULTIPLE CHOICE ANSWERS

1. b
2. b
3. d
4. a
5. a
6. d
7. d
8. d
9. b
10. d
11. b
12. b
13. c
14. a
15. d
16. d
17. b
18. d
19. a
20. b

ANSWERS TO PROBLEMS

1. The stockholder will be liable for none of the judgement, because stockholders not involved in running a corporation have no financial liability for the debts of the corporation.

2.
Pre Tax Earnings	$256,900	$256,900
Less:		
Corporate Tax(35%)	89,915	
Earnings/Dividends	$166,985	$256,900
Less:		
Personal Tax(30%)	50,096	77,070
Net	$116,889	$179,830

CHAPTER TWO

FINANCIAL BACKGROUND: A REVIEW OF ACCOUNTING, FINANCIAL STATEMENTS, AND TAXES

LEARNING OBJECTIVES

After studying this chapter you should understand the following terms and concepts:

1. the definition of an Accounting system and the double entry system of keeping records;
2. the difference between income and cash flow;
3. the information on the income statement and the balance sheet;
4. the relationship between depreciation expense and accumulated depreciation;
5. progressive tax systems, and marginal versus average tax rates;
6. how capital gains tax differs from ordinary income tax and why;
7. how to calculate taxes for single individuals and married couples;
8. how tax rates can affect investment decisions;
9. the tax liabilities of corporations;
10. how dividends paid to other corporations are taxed;

CHAPTER SUMMARY

This chapter provides a summary of accounting terms and concepts necessary for an understanding of Finance. Included is a discussion of the primary accounts reported on both the Income Statement and the Balance Sheet. Specific examples (e.g. credit sales, depreciation of a fixed asset) are shown to explain the different treatment that these transactions receive under accrual accounting and cash flow analysis. Methods for calculating federal tax liabilities for individuals and corporations are reviewed. Distinctions are made between the following tax concepts: (1) average and marginal tax rates; (2) taxation on ordinary income versus capital gains income; (3) progressive tax rate schedules as they apply to individuals and corporations.

CHAPTER REVIEW

ACCOUNTING SYSTEMS AND FINANCIAL STATEMENTS

1. **Accounting systems** are organized sets of rules that record every transaction a business makes that can be reported in financial terms (dollars in the U.S.). These transactions are then used to produce financial statements that reflect a business' performance for a specific period of time (an accounting period).

2. The majority of accounting systems use a **double entry** record keeping method where each entry has two sides. In general, one side shows **where money came from**, and the other side shows **what the business did** with the money.

THE INCOME STATEMENT

3. The **Income Statement** shows the earnings of a company for a specific period of time. Earnings are what is left from a company's revenues after all of the expenses (including the cost of goods sold, interest and taxes) have been subtracted. **Revenue** is the total receipts of a company that come from selling its products and/or services. **Cost of goods sold (COGS)** includes expenses that are closely associated with the production of products, the purchase of merchandise for resale or the provision of a service.

SALES REVENUE – COST OF GOODS SOLD = GROSS MARGIN
(OR GROSS PROFIT MARGIN)

SALES REVENUE
– COST OF GOODS SOLD
GROSS (PROFIT) MARGIN

Gross margin is a basic measure of profitability, concentrating on what this company spends to produce a product or deliver a service.

Expenses represent spending on activities other than the cost of goods sold, such as marketing and sales, human resources, and other staff functions not as closely related to production or the provision of a service.

GROSS (PROFIT) MARGIN
– EXPENSES
EARNINGS BEFORE INTEREST AND TAXES

Earnings before interest and taxes (EBIT) shows the profitability of the firm's operations before taking into consideration how the business is financed. Since the payment of interest (to bondholders) and the payment of dividends (to stockholders) both occur below this calculation on the income statement, EBIT, or **operating profit,** is completely focused on the success of the operating side of the business. The decision to finance a business with stocks or bonds is independent of the business' performance on EBIT.

$$
\begin{array}{c}
\textit{EBIT} \\
\underline{-\textit{INTEREST}} \\
\textit{EARNINGS BEFORE TAX} \\
\underline{-\textit{TAX}} \\
\textit{NET INCOME}
\end{array}
$$

Net income, also known as **earnings after tax**, is the bottom line for companies and represents the profit belonging to the owners of the business.

THE BALANCE SHEET

4. The **Balance Sheet** shows everything a company owns (assets) and everything a company owes (liabilities and equity) at a particular moment in time. The Balance Sheet typically displays assets on the left hand side of the statement and liabilities and equity on the right hand side. The fundamental rule for the Balance Sheet is that

$$ASSETS = LIABILITIES + EQUITY$$

Liquidity in the context of the balance sheet means how quickly an asset can be converted into cash or how quickly a liability will require cash. Both assets and liabilities are arranged on the balance sheet from the most liquid (at the top) to the least liquid.

Current assets are assets that are expected to become cash within one year. They include cash, accounts receivable, and inventory. **Cash** is defined as money in checking accounts and any currency on hand. **Accounts receivable** represent credit sales that have not yet been paid but are generally expected to be paid within 30 - 45 days. **Inventory** is product held for sale in the normal course of doing business. In a manufacturing company, inventory can be in one of three forms: **raw materials, work in process, or finished goods.**

Fixed assets are assets that are expected to have a useful life of more than one year and include items such as property, machinery, and equipment. Fixed assets are not treated as expenses to the business when they are purchased because their useful life will extend over multiple accounting periods. These assets are **depreciated,** which is a process that uses depreciation rates to recognize the cost of the asset over its useful life. **Depreciation expense** is found on the income statement and represents the current year's depreciation amount. Depreciation expense is a tax-deductible expense for corporations. **Accumulated depreciation** is subtracted from a fixed asset's cost and reported on the Balance Sheet to provide the **net book value** of the asset. Accumulated depreciation is the total of this year's and all previous years' depreciation expense.

Depreciation spreads the cost of an asset over the estimated useful life of that asset. **Straight-line depreciation** allows the same amount of depreciation expense to be taken each year, while **accelerated depreciation** methods allow more expense to be taken in the early years than in later years. Regardless of the depreciation method used, the total amount of depreciation expense will still equal the cost of the asset minus any salvage value. Because depreciation is a tax-deductible expense, accelerated depreciation methods allow for increased tax advantages in the early years of an asset's life.

On the left-hand side of the balance sheet:

ASSETS

CASH
+ACCOUNTS RECEIVABLE
+INVENTORY
CURRENT ASSETS

GROSS FIXED ASSETS

− ACCUMULATED DEPRECIATION
CURRENT ASSETS + NET FIXED ASSETS

CURRENT ASSETS + NET FIXED ASSETS = NET TOTAL ASSETS (NTA)

Liabilities represent debts or obligations of the company to outsiders. **Current liabilities** are items that require payment within one year and include: **accounts payable, accruals, notes payable, and short-term loans. Accounts payable** is also called **trade credit** and occurs when a firm makes purchases, often of inventory, on credit from a vendor. **Accruals** represent services that have been performed by others for the company but are not yet paid for, and for which no paperwork has been submitted.

Net Working Capital is defined as:

NET WORKING CAPITAL = CURRENT ASSETS − CURRENT LIABILITIES

Net working capital represents the sources of cash within the next year (current assets) less the uses of cash during the next year (current liabilities), and therefore represents the amount of money a business needs to operate on a day-to-day basis.

Long term debt consists of bonds and long term loans. A firm that uses debt for financing is said to be **leveraged.** The more debt a firm uses, the more highly leveraged it is said to be. The biggest problem with leverage is that interest charges are **fixed,** and they must be paid no matter how poorly the company may be performing. Failure to pay interest charges can force a business into bankruptcy.

Equity represents money that is supplied to the company by the owners through either direct investment or retained earnings. **Direct investment** is when an owner puts money directly into a business or when a corporation sells a share of stock either directly or through an intermediary to an investor. Equity investments are reflected in two stock accounts. One account is called **common stock** which represents the **par value** of each share multiplied by the number of outstanding shares. The other account represents the amount paid for stock over its par value and is called **paid in excess** or **additional paid-in capital.**

Retained Earnings comes from the profits of a business that aren't paid out to owners as dividends but rather are held for reinvestment in the business. This money is usually used by businesses to acquire assets. The balance in the retained earnings account is the cumulative profits not paid out in dividends since the business started.

If no dividends are paid out,

BEGINNING EQUITY + NET INCOME = ENDING EQUITY

When dividends are paid out,

BEGINNING EQUITY + NET INCOME – DIVIDENDS = ENDING EQUITY

Preferred stock is also classified as an equity and is included on the balance sheet in the equity section. **Total equity** is the sum of common and preferred equity.

LONG TERM DEBT + EQUITY = TOTAL CAPITAL

On the right-hand side of the balance sheet:

LIABILITIES

ACCOUNTS PAYABLE
+ACCRUALS
CURRENT LIABILITIES

LONG TERM DEBT
+EQUITY
TOTAL CAPITAL

CURRENT LIABILITIES + TOTAL CAPITAL = TOTAL LIABILITIES + EQUITY

TAXES

5. **Taxes** are levied by governments at three levels: federal, state, and local. Each tax must have a **tax base**, something that is taxed. The most common tax bases are income, wealth, and consumption. An **income tax** requires taxpayers to pay a percentage of their income to the taxing authority. Our federal government taxes income, as do most states and some local governments. A **wealth** tax is best exemplified by a tax on real estate charged by many cities and counties. A **consumption** tax is often in the form of a sales tax where the end user of a product pays a tax on purchases.

6. Since state taxes are a deductible expense for the calculation of federal taxes, the **total effective tax rate (TETR)** is calculated by:
federal tax rate + state tax rate(1 – federal tax rate) or

$$TETR = T_f + T_s (1 - T_f)$$

7. The **marginal tax rate** is the rate that a taxpayer will pay on the next dollar of income he or she earns. A **progressive tax system** is a system that charges a higher marginal tax rate when a taxpayer's income increases. **Tax brackets** are ranges of income where the tax rate stays constant. The **average tax rate** is the percent of total income that a taxpayer pays in taxes.

16   Chapter 2

8. **Ordinary income** is the result of normal money making activities such as earning a salary or receiving interest or dividends on investments. **Capital gains or losses** result when a taxpayer buys an asset (e.g. a stock, bond or a piece of equipment), keeps it for a period of time, and then sells it for either more or less than the purchase price. Traditionally our government has encouraged investment in stocks and bonds and by giving capital gains a favorable tax treatment.

9. **Personal income taxes** are paid by households. Different schedules exist for different kinds of households (e.g. single versus married filing jointly). **Deductions** are subtractions from taxable income permitted by the tax codes. **Exemptions** are fixed amounts that are allowed to be deducted for each person in a household. The federal government uses a progressive tax system to tax households. Investment decisions are influenced by how expected returns are taxed. For example, interest earned on bonds issued by corporations is taxable at the federal level, while interest on municipal bonds (issued by local government entities) is tax exempt at the federal level.

10. **Corporate taxes** are calculated on revenue minus the charges and expenses necessary to operate a business. The tax schedules used to calculate corporate taxes are also progressive, but they are different from personal tax schedules. The current federal tax system for corporations favors debt financing over equity financing, because interest payments made to debt investors are tax deductible expenses while dividend payments made to equity investors are not deductible. Dividends paid to corporations from other corporations are partially exempt from taxation by the corporations receiving the dividends.

TESTING YOUR UNDERSTANDING

TRUE-FALSE QUESTIONS

____1. Net income reflects the amount of cash actually flowing into a business.

____2. The double entry system of keeping records means that each transaction has two equal sides.

____3. Gross margin is sometimes called gross profit margin and is revenue minus COGS.

____4. Dividends are shown on the income statement while interest is not.

____5. Accounts receivables represent money that a company owes to its suppliers.

____6. When assets are overstated on the balance sheet, the firm's actual value is higher than indicated.

____7. The total depreciation expense for an asset over its life is always higher when an accelerated depreciation method is used than when the straight line method is used.

____8. The par value of common stock is used to separate the money received from the sale of stock into the common stock and paid-in excess accounts.

____9. Retained earnings represent the safety stock of cash for a corporation to be used in an emergency situation.

___10. Preferred stock is a cross between debt and common equity but is included in the equity section of the balance sheet.

___11. State tax rates are usually lower than federal tax rates.

___12. Most dividends paid by one corporation to another are exempt from taxes by the receiving company.

___13. Net book value and market value refer to the same amount.

___14. In any accounting transaction entry, total debits must equal total credits.

___15. When the term "fixed" is applied to assets, it means the asset is permanently located in one spot.

___16. Stretching payables is a common practice that never results in a penalty.

___17. Depreciation expense is a tax-deductible expense.

___18. Assets and liabilities are listed on the Balance Sheet in order of increasing liquidity.

___19. A company should never have more than 30 days of credit sales in receivables.

___20. A retailer will have no raw materials inventory.

___21. If all taxpayers pay the same tax rate, those with higher incomes pay higher taxes.

___22. Using accelerated versus straight-line depreciation can make a big difference in net income figures reported by two otherwise identical companies.

MULTIPLE CHOICE QUESTIONS

1. Current liabilities include:
   a. accruals and accounts payable.
   b. cash, inventory, and accounts receivable.
   c. long term debt.
   d. none of the above.

2. Taxing long term capital gains at a preferential rate:
   a. encourages investments in assets.
   b. encourages persons to hold investments for a longer time period.
   c. reflects a view that asset investment is desirable.
   d. all of the above.

3. We say that the US tax system favors debt financing of businesses over equity financing because:
   a. dividend payments are tax deductible.
   b. interest payments are tax deductible.
   c. dividend payments are not tax deductible.
   d. both b and c.

4. Losses can be carried back for _____ years and carried forward for as many as _____ years.
   a. 4, 10
   b. 2, 20
   c. 10, 4
   d. 3, 15

5. The three types of tax bases are:
   a. debt, asset, and equity.
   b. common stock, preferred stock, and retained earnings.
   c. federal, state, and local.
   d. income, consumption, and wealth.

6. A common consumption tax is:
   a. real estate tax imposed by the federal government.
   b. sales tax imposed by the federal government on cars and clothing.
   c. excise tax imposed by the federal government on alcohol, gas, and tobacco.
   d. none of the above.

7. Accruals include items such as:
   a. COGS and EBIT.
   b. payroll expenses and property tax.
   c. depreciation expense and accumulated depreciation.
   d. owner's equity.

8. The balance sheet can be thought of as an equation where:
   a. Assets = Liabilities + Equity.
   b. Assets – Liabilities = Equity.
   c. Assets – Equity = Liabilities.
   d. all of the above.

9. Which of the following represents current assets arranged in order of decreasing liquidity?
   a. cash, inventory, and accounts receivable
   b. cash, accounts payable, and inventory
   c. cash, accounts receivable, and inventory
   d. inventory, cash, and accounts receivable

10. COGS would include:
    a. labor and materials associated with production.
    b. marketing and sales expenses.
    c. accounting expenses.
    d. personnel costs.

11. When a firm sells its products on credit,
    a. it receives additional cash immediately.
    b. the sale is not recognized on financial statements.
    c. there is no immediate effect on the firm's cash position.
    d. none of the above.

12. When assets are overstated on the balance sheet, the firm's actual value is:
    a. unaffected.
    b. more than stated.
    c. less than stated.
    d. none of the above.

13. Because interest is shown on the income statement but dividends are not:
    a. a company with equity financing will always look weaker at the net income line.
    b. a company with debt financing will always look weaker at the net income line.
    c. a company with debt financing will always look stronger at the net income line.
    d. none of the above.

14. Which of the following may cause a difference between "income" and cash flow?
    a. cash sales
    b. credit sales
    c. depreciation expense
    d. both b. and c. may cause a difference

15. Which of the following is not a formula for net income?
    a. gross margin – expenses – interest expense – tax
    b. sales – cost of goods sold – interest expense – tax
    c. EBIT – interest expense – tax
    d. EBT – tax

16. Why is EBIT such an important number on the income statement?
    a. It shows how well the company has invested in other businesses
    b. It includes the effect of both state and federal tax rates
    c. It separates the operating and non-operating performance of the business
    d. It is the primary place for a business to analyze its interest expense

17. Which of the following is **not true**. If a fixed asset is fully depreciated,
    a. it has a book value of zero
    b. when it is sold, the company will always reflect a gain
    c. the sale of the asset could cause a tax increase or a tax decrease
    d. all of the above are true

18. Which of the following accounts is not part of equity?
    a. cash
    b. common stock
    c. preferred stock
    d. retained earnings

19. Which of the following may not be used in the process of reducing an individual taxpayer's total income to taxable income?
    a. interest on a home mortgage
    b. donations to charities
    c. personal exemptions
    d. ordinary dividends

20 Chapter 2

20. If Business A owns 40% of Business B, and Business B pays dividends to all of its shareholders, what percent of the dividends can be exempted from Business A's taxable income?
   a. none
   b. 70%
   c. 80%
   d. 100%

FILL-IN THE BLANK QUESTIONS

1. The two sides of an entry are called _____ and credits.

2. EBIT is also called _____.

3. If a person is interested in how much profit a company has earned during a certain period of time, he should look at the _____.

4. _____ is the speed with which an asset can be converted into cash or how quickly a liability will require cash.

5. _____ depreciation spreads out the cost of an asset evenly over the asset's useful life.

6. A company that is financed with debt is said to be _____.

7. _____ in a progressive tax system are the ranges of income where the tax rate is constant.

8. _____ interest is tax exempt while corporate bond interest is not.

9. Accounts payable represents _____.

10. The rate that a taxpayer will pay on the next dollar of earned income is called the _____.

11. Income, earnings, and _____ are usually used as synonyms.

12. When a receivable is determined to be uncollectible, it should be _____.

13. Earnings kept in the business are retained; earnings paid out are _____.

14. The original cost of an asset minus its accumulated depreciation is called its _____ value.

PROBLEMS

1. A taxpayer has $24,000 of taxable income and pays $4,250 in taxes. What is the taxpayer's average tax rate?

2. A single individual has a taxable income of $43,200. Based on Table 2.4, how much will she owe in taxes?

3. The Jones family earned $76,000 in salaries last year and $1,200 in interest and $300 in dividends. They paid mortgage interest of $4,200 and contributed $1,500 to charities. They have a nine-year old daughter. Assume a personal exemption rate of $2,900. What is their taxable income?

4. A corporation has taxable income of $26,244,116. What is its tax liability?

5. If a company had sales of $10,000 and a gross margin of $5,400, what was its COGS?

6. If the company listed above in problem 5 had expenses of $2,000, interest of $400, and taxes of $900, what was its net income?

7. If a $20,000 asset will be depreciated over 5 years at $4,000 per year, what is its net book value after 2 years?

8. What is a company's total current assets if the company has cash of $3,000, accounts receivable of $7,200, inventory of $5,600, and accounts payable of $3,400? What is its net working capital?

9. What will the total equity of a firm be that started out by selling 50,000 shares of $5 par value stock at $20 per share and then earns $100,000 and pays out $30,000 of the earnings as dividends?

10. The Smith's federal income tax rate is 20% and their state income tax rate is 6%. Calculate the Smith's total effective tax rate (TETR).

11. Johnson Corp. purchased a machine for $5,000 six years ago. They have been depreciating it on a straight line basis down to a salvage value of zero over its expected 20 year life. They just sold the machine for $3,800. Assuming a 40% tax rate, calculate the after-tax cash that Johnson Corp. will receive from the sale.

12. The Hawkins family had taxable income of $65,000, 24% of which was long-term capital gains. If the tax rate on ordinary income is 21% and the tax rate on long-term capital gains is 15%, calculate the Hawkins' total federal tax liability.

ANSWERS TO QUESTIONS

TRUE FALSE

1. f
2. t
3. t
4. f
5. f
6. f
7. f
8. t
9. f
10. t
11. t
12. t
13. f
14. t
15. f
16. f
17. t
18. f
19. f
20. t
21. t
22. t

FILL IN THE BLANKS

1. debits
2. operating profit
3. income statement
4. Liquidity
5. Straight line
6. leveraged
7. Tax brackets
8. Municipal bond
9. trade credit
10. marginal tax rate
11. profit
12. written off
13. distributed
14. net book

MULTIPLE CHOICE

1. a
2. d
3. d
4. b
5. d
6. c
7. b
8. d
9. c
10. a
11. c
12. c
13. b
14. d
15. b
16. c
17. c
18. a
19. d
20. c

ANSWERS TO PROBLEMS

1. 4250/24000 = 17.71%

2. $7,000 × 0.10 = $ 700.00
   ($28,400 - $7,000) × 0.15 =   3,210.00
   ($43,200 – $28,400) × 0.25 = $3,700.00
                                                    $7,610.00

3. $76,000
       1,200
         300
     77,500
    − 4,200
    − 1,500
     71,800
   − 8,700 (2,900 × 3)
   $63,100

4. $26,244,116 × .35 = $9,185,440.60

5. $10,000 – 5,400 = $4,600

6. $10,000 – 4,600 = 5,400 – 2,000 = 3,400 – 400 = 3,000 – 900 = $2,100

7. $20,000 – 8,000 = $12,000

8. Current Assets = $3,000 + 7,200 + 5,600 = $15,800
   Net Working Capital = $15,800 - $3,400 = $12,400

9. Common Stock (50,000 × $5)   250,000
   Paid in Excess (50,000 × 15)   750,000
   Retained Earnings (100,000 – 30,000)   70,000
                                                  $1,070,000

10. $TETR = T_f + T_s (1 – T_f)$
           = .20 + .06 (1 - .20)
           = .20 + .06 - .012 = .248 or 24.8%

11. Annual Depreciation $5,000/20 = $250
    Accumulated Depreciation $250 × 6 = $1,500
    Book Value $5,000 - $1,500 = $3,500
    Gain on Sale $3,800 - $3,500 = $300
    Tax on Gain $300 × .40 = $120
    After-tax Cash $3,800 - $120 = $3,680

12. $65,000 x .24 x .15 = $2,340 tax on capital gains
$65,000 x .76 x .21 = $10,374 tax on ordinary income
$2,340 + $10,374 = $12,714 total tax liability

CHAPTER THREE
CASH FLOWS AND FINANCIAL ANALYSIS

LEARNING OBJECTIVES

After studying this chapter you should understand the following concepts:

1. the definition of financial information, why it is important, who uses it, and where it originates;
2. the statement of cash flows and how to construct it;
3. what ratio analysis is and the information it provides;
4. how to develop common size statements;
5. how to calculate and analyze the ratios that are most commonly used for financial analysis;
6. the DuPont Equations and the relationships they analyze;
7. the limitations and weaknesses of ratio analysis.

CHAPTER SUMMARY

In this chapter, the concept of cash flow and the crucial difference between the emphasis in finance and the emphasis in accounting is introduced and thoroughly explained, as is the statement of cash flows, the document that details the movement of cash. Financial analysis through the use of ratio analysis is explored, and the categories of ratios and their calculations are demonstrated. The importance of recognizing not only the strengths of ratio analysis but also its limitations is stressed. This chapter concludes by emphasizing that financial analysts use these techniques not to provide answers but to provide indications of the need for further research and investigation.

CHAPTER REVIEW

FINANCIAL INFORMATION—WHERE DOES IT COME FROM, WHO USES IT, AND WHAT ARE WE LOOKING FOR?

1. **Financial information** refers to the results of business operations stated in monetary terms. This information is used both internally and externally by interested persons to make decisions concerning the firm. Primary users of this information are investors, creditors, and members of management. These users are interested in the firm's stability, its cash flows and its prospects for growth.

2. **Annual reports** are required of all publicly traded companies. They give historical financial information, guided by Generally Accepted Accounting Principles (GAAP) and information on future prospects. However, these reports are written by management, and their natural bias is to portray the future in a positive way. One of the functions of external financial analysts is to provide an objective review of company performance to help investors and creditors make investment decisions.

THE STATEMENT OF CASH FLOWS

3. The **statement of cash flows** shows the detailed movement of cash, where the money came from and how it was used. It is constructed from information from the **income statement** for the time period involved, and the **balance sheets** from the beginning of the period and the end of the period.

4. The statement of cash flows organizes cash flows into three different areas: (1) **Operating cash flows** which relates to the day-to-day running of the business (e.g. buying and selling inventory, paying invoices, collecting from customers); (2) **Investing cash flows** which relates to the purchase and sale of fixed (or financial) assets; and (3) **Financing cash flows** which relates to selling stocks and bonds and servicing those financial assets. The following rules are used when analyzing changes on the balance sheet during the period under study. Sources are cash inflows, and uses are cash outflows:

   ASSET INCREASE = USE OF CASH
   ASSET DECREASE = SOURCE OF CASH
   LIABILITY INCREASE = SOURCE OF CASH
   LIABILITY DECREASE = USE OF CASH

5. The **cash conversion cycle** shows that a business uses cash to purchase labor and inventory to make its products. The sale of those products results in a **receivable** that, when collected, results in cash that is used to begin the cycle again. The faster the products are produced and sold, the more times the cycle can be completed. This cycle highlights the activity in the operating portion of the statement of cash flows.

6. The **operating cash flows** are calculated by starting with Net Income, adjusting for all of the non-cash transactions that are included in the Net Income calculation and then adjusting for the changes in the balances of the current asset and liability accounts during the period under review. Depreciation (a non-cash expense) is added to Net Income to calculate Operating Income.

NET INCOME
+DEPRECIATION
OPERATING INCOME

Changes in the **current asset and current liability accounts** (except dividends payable) are added to operating income (using the source/use rules shown above) to calculate a net change in these accounts.

OPERATING INCOME
+NET CHANGES IN CURRENT ACCOUNTS
CASH FROM OPERATING ACTIVITIES

Cash from investing and financing activities are added to cash from operating activities to compute Net Cash Flow. Any of these amounts could be net cash inflows or net cash outflows, depending on the specifics of the business.

CASH FROM OPERATING ACTIVITIES
+CASH FROM INVESTING ACTIVITIES
+CASH FROM FINANCING ACTIVITIES
NET CASH FLOW

Net cash flow represents the difference between the cash balance at the beginning of the year and the end of the year.

BEGINNING CASH BALANCE
+NET CASH FLOW
ENDING CASH BALANCE

7. **Free cash flow** is defined as:

NET CASH FLOW
− FUNDS NEEDED FOR OTHER THAN OPERATING ACTIVITIES
FREE CASH FLOW

When free cash flow is negative, the firm has insufficient funds to meet these requirements or to pay dividends to common stockholders. A negative number means more borrowing is required or raising more equity capital through the sale of stock..

RATIO ANALYSIS

8. **RATIO ANALYSIS** is a standard technique used by financial analysts to compare and analyze information. Sets of numbers are used from one or more of the financial statements and compared to each other to form ratios. Ratios provide limited information when looked at on a stand-alone basis. They take on more value when they are compared to a firm's previous performance (**historical analysis**), the performance of other firms in the industry (**competitive analysis**), or the firm's planned performance (**budget analysis**).

9. **Common size statements** are used to compare companies of different size. Common size income statements are developed by expressing each line as a percent of total revenues. Common size balance sheets are developed by expressing each line as a percent of total assets.

10. Ratios are divided into five categories based on the type of issues they address: liquidity, asset management, debt management, profitability, and market value ratios.

    a) LIQUIDITY RATIOS deal with the short-term ability of the firm to pay its bills. These ratios are of special interest to creditors and suppliers.

    1) The **current ratio** measures the firm's capacity to meet current obligations.

    CURRENT RATIO = CURRENT ASSETS/CURRENT LIABILITIES

    2) The **quick ratio** subtracts inventory, which is often overvalued and more difficult to convert into cash, from other current assets. The quick ratio provides a higher level of assurance that a firm can meet current obligations.

    QUICK RATIO = (CURRENT ASSETS − INVENTORY) / CURRENT LIABILITIES

    b) ASSET MANAGEMENT RATIOS are indicators of how efficiently specific company assets are being managed or used.

    1) The **average collection period** tells how many days it takes a business to collect its money from credit sales. Management issues related to ACP performance include credit terms, credit and collection policies and the writing off of doubtful accounts.

    AVERAGE COLLECTION PERIOD = ACCOUNTS RECEIVABLE / AVERAGE DAILY SALES

    Or   *ACP = (ACCOUNTS RECEIVABLE/ANNUAL SALES) x 360*

    2) **Inventory turnover** measures how many times per year a firm uses its average inventory. Holding excess inventory is expensive and risky, so the higher the inventory turnover ratio, within reason, the less cost and less risk a company assumes. Too high a turnover may mean that customers' orders cannot be filled in a timely manner.

    INVENTORY TURNOVER = COST OF GOODS SOLD/INVENTORY

    An alternative (but less precise) formula for computing inventory turnover uses sales instead of cost of goods sold.

    INVENTORY TURNOVER = SALES/INVENTORY

3) **Fixed asset turnover and total asset turnover** ratios indicate how well a firm uses its assets to generate sales. When these numbers are too low (based on one of the comparison methods discussed above), the firm is not using its asset investment to the greatest benefit. While high is preferable to low, too high may mean that assets are being overstressed and may wear out prematurely.

FIXED ASSET TURNOVER (FAT) = SALES/FIXED ASSETS

TOTAL ASSET TURNOVER (TAT) = SALES/TOTAL ASSETS

c) **DEBT MANAGEMENT RATIOS** illustrate how well a business is using borrowed money.

1) The **debt ratio** tells what percent of a firm's assets are financed with borrowing. While higher debt ratios can generate higher returns for the owners of the business, they also increase the business' exposure to risk.

$$DEBT\ RATIO = \frac{LONG\ TERM\ DEBT + CURRENT\ LIABILITIES}{TOTAL\ ASSETS}$$

2) The **debt to equity ratio** compares long term debt to a firm's equity. Debt financing is riskier than equity financing because of its fixed repayment schedule and interest expense. This ratio is stated as a proportion rather than a percent.

DEBT TO EQUITY RATIO = LONG TERM DEBT/EQUITY

3) The **Times Interest Earned Ratio (TIE)** measures the number of times EBIT can cover interest.

$$TIMES\ INTEREST\ EARNED = \frac{EBIT}{INTEREST}$$

4) The **cash coverage ratio** takes into account an issue that the times interest earned ratio ignores — that interest is a cash payment but EBIT is not a good approximation of available cash. Adding depreciation to EBIT provides a better comparison between cash available to meet interest expense and the interest expense itself.

CASH COVERAGE = (EBIT + DEPRECIATION)/INTEREST

5) The **fixed charge coverage** ratio adjusts the times interest earned ratio to account for the additional fixed charges that companies incur to lease equipment. Businesses using leases to expand their asset base must cover these fixed charges in addition to interest expense.

$$FIXED\ CHARGE\ COVERAGE = \frac{EBIT + LEASE\ PAYMENTS}{INTEREST + LEASE\ PAYMENTS}$$

d) **PROFITABILITY RATIOS** are methods of evaluating the most fundamental and important indicator of a firm's success – its profits. These ratios compare net income to the following business measures: sales, assets and equity.

1) **Return on sales (ROS) or net profit margin** measures the overall profitability of the firm. This identifies what percent of sales (the top of the income statement) makes it all the way to the bottom of the income statement.

RETURN ON SALES = NET INCOME/SALES

2) **Return on assets** measures how well a firm uses its assets to produce income.

RETURN ON ASSETS = NET INCOME/TOTAL ASSETS

3) **Return on equity** is the most fundamental measure of profitability and measures the firm's ability to earn a return on the money that the owners have invested. When a firm has little or no debt, **ROE** and **ROA** will be very close. The greater the amount of debt a firm has, the higher **ROE** will be as compared to **ROA** in good times, and the lower **ROE** will be as compared to **ROA** in bad times.

RETURN ON EQUITY = NET INCOME/EQUITY

e) **MARKET VALUE RATIOS** vary from the above categories of ratios, which all are concerned with the internal management of the firm. Market Value ratios compare financial statement figures to the values the stock market places on the firm. Public attitudes and perceptions will influence how the market value is calculated, and a firm's management cannot directly control these factors. The market value of a firm is most closely reflected by the price of its stock.

1) The **price/earnings ratio** (P/E) compares the market price of the stock to the **earnings per share**, which is net income divided by the total number of outstanding shares of common stock. This ratio is very important to the stock market as it shows how much investors are willing to pay for a dollar of the firm's earnings. The P/E ratio is a function of a firm's expected growth.

P/E RATIO = STOCK PRICE/EARNINGS PER SHARE

2) The **market to book value ratio** is a comparison between the total value of the equity on a firm's balance sheet and its market value. A healthy firm is expected to have a market value that is higher than its book value.

MARKET TO BOOK VALUE RATIO = STOCK PRICE/BOOK VALUE PER SHARE

11. While each ratio measures a different type of performance, ratios are not necessarily independent of each other. The **DuPont Equations** illustrate meaningful relationships between certain ratios. The first **DuPont Equation** shows that a firm's ROA performance is a function of two other ratios: (1) managing its cost and expenses (ROS), and (2) generating a high amount of sales per dollar of assets (TAT).

DUPONT EQUATION

RETURN ON ASSETS = RETURN ON SALES × TOTAL ASSET TURNOVER

The **Extended DuPont Equation** explains that the way a business is financed can significantly affect the results of operations, causing them to be more favorable in good times and less favorable in bad times. The extended DuPont equation introduces the concept of the equity multiplier which is total assets divided by total equity. The more debt a company uses, the higher this ratio will be, and the more leverage the business is using to produce returns for its stockholders.

EXTENDED DUPONT EQUATION

RETURN ON EQUITY = RETURN ON ASSETS × TOTAL ASSETS/EQUITY

12. The best figures to use for comparing ratios are industry averages. These averages can be obtained from **Dun and Bradstreet, Robert Morris Associates,** and the **US Commerce Department's Quarterly Financial Report.**

13. Without taking away from the valuable information provided by ratio analysis, this technique does have some limitations and weaknesses that must be taken into consideration. Some of the more significant problems include: (1) Widely diversified companies make it difficult to meaningfully compare ratios to industry averages; (2) Companies may use "window dressing," a practice to make year-end balance sheets look temporarily better; (3) Within the scope of generally accepted accounting principles (GAAP) firms can have legitimate differences, and the impact of these differences can make comparisons between firms difficult; (4) Inflation can distort the value of assets.

TESTING YOUR UNDERSTANDING

TRUE-FALSE QUESTIONS

_____1. A negative free cash flow is actually a positive indicator for a firm.

_____2. An increase in fixed assets is a use of funds.

_____3. When a firm has a high amount of debt, its ROE and ROA should be almost identical.

_____4. Annual reports may contain some exaggerations.

_____5. In bad times, using a lot of debt is usually a good idea.

_____6. Inflation that occurs after the purchase of an asset will increase the asset's cost as reported on the balance sheet.

_____7. The DuPont equations express relationships between certain ratios.

_____8. Profitability ratios are generally expressed as percents.

32 Chapter 3

___9. Lease payments for equipment that is necessary for a firm to remain in business are regarded as fixed charges.

___10. Both auditors and accountants guarantee the accuracy of corporate financial information.

___11. Stockholders are likely to be interested in a firm's prospects for growth.

___12. Vendors and creditors are primarily interested in the same type of information from financial statements.

___13. In order for a ratio to have real value, it must be compared to other similar figures.

___14. Common size analysis gives financial managers a meaningful comparison of firms of different sizes.

___15. Only a beginning balance sheet for a company is used in computing ratios.

___16. If a company has a line of credit with a bank to cover temporary cash shortages, a relatively low current ratio is probably nothing to be concerned about.

___17. Customer dissatisfaction with a company's product is a common reason for them to pay late or not to pay at all.

___18. The lower the P/E, the better.

MULTIPLE CHOICE QUESTIONS

1. Comparing ratios for one firm to ratios for another firm in the same industry is a:
   a. competitive analysis
   b. historical analysis
   c. budget analysis
   d. trend analysis

2. Which of the following best expresses the effect of debt on a firm's performance?
   a. A firm with a high amount of debt will be more negatively impacted in good times than will a firm with no debt.
   b. A firm with a high amount of debt will be more positively impacted in good times than will a firm with no debt.
   c. A firm with a high amount of debt will be more negatively impacted in bad times than will a firm with no debt.
   d. both b and c.

3. The primary users of financial information are:
   a. creditors
   b. managers
   c. investors
   d. all of the above

4. The statement of cash flows is constructed from information from:
   a. income statement
   b. balance sheets
   c. income statement and balance sheets
   d. annual report

5. A firm with current assets of $2,000,000 and current liabilities of $1,000,000 will have a current ratio of:
   a. .5
   b. 2
   c. 1
   d. 1.5

6. Which category of ratios does management have the least capacity to control?
   a. Asset management
   b. Liquidity
   c. Market value
   d. Profitability

7. If you were a banker and were considering lending money to a firm for six months, which ratios would you be most concerned with?
   a. Fixed asset and total asset turnover
   b. Current and quick ratios
   c. Cash coverage and fixed charge coverage
   d. ROE and ROS

8. A firm with a high expected growth level should have:
   a. a high P/E ratio.
   b. a low P/E ratio.
   c. a higher than normal current ratio.
   d. a lower than normal current ratio.

9. A high average collection period (ACP) indicates:
   a. the firm is doing better than average in collecting credit sales.
   b. the firm may be too liberal in its credit policies.
   c. the firm is taking longer than the average to collect credit sales.
   d. both b and c.

10. Why does the quick ratio subtract inventory from current assets?
    a. Inventory may not convert to cash as quickly as other current assets.
    b. Inventory may be overstated and overvalued on the balance sheet.
    c. both a and b.
    d. none of the above.

11. The current ratio:
    a. is a liquidity ratio.
    b. measures the ability of a firm to pay its short-term obligations.
    c. should be above 1.0 for all firms.
    d. both a and b.

12. Financial analysts:
    a. often work for large brokerage firms.
    b. use their knowledge to predict a firm's performance.
    c. may make recommendations about stock and debt purchases.
    d. all of the above.

13. To build a statement of cash flows for an accounting period, you need:
    a. a balance sheet.
    b. an income statement.
    c. 2 balance sheets and an income statement.
    d. a balance sheet and 2 income statements.

14. In order to remain solvent, a firm must:
    a. have more money coming in than going out.
    b. have more money going out than coming in.
    c. must be making at least a 20% profit.
    d. must have at least as much money coming in as going out.

15. Holding too little inventory:
    a. can cause stockouts.
    b. results in a low inventory turnover.
    c. increases the chances of inventory spoilage and obsolescence.
    d. increases insurance costs.

16. The sale of new shares of common stock would appear in which section of the statement of cash flows?
    a. the operating section
    b. the investing section
    c. the financing section
    d. sale of stock does not appear on the statement of cash flows

17. Williams Co. had an accounts payable balance of $200,000 at the beginning of the month and $240,000 at the end of the month. This is an example of an increase in a(n) _____ account and is therefore a _____ of cash.
    a. asset; source
    b. asset; use
    c. liability; source
    d. liability; use

18. Which of the following activities is not part of the cash conversion cycle?
    a. purchase of raw materials
    b. sale of products
    c. collection of accounts receivable
    d. payment of dividends to stockholders

19. If cash is the only current asset/liability account whose balance changed during the accounting period, which of the following formulas should be used to calculate "cash from operations?"
    a. net income
    b. net income plus depreciation expense
    c. net income plus accumulated depreciation
    d. net income plus depreciation expense plus/minus the change in the cash account

20. Common size balance sheets can be used to analyze all of the following between companies except:
    a. comparative stock prices
    b. comparative use of inventory
    c. comparative use of fixed assets
    d. comparative use of debt and equity

FILL-IN THE BLANK QUESTIONS

1. Comparing different size firms in relative rather than absolute terms would be best accomplished by a _____ statement.

2. A decrease in a liability is a _____ of cash.

3. _____ is a term for a practice used by some corporations to make balance sheets look temporarily more favorable.

4. _____ is net income divided by the number of shares of outstanding common stock.

5. _____ ratios measure how well a firm is producing profits.

6. If a person is comparing ratios for the same firm from different time periods, he is performing a _____ comparison.

7. The _____ is expressed in days and shows how long it takes a company to collect its credit sales.

8. _____ ratios illustrate how a business uses borrowed money.

9. Another name for the return on sales ratio is _____.

10. The _____ ratio tells how much investors are willing to pay for a dollar of the firm's earnings.

36   Chapter 3

11. Cash flow statements show _____ numbers in parentheses.

12. A liquidity measure that does not depend upon inventory is the _____ ratio.

PROBLEMS

1. A firm has total current assets of $3,450,000, total current liabilities of $1,750,000, and inventory of $425,000. What is its current ratio? What is its quick ratio?

2. A firm has an average collection period of 90 days as compared to an industry average of 60 days. Explain what this means. What does this ratio indicate this firm should investigate?

3. Use the following information to calculate ROA and ROE using the DuPont equations:

   ROS = 14%
   TOTAL ASSETS = $60M
   TOTAL ASSET TURNOVER = 1.2
   EQUITY = $45M

4. What is the free cash flow for this firm, and what will this firm need to do, based on your answer?

Cash from operating activities	$4,000
Cash from investing activities (replacing fixed assets)	(2,000)
Cash from financing activities (paying preferred stock dividends)	(1,000)
Cash from financing activities (paying common stock dividends)	(2,000)

5. A firm has a Current Ratio of 1.9 and the industry average is 1.51. This same firm has a quick ratio of .95 compared to an industry average of .98. Do either of these ratios indicate an area of concern? Where do you think there might be a problem?

6. A firm has sales of $300,000, fixed assets of $60,000, and total assets of $250,000. What is its fixed asset turnover ratio? What is its total asset turnover ratio?

7. Firm A has a times interest earned ratio of 7, while Firm B has a times interest earned ratio of 20. Which firm would a bank consider as the safer risk to loan money? Why?

8. What is a firm's P/E ratio if it has net income of $200,000, and 20,000 shares of common stock outstanding, currently selling for $30 a share?

9. The following table shows the beginning and ending balances for all of the current asset and liability accounts for the past year. What are the total sources and uses of cash resulting from changes in these accounts?

($-000)	Beginning	Ending
Cash	500	560
Accounts Receivable	650	720
Inventory	945	890
Accounts Payable	350	415
Accruals	300	268

10. Use the information from problem 9. If this company had a Net Income of $450,000 and depreciation expense of $135,000, calculate "Cash from Operating Activities."

11. Use the information from problem 9. If this company had sales of $5 million and a gross margin of 36%, calculate inventory turnover using both methods based on the end-of-year information.

12. Below are selected items from a company's end-of-year balance sheet:

Total Assets   4,500
Long Term Debt   1,400
Total Equity   2,700

Calculate the debt ratio and the debt/equity ratio.

ANSWERS TO QUESTIONS

TRUE-FALSE

1. f
2. t
3. f
4. t
5. f
6. f
7. t
8. t
9. t
10. f
11. t
12. t
13. t
14. t
15. f
16. t
17. t
18. f

FILL IN THE BLANKS

1. common size
2. use
3. Window dressing
4. Earnings per share
5. Profitability
6. historical
7. average collection period
8. Debt management
9. net profit margin
10. price/earnings ratio
11. negative
12. quick

MULTIPLE CHOICE

1. a
2. d
3. d
4. c
5. b
6. c
7. b
8. a
9. d
10. c
11. d
12. d
13. c
14. d
15. a
16. c
17. c
18. d
19. b
20. a

ANSWERS TO PROBLEMS

1. Current ratio = $3,450,000/$1,750,000 = 1.97
   Quick ratio = $3,450,000 − $425,000/$1,750,000 = 1.73

2. This firm is taking 90 days to collect its credit sales while other firms in the same industry are taking only 60 days.

   The firm should look into its credit collection policies to see if they are extending credit to customers who are not credit worthy, or who are taking advantage of their lax collection policies. Taking 50% longer to collect credit is expensive and risky. It's likely that most customers are paying on time, but a few accounts are very old and probably uncollectable.

3. DuPont Equation: ROA = ROS × TAT
   ROA = 0.14 × 1.2 = 0.168 = 16.8%
   Extended DuPont Equation: ROE = ROA × Total Assets/Equity
   ROE = 0.168 × ($60 million / $45 million) = 22.4%

4.
Cash from Operating Activities	4,000
Cash from Investing Activities	(2,000)
Cash from Financing Activities (pref. stock)	(1,000)
Free Cash Flows	1,000
Funds needed for common stock dividends	(2,000)
Net cash flows	(1,000)

   This firm has positive free cash flows which means that it is generating sufficient cash from operations to meet its asset replacement and preferred stock commitments. However, total cash flows are negative, and this condition cannot continue indefinitely. The firm must looks for ways to improve cash flows or be faced with reducing or eliminating dividends.

5. Current ratio is higher than the industry average, but the quick ratio is right on the industry average. Assuming that the industry average is representative of the industry, this firm is probably experiencing a problem with excess inventory investment. The only difference between these ratios is the subtraction of inventory, so this is where an investigation should be centered.

6. $\dfrac{300,000}{60,000} = 5.0$ Fixed Asset Turnover

   $\dfrac{300,000}{250,000} = 1.2$ Total Asset Turnover

7. Firm B. The more times earnings cover existing interest, the safer it is for that firm to take on more additional debt because it has more earnings with which to pay interest expense.

8. $\dfrac{\$200,000}{20,000 \text{ shares}} = \$10$ Earnings per Share (EPS)

   $\dfrac{\$30 \text{ market price}}{\$10} = 3$ P/E ratio

40 Chapter 3

$10 EPS

9. The Cash account is not used.
Accounts Receivable is a $70 use of cash
Inventory is a $55 source of cash
Accounts Payable is a $65 source of cash
Accruals is a $32 use of cash
Therefore sources total $120 and uses total $102

10. Cash fro Operating Activities = Net Income + Depreciation + Net Changes in the Current Asset/Liability accounts

$450,000 + $135,000 + $120,000 (sources) - $102,000 (uses) = $603,000

11. With a gross margin of 36%, COGS must be $5 million x (1 - .36) = $3.2 million

Inventory Turnover (using Sales) = $5,000,000/$890,000 = 5.62 times

Inventory Turnover (using COGS) = $3,200,000/$890,000 = 3.60 times

12. In order for the balance sheet to balance, current liabilities must equal $400

$4,500 - $1,400 - $2,700 = $400 (current liabilities)

Debt Ratio = ($400 + $1,400)/$4,500 = 40.0%

Debt/Equity Ratio = $1,400/$2,700 = .52

CHAPTER FOUR

THE FINANCIAL SYSTEM AND INTEREST

LEARNING OBJECTIVES

After studying this chapter you should understand the following terms and concepts:

1. the three sectors of the financial system and the relationship of savings and investment;
2. the classification of financial markets;
3. the definitions and functions of the primary and secondary markets;
4. the functions that investment banks and financial intermediaries play in financial markets;
5. the stock market and how stock exchanges function;
6. the components of interest rates and the relationships between the interest rates and the stock market, the economy, and debt markets;
7. the relationship between Federal Government securities and the risk-free rate;
8. the term structure of interest rates and the yield curve;
9. three theories that help explain the shape of the yield curve: the Expectations Theory, the Liquidity Preference Theory, and the Market Segmentation Theory.

CHAPTER SUMMARY

In this chapter, the roles of the three segments of the economy (consumption, production and government) are introduced, along with a more in depth look at financial assets and financial markets and the roles that they play in facilitating the movement of cash between these three segments. The stock market and stock exchanges are examined in great detail, the relationship between stock market returns and interest rates is established. The concept of how interest rates are developed is discussed from two related views. The first views the way the marketplace sets interest rates, using traditional supply and demand models; the second views the conceptual components of interest rates and introduces the concept of risk-free rates and risk components that would be considered by a potential investor.

CHAPTER REVIEW

THE FINANCIAL SYSTEM

1. The **financial system** of an industrialized society is composed of three sectors. The **consumption sector** is concerned with individuals and households buying and using products and services that have been created by the **production sector.** The **government sector** provides services used by the consumption and production sector and collects taxes from both. Persons move from sector to sector and can operate simultaneously in more than one sector. Money also moves freely among the sectors.

2. **Financial markets** provide a method for consumer savings (the portion of income not used for consumption) to be used for financing business projects (e.g. buying large pieces of equipment). Companies that need money issue stocks and bonds that are purchased by consumers with their savings.

3. Projects financed by businesses through borrowing (issuing bonds) are said to be **debt financed**, while projects financed through the sale of stock or from retained earnings are said to be **equity financed.** **Term** refers to how much time elapses between the beginning and the end of financial investments or projects. **Short-term financing** must be repaid within one year, and **long-term financing** is for more than one year. Stocks have no repayment date (the issuing company has no obligation to repurchase the stock they issue), and thus have an indefinite term and are considered long-term financing.

4. **FINANCIAL MARKETS** are classified according to term and purpose.

    a) **Capital markets** are the financial markets that trade in stocks and long-term debt securities.

    b) **Money markets** are the financial markets that deal with the short-term requirements of companies through debt instruments known as **notes, commercial paper, and bills.** The federal government is the most active participant in issuing short-term debt to cover its annual budget deficit.

    c) **Primary markets** deal with new issues of stocks and bonds transacted between the issuer and the individual investor.

    d) **Secondary markets** handle the sale of securities between investors after the initial purchase from the issuing firm. Most transactions occur in these markets.

5. **Investment bankers** usually facilitate the **direct transfer** of newly issued securities by bringing the sellers and the buyers together. In an **indirect transfer**, a **financial intermediary**, such as a **mutual fund**, pools money that is collected from numerous individuals and buys an assortment of stocks and bonds. The mutual fund then issues a new financial asset, shares in the mutual fund, to the individual investors. Mutual funds and other intermediaries such as **pension funds, insurance companies, and banks,** are called **institutional investors** and own about 25% of the stocks listed on the major stock exchanges while transacting about 75% of all trades.

THE STOCK MARKET AND STOCK EXCHANGES

6. The **stock market** is a network of exchanges and brokers who assist people in buying and selling securities. Each **stock exchange** has a limited number of seats that are sold to **brokerage firms**. The purchase of a seat allows the brokerage firm to do business on that exchange. **Investors** are the customers of **brokers**, who place the customers' buy and/or sell orders. Brokers make a commission each time they buy or sell securities. The **New York Stock Exchange** is the largest in the United States and handles about 85% of all the stock trading activity in this country. Other stock exchanges include the **American Stock Exchange (AMEX)** and numerous regional exchanges. Most large corporations are listed on one of the larger stock exchanges, but the stock for some large corporations and many smaller corporations is traded on the **National Association of Securities Dealers Automated Quotation System (NASDAQ),** a loosely organized network of brokers.

7. **Privately held or closely held** companies do not sell their stock to the general public. If a company wants to raise a large amount of money by selling stock to lots of investors, it offers its securities for sale to the general public and becomes a **public company or publicly traded company**. The first time a company sells stock to the general public is called an **initial public offering (IPO)**. The process of "going public" is closely monitored by the **Securities and Exchange Commission (SEC)**, an arm of the federal government established in 1934.

INTEREST

8. When an investor purchases a **bond** from a business, it is lending that amount of money (typically in multiples of $1,000) to the business. In return, the investor expects to receive money from the business according to the terms of the bond. The amount of money the issuer of a security pays to the investor on a periodic basis for the use of his or her money is called **interest**, expressed as a percent. The rate of interest received by the purchaser will depend upon the type of the bond, its maturity date, the riskiness of the investment, and the market rate of interest. The date on which a bond must be repaid by the issuer is known as its **maturity date**. Bonds are **non-amortized debt**, meaning that only interest is paid during the life of the loan. Issuers usually pay interest twice a year with the principal being repaid entirely on the maturity date.

9. There is a relationship between the interest rate that bonds pay and the return that a person will receive from an investment in stocks. Because investments in bonds are safer than investments in stocks (bonds must be repaid while dividends paid to stockholders are optional), stocks will usually have to offer higher returns than bonds to get persons to invest in them instead of bonds.

10. **Interest rates** also have an effect on the general economy. **Low** interest rates encourage people to borrow money and to make purchases such as cars and new homes. This purchasing activity encourages business to invest in more projects to allow them to produce more products. When interest rates are **high**, borrowing becomes too expensive, and people cut back on their purchasing. This in turn means that businesses will produce less, lay off instead of hire workers, and the economy can become depressed.

11. There are **supply** and **demand** curves for money, just like those for products and services. When money is in ample supply, the price **(interest rate)** will be lowered. When money is in

short supply, the price will be higher. When the demand for money exceeds the supply, the price of money will be driven up. When the demand for money is less than the supply, the price will fall. The demand for money from individuals is determined in part by how optimistic they feel about the future; optimistic consumers purchase lots of products. The supply of money is determined by the amount of money that people are saving rather than spending.

THE COMPONENTS OF AN INTEREST RATE

12. An **interest rate model** is composed of two major components. The first component is the **base rate**, which is the rate that people would expect in return for a "no risk" investment. Included in the base rate are components to account for a "real return" (the return that would exist in a perfect economy with no inflation) and a component to offset the effects of inflation. The second component is the **risk premium,** which includes amounts required by lenders to compensate them for assuming the risk that they may receive less than the full amount of the principal and interest. Higher perceived risk regarding the loan will result in higher interest rates.

13. Different kinds of risks are assumed by lenders.

    a) **Default risk** represents the chance that the borrower will not be able to pay the interest during the life of the loan or repay the principal upon maturity. A lender could lose all or part of his investment. The longer the term of the loan, the greater the chance that default can occur.

    b) **Liquidity risk** occurs when there is no market for the sale of the security before its maturity date, so if the lender must sell the security earlier than its maturity, he or she can lose some of the investment.

    c) **Maturity risk** is concerned with fluctuations in interest rates that can occur over time. When interest rates increase after a bond has been purchased, the investor will lose money if the security is sold prior to maturity. Because interest rates fluctuate much more over long periods of time, this type of risk increases as the term of the security increases.

14. The **risk-free rate** of interest is the rate paid by the federal government on short-term debt securities (e.g. 90-day treasuries) and is used as a surrogate for the base rate, discussed above.

15. Interest rates vary depending upon the term of the debt, and the relationship between the term and the interest rate is known as the **term structure**. A **yield curve** is a graph of the term structure. A **normal yield curve** slopes upward and to the right. This slope is because short-term rates are usually lower than long-term rates. If short-term rates happen to be higher than long-term rates, the yield curve is **inverted**. Various theories have evolved to help explain the shape of the yield curve. The **Expectations Theory** says that the yield curve slopes up or down based on what people expect to happen to interest rates in the future. The **Liquidity Preference Theory** says that because short-term loans are more liquid, they are preferred by investors. This short term preference results in the need to offer incentives in the form of higher rates to encourage investment in long-term loans. The **Market Segmentation Theory** says that debt markets are segmented by the terms of the loan, and that each segment has its own set of supply and demand curves.

TESTING YOUR UNDERSTANDING

TRUE-FALSE QUESTIONS

_____1. A person may participate in only one sector of the economy at any one time.

_____2. Short-term financing includes temporary loans to businesses to cover temporary operating shortages.

_____3. Capital markets deal only in short-term securities.

_____4. The federal government uses short-term debt to finance its budget deficit.

_____5. The liquidity preference theory explains the normal yield curve by theorizing that investors prefer ready liquidity, and therefore prefer long-term debt because it is more liquid.

_____6. The risk of default is higher for long-term debt than for short-term debt.

_____7. Long-term government securities set the risk-free rate.

_____8. The most creditworthy firms will have to pay a lower default risk premium than will riskier firms.

_____9. Business financing for large projects comes almost exclusively from operating funds.

_____10. Stocks have no specific repayment date and so are treated as long-term capital.

_____11. A security is traded in the primary market when it is issued and purchased for the first time.

_____12. The purpose of a prospectus is disclosure.

_____13. Stockbrokers receive commissions only when they sell securities.

_____14. It is a simple and short procedure to shift from being a privately held to a publicly held corporation.

_____15. There are three sectors in an industrialized economy.

_____16. People usually spend their entire incomes on consumption.

_____17. Bonds are considered exclusively to be short-term financing.

_____18. In traditional financial markets, the majority of transactions are in the primary market.

_____19. New securities are usually marketed directly to the public by the issuing firm.

_____20. Mutual funds are influential in setting prices and trends in the secondary market.

_____21. Securities markets are regulated only by the ethics of those who are involved.

46   Chapter 4

____22. When the SEC approves a prospectus, it is endorsing the security as a good investment opportunity.

____23. Mutual funds frequently purchase IPOs.

____24. Most business and governmental debt is non-amortized.

____25. Stocks have to offer higher returns than debt investments to induce most people to invest in them.

MULTIPLE CHOICE QUESTIONS

1. According to the expectations theory, if investors expect interest rates to stay flat for the next 10 years:
   a. the yield curve will gradually slope increasingly upward for each of the next 10 years.
   b. the yield curve will drop dramatically and continue to fall for each of the next 10 years.
   c. the yield curve will remain flat indefinitely.
   d. none of the above.

2. The federal government has no default risk because:
   a. there will always be a federal government.
   b. there is always a market for the federal government's obligations.
   c. the federal government can print money.
   d. both b and c.

3. The three segments of an industrial economy are:
   a. consumer, producer, and government.
   b. stockbrokers, stock exchanges, and stock markets.
   c. investment bankers, banks, and mutual funds.
   d. inflation, deflation, and stagnation.

4. The three sources of risk are:
   a. personal, professional, and ethical.
   b. business, economic, and government.
   c. default, liquidity, and maturity.
   d. none of the above.

5. Mutual funds:
   a. act as financial intermediaries.
   b. pool money from a number of different individuals.
   c. have a great deal of influence in stock and bond markets.
   d. all of the above.

6. Financial intermediaries include:
   a. doctors and lawyers.
   b. pension and mutual funds.
   c. insurance companies and banks.
   d. both b and c.

7. The New York Stock Exchange:
   a. handles only 25% of all stock transactions in the US.
   b. is the smallest of all US stock exchanges.
   c. deals in the securities of the smallest corporations in the US.
   d. none of the above.

8. The stock of privately held corporations:
   a. is severely restricted by federal regulations, cannot be transacted across state lines, and can be issued to a limited number of stockholders.
   b. always provides enough funds to finance huge capital projects.
   c. must be offered for sale to the general public.
   d. none of the above.

9. Initial public offerings:
   a. are considered quite risky.
   b. are primary market transactions.
   c. are frequently purchased by mutual funds.
   d. all of the above.

10. A bond with a 20 year term:
    a. is considered long term.
    b. will mature ten years from the current date.
    c. is usually amortized.
    d. all of the above.

11. High interest rates:
    a. tend to stifle the economy.
    b. discourage borrowing.
    c. both a and b.
    d. none of the above.

12. Short-term debt instruments include:
    a. bills.
    b. commercial paper.
    c. notes.
    d. all of the above.

13. Our national debt:
    a. is the same as the federal deficit.
    b. is comprised of both long- and short-term borrowing.
    c. is comprised only of long-term borrowing.
    d. is non-existent because of the current budget surplus.

14. Corporate financial managers are concerned about secondary stock market transactions because:
    a. that is when the issuing company gets its money.
    b. this is where the par value of the stock is determined.
    c. senior managers' compensation is usually tied to stock price.
    d. all of the above.

48   Chapter 4

15. Most demand curves are:
    a. downward sloping to the right.
    b. a straight vertical line.
    c. upward sloping to the right.
    d. a straight horizontal line.

16. The cash flow from the consumption sector to the production sector occurs for which of the following reasons?
    a. purchase of goods and services; purchase of securities
    b. purchase of goods and services; payment of wages
    c. payment of wages; purchase of securities
    d. purchase of securities; payment of interest and dividends

17. Which of the following markets deal with the sale of stock from the company to individual stockholders?
    a. capital and primary markets
    b. capital and secondary markets
    c. money and primary markets
    d. money and secondary markets

18. The vast majority of IPO's are handled as:
    a. direct transfers
    b. direct transfers through a financial intermediary
    c. indirect transfers through a financial intermediary
    d. all of the above methods handle an equal proportion of IPO's

19. "Going Public" requires:
    a. approval from the SEC
    b. the issuance of a prospectus
    c. disclosure of important facts that would be of interest/concern to potential investors
    d. all of the above

20. By reading a stock quotation in the paper, you can determine:
    a. the price of a stock exactly one year ago
    b. the price of a stock at the beginning of the calendar year
    c. the current price of the stock
    d. both b. and c. are true

FILL-IN THE BLANK QUESTIONS

1. The _____ theory says that each segment of the debt market has its own supply and demand picture.

2. A _____ yield curve is upward sloping to the right.

3. The premium paid by borrowers to cover the risk that not all of the principal and interest will be repaid is called the _____ premium.

4. Economists say that savings = _____.

5. _____ refers to the length of time between the start of an investment or project and the end.

6. _____ markets trade in short-term debt.

7. _____ are members of stock exchanges.

8. _____ means that investors must be given complete information about companies whose stock is offered for sale.

9. When a company offers its stock for sale to the public for the first time, this is called an _____.

10. When individuals feel optimistic about the economy, they borrow _____ money.

11. _____ matches the term of a project with the term of its financing.

12. Most of the money that supports the day-to-day operations of a firm is generated by _____.

13. When the government spends more than it takes in, there is a federal _____.

14. When the individual owner of a stock sells it to another individual, this is a _____ market transaction.

15. A _____ gives detailed information about a firm's business, financing, and background of principal officers.

16. _____ debt is when the principal and interest is paid back over the life of the loan.

PROBLEMS

1. According to economists, if savings equal $5 trillion and spending equals $100 trillion, what will investment equal?

2. Inflation is expected to be 3.0% this year, 4.0% next year, 5.0% in year 3 and a steady 4.0% after that. The Pure Interest Rate is 2.5%. The Liquidity Risk Premium is zero for corporate bonds under three years and 0.5% for bonds with terms of three years or more. The Default Risk Premium is 1.0% for corporate bonds. The Maturity Risk Premium is calculated by using the following formula: 0.2%(t – 1), where t = the term of the bond. Using the Interest Rate Model, develop the term structure for a corporate bond and for a federal government bond for bonds with terms of 1 through 10 years.

3. Use Figure 4.7 on page 127 of the text. The figure shows that the yield percentage for GM stock on that date was 6.5%. Can that information be derived from other information on the figure? How?

4. See Figure 4.7 on page 127 of the text. What was the GM stock price on January 1, 2003?

5. If inflation is expected to be 3.0% per year for the next three years and 4.0% per year thereafter, and the real risk free rate is estimated to be 2.4%, calculate the base rate component for each of the following securities: 4-year; 6-year; 10-year.

6. If inflation is not expected to change from its current level for the foreseeable future, would you expect to see a normal or an inverted yield curve for a series of bonds issued by a stable corporation? Why?

ANSWERS TO QUESTIONS

TRUE-FALSE
1. f
2. t
3. f
4. t
5. f
6. t
7. f
8. t
9. f
10. t
11. t
12. t
13. f
14. f
15. t
16. f
17. f
18. f
19. f
20. t
21. f
22. f
23. t
24. t
25. t

MULTIPLE CHOICE
1. c
2. c
3. a
4. c
5. d
6. d
7. d
8. a
9. d
10. a
11. c
12. d
13. b
14. c
15. a
16. a
17. a
18. b
19. d
20. d

FILL IN THE BLANKS

1. market segmentation
2. normal
3. default risk
4. investment
5. Term
6. Money
7. Brokers
8. Disclosure
9. Initial Public Offering
10. more
11. Maturity matching
12. sales
13. deficit
14. secondary
15. prospectus
16. Amortized

52 Chapter 4

ANSWERS TO PROBLEMS

1. $5 trillion

2. The federal government bond will consist of the base rate (the Pure Rate plus the Inflation component) and the Maturity Risk Premium. The corporate bond will include the base rate and all of the risk components. The components are listed below:

Term	Inflation	Pure Rate	Maturity	Liquidity (corp. only)	Default (corp. only)	Fed	Corp
1	3.0%	2.5%	0.0%	0.0%	1.0%	5.5%	6.5%
2	3.5	2.5	0.2	0.0	1.0	6.2	7.2
3	4.0	2.5	0.4	0.5	1.0	6.9	8.4
4	4.0	2.5	0.6	0.5	1.0	7.1	8.6
5	4.0	2.5	0.8	0.5	1.0	7.3	8.8
6	4.0	2.5	1.0	0.5	1.0	7.5	9.0
7	4.0	2.5	1.2	0.5	1.0	7.7	9.2
8	4.0	2.5	1.4	0.5	1.0	7.9	9.4
9	4.0	2.5	1.6	0.5	1.0	8.1	9.6
10	4.0	2.5	1.8	0.5	1.0	8.3	9.8

3. DIV/CLOSE = 2.00/30.68 = .065 = 6.5%

4. Beginning of year price = Close / (1 - .168)
   = 30.68 / .832
   = 36.875

5. 4-year (3 + 3 + 3 + 4)/4 = 3.25 + 2.4 = 5.65%

   6-year (3 + 3 + 3 + 4 + 4 + 4)/6 = 3.5 + 2.4 = 5.9%

   10-year (3 + 3 + 3 + 4 x 7)/10 = 3.7 + 2.4 = 6.1%

6. Since inflation is not expected to change and we don't know anything about the real risk free rate, we need to look at the risk components to determine the answer. If a corporation is stable and has a long, successful trading history, liquidity risk should not be much of an issue and would not be a primary driver of the yield curve. Even with a good history, however, the longer the term of the bond, the greater the possibility that default might become an issue. Therefore, you would expect the default risk premium to increase over time. Maturity risk always increases with time because the likelihood that interest rates will rise at some time in the future becomes greater as the term increases. Therefore, both the maturity and default risk premiums will tend to increase over time which will result in a normal yield curve.

CHAPTER FIVE

THE TIME VALUE OF MONEY

LEARNING OBJECTIVES

After studying this chapter you should understand the following terms and concepts:

1. the time value of money (TVM) and how to solve problems involving present and future value using both the table and calculator methods;
2. ordinary annuities, annuities due and how to solve TVM problems including annuities;
3. compound interest, effective annual rates (EAR) and how to use them in TVM problems;
4. amortized loans (e.g. mortgage loans) and how they are calculated;
5. perpetuities, continuous compounding, multi-part problems, uneven streams, and imbedded annuity problems.

CHAPTER SUMMARY

This chapter concentrates on the concept of the time value of money–the idea that a dollar received today is more valuable than a dollar received at some point in the future. Problems involving the present and future value of individual amounts and of annuities are carefully explained and solved. The effect of the interest rate and interest rate compounding on the value of money is explained and demonstrated through various examples. The concepts expressed in this chapter are of vital importance to the understanding of the field of finance, and the student should carefully follow the instructions for problem-solving presented throughout the chapter.

CHAPTER REVIEW

1. The **time value of money** (TVM) is the concept that treats money as having two dimensions: (1) a dollar amount, and (2) a specific time at which the money is received or spent. The fundamental assumption underlying TVM is that "money received today is more valuable than money received at some point in the future, because today's money can be invested and

grow by earning interest for a longer period of time." Closely related to this idea is the understanding that if a person wants to accumulate a particular amount of money at a future date, the interest rate paid on the original amount invested will determine how much must be invested in order for it to grow to the required future amount. The higher the interest rate received, the less money that must be originally invested to grow to the desired amount.

AMOUNT PROBLEMS

2. An **amount** refers to a single amount of money that will grow into a larger sum in the future because of earning interest. **Amount** problems involve two important and related concepts: **present value** and **future value.**

3. **"Future value of an amount"** problems determine how much an amount of money deposited today will be worth at some specified time in the future. The future value will be determined by how much is originally deposited; how long the money remains on deposit; and how often the interest will be paid and at what rate. This amount can be calculated by using the formula,

$$FV_n = PV[FVF_{k,n}]$$

where the future value factor (FVF) is determined by the interest rate per period (k) and the number of periods the amount is on deposit (n). These factors can be found in Table A-1 in the text. The formula can also be stated as

FUTURE VALUE OF AN AMOUNT = AMOUNT DEPOSITED × TABLE FACTOR

This is a simple problem to solve when only one sum of money is deposited, but the calculations become more complicated when multiple sums are involved. When more than one amount is involved, separate calculations must be performed for each amount, and then the answers are added together to get the future value of the various amounts.

4. The **opportunity cost rate** is defined as the rate of interest at which a person could have invested his or her money. The opportunity cost will vary from person to person depending upon his or her investment opportunities.

5. **"Present value of an amount"** problems compute the value of a specified future amount of money in today's terms. If a person wants to have a certain amount of money in five years, he or she will want to know what must be invested today so that it will grow to the desired amount in the time available. The amount that must be deposited today is the **present value** of that future amount. The amount that must be deposited today will also depend upon the following: the value of the future amount, how long the money will remain on deposit, and how often interest will be paid and the rate of that interest.

As with future value calculations, present value amounts may be calculated by using the formula

$$PV = FV_n(PVF_{k,n})$$

where the present value factor (PVF) is determined by the interest rate per period (k) and the number of periods the amount is on deposit (n). These factors can be found in Table A-2 in the text. The formula can also be stated as:

PRESENT VALUE OF AN AMOUNT =
FUTURE AMOUNT DESIRED × TABLE FACTOR

6. **Financial calculators** provide the simplest way to solve most TVM problems, particularly those involving numbers whose values fall in-between the values listed on the tables.

ANNUITY PROBLEMS

7. **Annuities** are defined as a series of equal payments that occur at equal intervals for a specified period of time. **Annuity problems** are more difficult to visualize and can often be more easily understood through the use of **time lines**. Time lines are one way to graphically present the timing and amount of cash flows that relate to a specific problem.

    Annuity payments occur once per period (e.g. once a year or once a month). Annuities can have different characteristics based on when the payment occurs during the period. If the payment occurs at the end of the period, then the annuity is called an **ordinary annuity.** Annuities whose payments occur at the beginning of the period are called **annuities due.** Since payments occur sooner with an annuity due, they are more attractive to the recipient of the payment and less attractive to the payer.

8. **"Future and present value of annuities"** problems are solved in much the same way as future and present value amount problems discussed above. A common application for the future value of an annuity would be to determine how much money could be accumulated over a period of time by making regular deposits in an interest bearing account (e.g. $100/month for 10 years in an account paying 8% per year). The formula for the future value of an annuity is

    $$FVA_n = PMT[FVFA_{k,n}]$$

    where PMT represents the regular deposit (payment) and the future value factor for the annuity (FVFA) is determined by the interest rate per period (k) and the number of periods the amount is on deposit (n). These factors can be found in Table A-3 in the text.

9. A common application for the present value of an annuity is for amortized loans, such as a car loan or a home mortgage, where the principal is paid off gradually during the life of the loan. In this case a borrower might want to know how large a home mortgage could be supported based on an estimated monthly payment (e.g. how large a loan could a borrower get for 30 years, monthly payments, if interest rates are 6% and the borrower can make $1,000 payments every month). The formula for the future value of an annuity is

    $$PVA_n = PMT[PVFA_{k,n}]$$

    where PMT represents the regular payment and the present value factor for the annuity (PVFA) is determined by the interest rate per period (k) and the number of periods of the loan (n). These factors can be found in Table A-4 in the text.

10. Annuities typically do not last forever. If the series of equal payments at equal intervals continues forever, it is called a **perpetuity**. The formula for calculating the present value of a perpetuity is as follows:

$$PV_P = PMT/k$$

Where **PMT** is the amount of the equal payment and **k** is the interest rate. This formula is most often used to calculate the price of preferred stock, or to calculate the value of a fair price for a company using the present value of the company's earnings into perpetuity.

11. A **sinking fund** is a special account set up and regularly paid into by borrowers, and dedicated to repaying a bond's principal. Bonds are non-amortized debt, which means that borrowers make only interest payments until the maturity date when the principal is due. When bonds mature, a great deal of money becomes due, and there is often justifiable concern as to whether a company will have the large amounts needed to pay off the debt. The sinking fund is a solution to this problem.

12. Interest rates are usually paid more than once a year; this is known as **compounding**. Compounding is important because after the first compounding period, the investor is earning interest not only on the principal but also on the previously earned interest. The more often interest is compounded, the better off the investor will be but the more it will cost the borrower. In order to use the present and future value tables when interest is compounded more than once a year, adjustments must be made to the number of periods and to the rate used.

NUMBER OF PERIODS = NUMBER OF YEARS × NUMBER OF TIMES A YEAR COMPOUNDING OCCURS

RATE = INTEREST RATE/NUMBER OF TIMES A YEAR COMPOUNDING OCCURS

13. Because compounding will affect the amount of interest a person pays or receives, the nominal or stated interest rates may make comparisons between loan terms difficult (e.g. 8.5% compounded quarterly vs. 8.35% compounded monthly) The percentages used in the previous example are called the **annual percentage rates** or the **nominal rates**. Lenders are required to state the **effective annual rate (EAR),** which is the annually compounded interest rate that pays the same interest as a lower rate compounded more frequently. In other words, it is the rate which regardless of the stated interest (e.g. 12% compounded monthly), equates to the rate if the interest was only compounded annually. In this case of 12% compounded monthly, the EAR would be 12.68%.

The EAR allows comparison between loans that are compounded differently. As a quick method of comparing the same rate but when compounding occurs more frequently, the more often compounding occurs with the same nominal rate, the higher the EAR will be. At a 12% nominal interest rate, the borrower will pay less interest with less frequent compounding, while the lender will collect more interest when the interest is compounded more frequently.

14. **Mortgage loans** or **mortgages** are used to buy real estate such as homes or office buildings. A mortgage is an amortized loan, typically with monthly compounding and payments that may be spread out over as long as 30 years. During the early years of the loan, most of the payment will be devoted to interest, while during the last years of the loan, most of the payment will go to

repay the principal. Because mortgage interest is tax deductible, homeowners will have larger tax deductions during the early years of the mortgage.

15. Many problems will involve multiple parts that require combining two or more time value of money techniques. Time lines to graphically represent the various parts of the problem will assist in solving these types of problems. The separate parts are resolved sequentially, and then their answers are combined to achieve a final answer for the problem.

16. When problems involve uneven streams of payments, which is the most common way for persons to pay into retirement or savings plans over their lifetime, the annuity method of calculating future value cannot be used. Each payment must then be handled as an individual problem to come up with an accurate solution. When uneven streams of payments have sections of even streams of payments, this is called an **imbedded annuity**. The section that contains the even stream of payments may be treated as an annuity in order to reduce the number of separate calculations that are required to solve the problem. Many financial calculators and/or computers have the capability to solve problems with uneven cash streams. These techniques are particularly important in capital budgeting, discussed in Chapters 10 and 11.

TESTING YOUR UNDERSTANDING

TRUE-FALSE QUESTIONS

____1. All persons will have the identical opportunity cost rate.

____2. A perpetuity may be thought of as an annuity that continues forever.

____3. The Truth in Lending Act requires that lenders disclose the EAR.

____4. The present value of a future amount will be higher with a higher interest rate.

____5. Present value and future value problems in real-life often require combining two or more time value problems.

____6. Most annuities are categorized as annuities due.

____7. In order to calculate the future value of a perpetuity, one need only to consult an existing table.

____8. Lenders prefer less frequent compounding; borrowers prefer more frequent compounding.

____9. When the compounding period is one year and the interest is compounded annually, the EAR and the nominal rate of interest will be the same.

____10. Mortgage interest is tax deductible for individuals.

____11. During the final years of a mortgage loan, most of the payments go toward the paying of interest.

____12. The present value of a future amount is smaller when interest rates decrease.

58   Chapter 5

____13. A sinking fund protects investors or lenders from big losses.

____14. Interest rates are usually compounded annually.

____15. When no compounding period is mentioned, quarterly compounding should be assumed.

____16. The frequency of compounding affects the actual amount of interest being paid.

____17. Amortized loans usually have payments that vary periodically over the loan's life.

____18. Mortgage loans are structured so that halfway through a 30-year loan, half of the loan has been paid off.

____19. The future value of a perpetuity makes no sense because the payments never end.

____20. Problems involving uneven streams of payments require that each payment be handled as an individual amount.

MULTIPLE CHOICE QUESTIONS

1. Financial calculators:
    a. make most computations easier.
    b. eliminate the need to understand the concepts behind time value.
    c. are used almost exclusively in real-life.
    d. a and c only.

2. The continuous compounding of interest:
    a. is mathematically impossible.
    b. can easily be calculated without a calculator.
    c. requires a calculator to calculate.
    d. none of the above.

3. The future or present value of an amount depends upon:
    a. the interest rate.
    b. the number of periods.
    c. number of times per year compounding occurs.
    d. all of the above.

4. When a firm is valued at the present value of its annual earnings divided by the relevant interest rate:
    a. this is called the Capitalization of Earnings.
    b. the firm is being valued as a perpetuity.
    c. a and b.
    d. none of the above.

5. In which case will an investor receive the most interest:
   a. 10%, compounded annually.
   b. 10%, compounded monthly.
   c. 10%, compounded continuously.
   d. 10%, compounded daily.

6. When a banker quotes an interest rate of 8% compounded semiannually, he is quoting the:
   a. nominal rate.
   b. APR.
   c. EAR.
   d. both a and b.

7. Annuities:
   a. are a stream of equal payments at unequal time intervals.
   b. are a stream of equal payments at equal time intervals.
   c. are a stream of equal payments that continue forever.
   d. all of the above.
   e. none of the above.

8. Sinking funds:
   a. are a series of equal payments.
   b. are made to an account designated to pay off a bond's principal.
   c. help to reassure bondholders that a company can repay a bond's principal at maturity.
   d. all of the above.

9. At 12% interest compounded quarterly for 5 years, what is the interest rate and the number of periods that will be computed before a present or future value table can be used?
   a. 12%, 5 periods
   b. 6%, 10 periods
   c. 3%, 20 periods
   d. 4%, 15 periods

10. Mortgage loans:
    a. are used to purchase real estate.
    b. are primarily long term.
    c. usually have more than half the balance remaining when the loan is half-way to maturity.
    d. have tax deductible interest.
    e. all of the above.

11. The basic rule of the time value of money is:
    a. investments will always be worth more tomorrow than they are today
    b. it's always wiser to save a dollar for tomorrow than to spend it today
    c. a dollar in hand today is worth more than a dollar promised at some time in the future
    d. all of the above express an aspect of the basic rule of time value of money

12. The present value of a future amount:
    a. will always be less than the future amount
    b. can be calculated precisely if the discount rate and number of periods is known
    c. is worth less than the future value
    d. both a. and b. above are true

13. Which of the following formulas is the correct way to express a future value two years into the future based on a present value and an interest rate? $FV_2 =$
   a. $PV(1+k) + PV(1+k)(k)$
   b. $PV(1+k)(1+k)$
   c. $PV(1+k)^2$
   d. all of the above are correct

14. If you want to know how much money you will have at the end of 15 years if you make quarterly deposits in a bank that pays 6% interest compounded quarterly, you should go to Table A-3 and look up the value for n = _____ and k = _____.
   a. 15, 6%
   b. 15, 1.5%
   c. 60, 6%
   d. 60, 1.5%

15. If you use a financial calculator to solve a mortgage problem and you are given the amount of the loan, the interest rate and the term of the loan, you will be solving for:
   a. n
   b. I/Y
   c. PV
   d. FV
   e. PMT

16. When comparing an annuity due with an ordinary annuity with the same payment and duration, the annuity due will always have a _____ present value and will always have a _____ future value.
   a. higher; higher
   b. higher; lower
   c. lower, higher
   d. lower, lower

17. Which of the following terms mean the same thing
   a. APR, EAR, nominal rate
   b. APR, annual rate, nominal rate
   c. EAR, annual rate, nominal rate
   d. APR, EAR, annual rate

18. With amortized loans, such as a mortgage:
   a. interest is always more than half of the payment amount
   b. return of principal is always more than half of the payment amount
   c. the proportion of interest to the total decreases later in the payment schedule
   d. the proportion of interest to the total increases later in the payment schedule.

19. An imbedded annuity is:
    a. an annuity that starts at the beginning of a stream of payments but doesn't continue for the entire payment stream
    b. an annuity that starts during a payment stream (not at the beginning) and continues to the end of the payment stream
    c. an annuity that starts after the beginning of a payment stream and concludes before the end of the payment stream
    d. all of the above describe imbedded annuities

20. A perpetuity:
    a. has infinite value because the payments continue forever
    b. can be valued (PV) if the payment amount and interest rate are known
    c. don't exist in the financial world
    d. none of the above are true

FILL IN THE BLANK QUESTIONS

1. An _____ is a single sum of money that grows with interest over time to a larger sum.

2. When a credit card company quotes an annual rate of 10% compounded monthly, the EAR will be _____ than the quoted rate.

3. If a person wants to know what an amount deposited today at 4% will be worth in 4 years, he is asking its _____ value.

4. An _____ annuity has payments that occur at the end of the time periods

5. Debt is _____ when the principal is paid off during the life of the loan.

6. When a person wants to know what he must deposit today so that in 5 years he will have $5,000, he is asking its _____ value.

7. Preferred stock is valued as a _____.

8. _____ are specially designated funds into which the company deposits money so that a bond can be paid off at maturity.

9. A dollar received today is worth _____ than a dollar received one year from today.

10. _____ is earning interest on previously earned interest.

11. The _____ is the same as the nominal rate.

PROBLEMS

1. If a person deposits $11,500 in the bank today, what will the money be worth in 3 years at 8% if it's a.) compounded semi-annually; b.) compounded quarterly; and c.) compounded annually.

2. What is the EAR for 8% if a.) compounded annually; b.) compounded semi-annually; and c.) compounded quarterly.

3. What is the present value of an ordinary 12-year annuity that pays $1,000 per year when the interest rate is 7%?

4. How much must a person put into the bank today if he wants $50,000 in 5 years at 6% compounded a.) annually and b.) semi-annually.

5. The Abrakadabra Corporation issues preferred stock that pays a quarterly dividend of $3.50 indefinitely. Investors could invest their money at 6% compounded quarterly. For how much will the preferred stock sell?

6. Using the Capitalization of Earnings technique, what is a fair valuation for a company that consistently has earnings after taxes of $4,000,000 when interest rates are 8%? What if interest rates instead were 9%?

7. Candace is selling an apartment building for $220,000. She will pay 10% down and $19,800 a year for 10 years. What is the real purchase price if she could get an interest rate of 5% on invested money?

8. How many years does it take money invested at 9% to double?

9. Allright Corporation started making sinking fund deposits of $20,000 today. Its bank pays 6% compounded semi-annually and the payments will be made every six months for 20 years. What will the fund be worth at the end of that time?

10. Billy thinks he can save enough to deposit $1,200 in the bank at the end of each year for the next 30 years. How much will he have if the bank pays 6% interest, compounded annually?

11. See the previous problem. If instead, Billy can deposit $100 per month in the bank, and the bank compounds interest monthly, how much will Billy have at the end of 30 years? What is the effective annual interest rate (EAR) that Billy will be earning?

12. Barbara and Mike just borrowed $200,000 to purchase a home. The bank gave them a 6% interest rate on a 15 year mortgage. How much will their monthly mortgage payments be? How much less would their payments be if the mortgage was a 30 year mortgage?

ANSWERS TO QUESTIONS

TRUE-FALSE

1. f
2. t
3. t
4. f
5. t
6. f
7. f
8. f
9. t
10. t
11. f
12. f
13. t
14. f
15. f
16. t
17. f
18. f
19. t
20. t

FILL IN THE BLANKS

1. amount
2. higher
3. future
4. ordinary
5. amortized
6. present
7. perpetuity
8. Sinking Funds
9. more
10. Compounding
11. APR

MULTIPLE CHOICE

1. d
2. c
3. d
4. c
5. c
6. d
7. b
8. d
9. c
10. e
11. c
12. d
13. d
14. d
15. e
16. a
17. b
18. c
19. d
20. b

ANSWERS TO PROBLEMS

1. a. FV = $11,500 [FVF$_{4, 6}$] = $11,500 (1.2653) = $14,550.95

    b. FV = $11,500 [FVF$_{2, 12}$] = $11,500 (1.2682) = $14,584.30

    c. FV = $11,500 [FVF$_{8, 3}$] = $11,500 (1.2597) = $14,486.55

2. a. EAR = 8/100 = 8%

    b. EAR = 8.16/100 = 8.16%

    c. EAR = 8.24/100 = 8.24%

3. PVA = $1,000[PVFA$_{7, 12}$] = $1,000 (7.9427) = $7,942.70

4. a. PV = $50,000[PVF$_{6, 5}$] = $50,000 (0.7473) = $37,365

    b. PV = $50,000 [PVF$_{3, 10}$] = $50,000 (0.7441) = $37,205

5. $\dfrac{3.50}{.015}$ = $233.33

6. $\dfrac{\$4,000,000}{.08}$ = $50,000,000

    $\dfrac{\$4,000,000}{.09}$ = $44,444,444

7. Effective price = 10% down payment + PVA
    = $22,000 + $19,800[PVFA$_{5, 10}$]
    = $22,000 + $19,800 (7.7217)
    = $22,000 + $152,889.66
    = $174,889.66

8. FV = PV[FVF$_{9, n}$]
    $2 = $1 [FVF$_{9, n}$]
    FVF$_{9, n}$ = 2.0000
    Search Table A-1 in the 9% column. The closest factor to 2.000 is 1.9926 for 8 years.

9. FVA = $20,000[FVFA$_{3, 40}$](1.03)
    = $20,000 (75.4013)(1.03)
    = $1,553,266.78

10. PMT =   1,200
    n =   30
    I/Y =   6
    PV =   0
    FV = ? = $94,869.82

11. PMT = 100
    n = 360
    I/Y = .5
    PV = 0
    FV = $100,451.50

    EAR = $(1 + .06/12)^{12} - 1 = .0617$ or 6.17%

12. PV = 200,000
    n = 180
    I/Y = .5
    FV = 0
    PMT = ? = $1,687.71

    PV = 200,000
    n = 360
    I/Y = .5
    FV = 0
    PMT = ? = $1,199.10

    Difference = $1,687.71 - $1,199.10 = $488.61

CHAPTER SIX

THE VALUATION AND CHARACTERISTICS OF BONDS

LEARNING OBJECTIVES

After studying this chapter you should understand the following concepts:

1. the difference between the valuation of real assets and financial assets;
2. what the terms investment and return on investment mean;
3. bond valuation, terminology, and practice;
4. maturity risk and the factors with which it is associated;
5. how to calculate the yield of a bond when it sells at a given price;
6. call provisions and their effect on bond prices;
7. features of convertible bonds and their impact on diluted EPS;
8. features of bonds and bond agreements not directly related to pricing.

CHAPTER SUMMARY

This chapter examines in great detail the process of how financial assets, particularly bonds, are valued and what factors directly and indirectly affect their prices. Bond value is related to the time value of money concept that we studied in Chapter 5, so a brief review of the present value of an amount and of an annuity may be helpful in understanding this chapter. The terminology referring to bond valuation is introduced and used throughout the chapter, and it is essential that the student study and understand these terms before continuing with the remainder of the chapter. The chapter concludes with an explanation of various types of call provisions, convertible bonds along with other factors that are only indirectly associated with bond valuation.

CHAPTER REVIEW

THE BASIS OF VALUE

1. Unlike real assets that provide service, **financial assets** are pieces of paper that must rely on something else to give them value. Financial assets receive their value from the value of the future cash flows they are expected to return. Because the amounts of interest and repayment are cash flows that will be received at some future date, the value of a security is calculated to be the **present value of these future cash flows.**

    a.) **Investing** is defined as using a resource in a manner that provides future benefits as opposed to immediate satisfaction. For most people this equates to saving money rather than immediately spending it. In order to persuade people to postpone immediate gratification, it is necessary to convince them that their money will be put to work to earn more money during the time it is invested. When people choose to buy stock, they are making an **equity investment.** The most common way to make a **debt investment** is to purchase bonds.

    b.) **Return** is what an investor receives for making an investment. It can be expressed in either dollars or percents. If an investment is held for one year:

    RATE OF RETURN = INTEREST RECEIVED/AMOUNT INVESTED

    If instead of knowing the amount invested and the interest received, a person knows the interest amount and the interest rate, the formula can be modified to solve for the value of a one year investment:

    PRESENT VALUE OF INVESTMENT = INTEREST AMOUNT/(1+INTEREST RATE)

    OR

    $$PV = \frac{FV_1}{(1+k)}$$

    The terms **yield** and **rate of return** are used interchangeably.

BOND VALUATION

2. **Bonds** represent a debt relationship. Companies can raise large amounts of money by borrowing small amounts of money from numerous lenders. This is often done by issuing bonds. The time period of the bond is known as its **term**. A bond is a legal **promissory note** that matures on the last day of its term, when the **par value** or **face value** or **maturity value** of the bond will be repaid. Interest payments are paid to the borrowers throughout the term, usually in semiannual payments. Bondholders have extended credit to the borrowing organization so they are regarded as **creditors** of the company.

3. The **coupon rate** of a bond is the interest rate that is set at the time the bond is issued. These rates and **coupon payments** are fixed throughout the term of the bond. When the bond is sold by the issuing company to an original investor for the first time, this transaction occurs in the primary market. Any subsequent selling or buying of the bond occurs in the secondary market.

4. Bond interest rates are fixed throughout their term, but market interest rates fluctuate all the time. The only way a bond with a fixed interest rate can be resold on the secondary market is if the price that the bond will be sold for is allowed to vary as market interest rates go up or down.

5. There is an **inverse relationship** between the value of bonds and market interest rates. When market interest rates increase and exceed the interest rate paid by a particular bond (e.g. the coupon rate) the price that investors will pay for that bond *decreases*. When market interest rates decrease and pay less than the interest rate paid by a particular bond, the price that investors will pay for that bond *increases*. Remember,

WHEN MARKET INTEREST RATES *INCREASE*, BOND VALUES *DECREASE*.

Bonds selling for more than their face value are said to be trading at a **premium**, while bonds selling below their face value are said to be selling at a **discount.**

6. The price of a bond is the present value of its expected future cash flows, or the present value of its interest payments and the single amount it will repay upon maturity. The interest payments are a stream of even amounts paid at equal intervals and can be valued as an annuity. So the formula for bond valuation is:

PRESENT VALUE OF BOND = PRESENT VALUE OF INTEREST PAYMENTS + PRESENT VALUE OF PRINCIPAL REPAYMENT

Or

$$P_B = PMT[PVFA_{kn}] + FV[PVF_{kn}]$$

7. There are two interest rates associated with pricing a bond. The coupon rate is fixed and is used **ONLY** to calculate the amount of the interest payments. The current market interest rate on comparable bonds is the discount rate used to calculate the present value of the principal repayment and the present value of the interest payments.

8. **Maturity risk, price risk,** and **interest rate risk** are terms associated with the risk investors face if they purchase a bond with a fixed interest rate when there is the chance that market rates will increase. If market rates increase and the investor has to sell the bond to someone else, the bond will be sold at a loss. The longer the term of a bond, the higher the risk, because the price of long-term bonds fluctuates more with interest rate changes than do short-term bonds.

9. Sometimes the issuer of bonds would like to pay off the debt early. This usually happens when the interest rate on the bond is much higher than current market rates, and issuers could pay off the existing bonds by issuing bonds that carry a lower interest rate (e.g. the current market rate).

   a) **Call provisions** are clauses in bond agreements that give the issuing organizations **the right** to pay off bonds before their maturity date, under certain circumstances. Bondholders may not be enthusiastic about such provisions, because if they have a bond that pays 12% and market rates have dropped to only 8%, they will want to continue to collect their 12%

interest for all the years until the bond is scheduled to mature.

b) In order to appease bondholders, call provisions usually include **call premiums**, which are extra amounts that must be paid to bondholders if the bond is called in before its maturity date.

c) In addition, **call protection** specifies that bonds cannot be called in for a certain number of years after they are issued. Bonds that contain call provisions often pay a higher interest rate to compensate bondholders for the uncertainties associated with the call provisions.

d) In order to calculate the price (present value) of a bond with a call provision, a determination must be made as to the likelihood of the call being exercised. If the call won't be exercised, then the price of the bond is determined by the present value of all the future cash flows up to maturity. If the bond is likely to be called (e.g. if the current market rate is below the coupon rate on the bond), then the price is determined by the present value of the bond's cash flows up to the call date. These are the only future cash flows that are likely to occur if the bond is called.

CONVERTIBLE BONDS

10. **Convertible bonds** can, **at the option of the owner**, be converted from debt into a specified number of shares of stock. This usually happens when the stock price increases enough so that the shares of stock will be worth more than the bond. Convertible bonds usually carry a lower coupon rate than comparable bonds without the convertible feature because of the potential advantages that will accrue to the bondholder. Conversion prices are usually set 15% to 30% above the stock's market price at the time the conversion is issued. The conversion ratio is calculated as follows:

**CONVERSION RATIO = BOND'S PAR VALUE/CONVERSION PRICE
= SHARES EXCHANGED**

a) Convertible bonds offer the following advantages to the issuing companies: (1) may allow companies that otherwise might have difficulty raising debt to do so; (2) may be viewed as a way to sell equity at above the market price; (3) since convertible bonds are viewed by investors as purchasing equity, investors require less restrictions than on other debt.

b) Convertible bonds offer the following advantages to buyers: (1) the opportunity to participate in stock price appreciation; (2) protection against the downside risk associated with the investment in stock.

c) Convertible bonds usually contain call provisions so that bondholders can't continue to take advantage of both interest payments and the potential to receive stock appreciation. Call provisions also help companies manage their capital structure.

d) Calculating the value of a convertible bond is complicated because it is a function of all of the following: (1) the value of the bond without the convertible feature; (2) the value of the stock that would be received upon conversion; (3) the current interest rate in the market.

e) Since convertible bonds can be converted to stock at the bondholder's discretion, it is important for current stockholders to know how many additional shares might become outstanding as a result of bond conversions. FASB has required that companies calculate "diluted earnings per share" which, among other things, includes the effect on earnings of the potential additional outstanding shares that might result from bond conversions. Stockholders can compare regular EPS to diluted EPS to determine the potential effect of convertible bonds on their investment.

INSTITUTIONAL CHARACTERISTICS OF BONDS

11. **Bearer bonds** belong to whoever has physical possession of the securities, which makes them vulnerable to theft or loss. **Registered bonds** are recorded with a transfer agent, and only the owner of record may sell them.

    a.) **Secured bonds** are backed by the assets of the issuing company. If the borrower should default on the bond, the bondholders can take possession of the assets and sell them to recover all or part of their investment. Bonds secured by real estate are called **mortgage bonds**.

    b.) **Debentures** are bonds that are not secured by assets, but only by the reputation and creditworthiness of the issuing company. They pay higher yields than secured bonds because they are riskier.

    c.) Debt that is **subordinated** has a lower priority for repayment than does other debt. A debt with priority over subordinated debt is known as **senior debt.** Subordinated debt is also riskier than senior or unsubordinated debt, and so requires a higher rate of return.

    d.) **Junk bonds** are issued by companies that are not in good financial health. They pay relatively high interest rates because they are risky investments.

    e.) **Zero coupon bonds** pay no interest throughout the term of the bond. These bonds sell for a much lower price than bonds with the same face value and that make interest payments throughout their life. US Savings Bonds are the most common example of zero coupon bonds. However, zero coupon bonds issued by corporations have one significant tax disadvantage. Even though no interest is paid, bondholders must recognize interest income related to the increase in the value of the bonds as they approach maturity. That means that zero coupon bondholders must recognize income even though they don't receive any cash related to their interest income.

12. **Quality ratings** are assigned to bonds that reflect their chances of going into default. The higher the ratings, the less the chance of going into default. Bond rating agencies such as Moody's and Standard and Poor's rate bonds by studying the financial conditions of the issuing companies and market conditions in general. Bond ratings are based on financial numbers and information, but also depend upon the subjective evaluation of the analyst and the rating agency. A "AAA" rating by Standard and Poor's and a "Aaa" rating by Moody's represent the highest ratings. The higher the rating, the lower the risk, the lower the required rate of return and the lower interest expense incurred by the issuing company. Conversely, the lower the rating, the

higher the risk, the higher the required rate of return and the higher interest expense incurred by the issuing company. During high market interest rates (which are associated with difficult times) and recessions (when marginal companies tend to have high failure rates) there tends to be a bigger spread between yields of low-risk bonds and yields of high-risk bonds.

Institutional investors purchase most bonds and by law are restricted from purchasing anything less than **investment grade bonds** (e.g. "Baa for Moody's and "BBB" for Standard and Poor's). A firm whose bonds are not rated as investment grade will find a very limited market for its debt.

13. **Bond indentures** are restrictions that govern the activities of the borrowers until the debt is paid off. These covenants restrict the actions of firms that might make the firm riskier and which would affect the rating and price of the firm's bonds. Typically such restrictions would include the maintenance of certain levels for financial ratios or limitations on further borrowing. The **trustee** named for each bond issue administers and enforces the indentures on behalf of the bondholders. **Sinking funds** are also a method used to make sure that the money needed for repayment is there at the maturity date of the debt.

TESTING YOUR UNDERSTANDING

TRUE-FALSE QUESTIONS

____1. Zero coupon bonds require the semi-annual payment of interest to the bondholder.

____2. A security will usually sell in financial markets for very close to the present value of its expected future cash flows.

____3. An investor sacrifices immediate consumption for future benefits.

____4. It is usually easier for a company to borrow smaller amounts from numerous investors than a large amount from one investor.

____5. A bond is a promissory note.

____6. Bonds normally sell for their face value in the secondary market.

____7. Previously issued bonds' interest payments vary with market interest rates.

____8. Bonds secured by real estate are called mortgage bonds.

____9. Debentures are less risky than secured bonds, because they are secured by specific assets of the company.

____10. Firms that issue bonds can raise large amounts of money by spreading the loan out among a number of lenders.

____11. Bonds are amortized debt.

____12. All bonds contain coupons which must be detached and sent in so that the interest check can be mailed.

____13. When market interest rates have changed, there are two interest rates associated with pricing a bond – the coupon rate and the current market rate.

____14. When people refer to a bond's yield, they are usually referring to its yield to maturity.

____15. Bond issuers are more likely to want to pay off their indebtedness early when market interest rates have risen a great deal since the bonds were issued.

____16. Investors who buy bonds tend to like call provisions.

____17. When a bond has a call provision, the company still has to make a decision as to whether or not to exercise the call.

____18. Convertible bonds generally must be issued at higher interest rates than regular bonds.

MULTIPLE CHOICE QUESTIONS

1. Bond ratings:
   a. impact the rate of return the bond must offer.
   b. affect the market for a company's debt.
   c. are based on financial analysis and subjective evaluation.
   d. all of the above.

2. Investment grade bonds:
   a. are considered to be substandard.
   b. may be purchased by institutional investors.
   c. are defined as junk bonds.
   d. none of the above.

3. Bond indentures:
   a. are intended to protect bondholders.
   b. may restrict further borrowing by the issuing firm.
   c. may require the maintenance of certain financial ratio levels.
   d. all of the above.

4. Market interest rates and bond valuations:
   a. have an inverse relationship.
   b. vary upward together.
   c. have no relationship.
   d. vary downward together.

74   Chapter 6

5. Call provisions:
   a. are disliked by investors.
   b. generally include a call premium.
   c. both a. and b. above.
   d. none of the above.

6. Senior debt:
   a. is subordinated to subordinated debentures.
   b. has a higher priority for repayment than subordinated debt.
   c. is riskier than subordinated debentures.
   d. both a and c.

7. Convertible bonds:
   a. can be converted into a specific number of shares of common stock.
   b. are generally converted into stock when the stock's price decreases.
   c. are considered to be an unattractive feature that requires a higher yield.
   d. both b and c.

8. Bondholders generally utilize the conversion privilege on a convertible bond when:
   a. the stock price rises enough to make the converted shares worth more than the bond.
   b. when the stock price falls enough to make the converted shares worth less than the bond value.
   c. when the stock price remains constant for a long period of time.
   d. none of the above.

9. Debentures:
   a. are unsecured debt.
   b. rely on the general creditworthiness of the issuing firm.
   c. are more risky than secured debt.
   d. all of the above.

10. Transfer agents:
    a. are often banks.
    b. keep track of the owners of securities.
    c. are associated with bearer bonds.
    d. a and b only.

11. A bond:
    a. is non-amortized debt.
    b. is a promissory note.
    c. has a par or face value.
    d. all of the above.

12. A bond selling for its face value is said to be trading:
    a. at a premium.
    b. at par value.
    c. at a discount.
    d. at a bargain.

13. Call protections:
    a. prevent call provisions from ever being executed.
    b. determine the amount of premium that must be paid if call provisions are executed.
    c. prevent call provisions from being executed for a specified period of time after the bond is issued.
    d. none of the above.

14. Subordinated means:
    a. debts are secured by specific assets.
    b. debts have lower priority for repayment.
    c. debts have higher priority for repayment.
    d. none of the above.

15. The most common example of a zero coupon bond is:
    a. a U.S. Savings Bond.
    b. a convertible bond.
    c. a subordinated bond.
    d. a senior bond.

16. The value of a bond is equal to:
    a. the sum of the interest payments over the life of the bond
    b. the sum of the interest payments and par value over the life of the bond
    c. the PV of the interest payments over the life of the bond
    d. the PV of the interest payments and the return of principal over the life of the bond

17. For an annual bond, the interest payment is calculated by multiplying:
    a. the coupon rate times the market value of the bond
    b. the coupon rate times the par value of the bond
    c. the market rate times the market value of the bond
    d. the market rate times the par value of the bond

18. If a $1,000 8% semiannual bond matures, how much money will the bondholder receive as a final payment?
    a. $1,000
    b. $1,040
    c. $1,080
    d. Cannot be determined without knowing the term of the bond

19. A 15-year, 8% semiannual bond was issued four years ago. The market rate is now 7.5% for comparable bonds. Without doing the calculation, you would expect the PV of the bond to be:
    a. slightly less than $1,000
    b. slightly more than $1,000
    c. a lot less than $1,000
    d. a lot more than $1,000

76   Chapter 6

20. In comparing an 8-year bond to a 30-year bond issued at the same time with the same coupon rate, if the market rate has increased since the bonds were issued:
   a. the value of the 8-year bond will have increased more than the value of the 30-year bond
   b. the value of the 30-year bond will have increased more than the value of the 8-year bond
   c. the value of the 8-year bond will have decreased more than the value of the 30-year bond
   d. the value of the 30-year bond will have decreased more than the value of the 8-year bond

FILL-IN THE BLANK QUESTIONS

1. US Savings Bonds are the most common examples of _____ bonds.

2. Bonds are _____ debt, which means that there are no repayments of principal until maturity.

3. Bond interest payments may be treated as an _____ when bonds are valued.

4. A bond's principal is always equal to its _____ value.

5. Two other names for maturity risk are _____ risk and _____ risk.

6. A _____ is a clause in bond agreement that gives the issuing organization the right to pay off the bond prior to its maturity date.

7. Borrowing money at lower interest rates and using it to retire higher interest debt is known as _____.

8. Costs associated with issuing new bonds are known as _____ costs.

9. Bonds that sell for prices far below the prices associated with the valuation techniques are usually much _____ risky than average.

10. _____ bonds are more susceptible to loss or theft than are registered bonds.

11. _____ bonds are backed by the value of specific assets of the company.

12. Bonds selling above their face value are said to be trading at a _____.

13. Bonds selling below face value are said to trade at a _____.

14. The _____ of a bond is the annual interest payment divided by the bond's current price.

15. The longer the term, the _____ the maturity risk.

16. _____ must be paid to bondholders if call provisions are executed.

17. A call premium is also known as a _____.

PROBLEMS

FOR ALL PROBLEMS, ASSUME SEMI-ANNUAL INTEREST PAYMENTS.

1. What will a person be able to sell a newly issued 10-year, $1,000 bond paying 6% interest for, if a few days after the purchase market interest rates increase to 10%?

2. A corporation issued a 6%, 15-year bond, ten years ago. At that time it sold for its $1,000 face value. Today comparable bonds are yielding 10%. What must the bond sell for today to yield 10% to the buyer? What is its current yield?

3. A corporation issued a 12%, 20-year bond, 14 years ago. At the time of issue, it sold for its face value of $1,000. Today comparable bonds are yielding 8%. What will the bond sell for today to yield 8% to the buyer? What is its current yield?

4. A $1,000, 20-year bond was issued 8 years ago with a call provision that allows it to be retired any time after the first 10 years with the payment of an additional year's interest. The bond's coupon rate is 14%, and interest rates on comparable bonds today are 8%. What is the bond worth today if it did not have a call feature? What is the bond worth today with the call feature?

5. Tomorrow a company is issuing a 10-year bond with a face value of $5,000 that will pay a 10% coupon rate. Market interest rates have increased to 12%. What will each bond sell for?

6. What is the current yield of a bond that pays $20 in annual interest and is selling for $500?

7. A corporation issued a $5,000, 20 year bond, five years ago at 10% interest. Comparable bonds yield 8% today. What should the bond sell for today?

8. Before calculating the selling price of the bond in problem 7, what did you know about today's value of the bond compared to its face value? Why?

9. A $5,000 bond is convertible into 100 shares of stock. The price of the stock is currently $80 a share. If the bondholder converts the bond into stock, what is the gain/loss?

10. A company had net income of $1,000,000 with 200,000 outstanding shares. Assume that 500, 8% convertible bonds can be converted to 30 shares of common stock each. If this is the only adjustment to EPS, calculate the company's diluted EPS, assuming a 40% tax rate.

ANSWERS TO QUESTIONS

TRUE-FALSE

1. f
2. f
3. t
4. t
5. t
6. t
7. f
8. f
9. t
10. f
11. t
12. f
13. f
14. t
15. t
16. f
17. f
18. t
19. f

FILL IN THE BLANKS

1. zero coupon
2. non-amortized
3. annuity
4. face
5. price, interest rate
6. call provision
7. refunding the debt
8. flotation
9. more
10. bearer
11. Secured
12. premium
13. discount
14. current yield
15. greater
16. Call premiums
17. call penalty

MULTIPLE CHOICE

1. d
2. b
3. d
4. a
5. c
6. b
7. a
8. a
9. d
10. d
11. d
12. b
13. c
14. b
15. a
16. d
17. b
18. b
19. b
20. d

ANSWERS TO PROBLEMS

1. $P_B = 30[PVFA_{5,20}] + 1,000[PVF_{5, 20}]$
   $= 30 (12.4622) + (0.3769)$
   $= 373.87 + 376.90$
   $= 750.77$

2. $P_B = 30[PVFA_{5, 10}] + 1,000[PVF_{5, 10}]$
   $= 30 (7.7217) + (0.6139)$
   $= 231.65 + 613.90$
   $= 845.55$

   Current yield $= \dfrac{60}{845.55} = 7.1\%$

3. $P_B = 60[PVFA_{4,12}] + 1000[PVF_{4, 12}]$
   $= 60 (9.3851) + (0.6246)$
   $= 563.10 + 624.60$
   $= 1187.70$

   Current yield $= \dfrac{120}{1187.70} = 10.1\%$

4. $P_B = 70[PVFA_{4,24}] + 1000[PVF_{4, 24}]$
   $= 70 (15.2470) + (0.3901)$
   $= 1067.29 + 390.10$
   $= 1457.39$

   $P_B = 70[PVFA_{4,4}] + 1140[PVF_{4, 4}]$
   $= 70 (3.6299) + 1140(0.8548)$
   $= 254.09 + 974.47$
   $= 1228.56$

5. $P_B = 250[PVFA_{6,20}] + 5000[PVF_{6, 20}]$
   $= 250 (11.4699) + 5000(0.3118)$
   $= 2867.48 + 1559.00$
   $= 4426.48$

6. $\dfrac{\$20}{\$500} = 4\%$

7. $P_B = 250[PVFA_{4, 30}] + 5,000[PVF_{4, 30}]$
   $= 250 (17.2920) + 5,000 (0.3083)$
   $= 4,323 + 1,541.50$
   $= 5,864.50$

8. The current market value would be higher than the face value because the interest rate had dropped and there is an inverse relationship between bond prices and interest rates.

9. Stock value $= \$80 \times 100$ shares $= \$8,000$
   Bond value $= \underline{5,000}$
   Gain $= \$3,000$

10. Increase in Net Income: $500,000 x 8% x .6 = $24,000
Increase in Shares: 500 x 30 = 15,000 shares

Diluted EPS = ($1,000,000 + $24,000)/(200,000 + 15,000) = $4.76

CHAPTER SEVEN

THE VALUATION AND CHARACTERISTICS OF STOCKS

LEARNING OBJECTIVES

After studying this chapter you should understand the following terms and concepts:

1. common stock ownership and how to calculate its return on investment;
2. the differences between cash flows from stocks and cash flows from bonds;
3. how to use the constant (Gordon) growth and two-stage growth models to value common stock;
4. why some stocks do not pay dividends and how these types of stock are valued;
5. how corporations are organized and who controls their activities;
6. the characteristics of preferred stock, how it differs from both bonds and common stock and how it is valued;
7. the two basic approaches to securities analysis – fundamental analysis and technical analysis;
8. the Efficient Market Hypothesis
9. how stock options and warrants function in financial markets

CHAPTER SUMMARY

While the previous chapter looked at debt securities, this chapter takes an in-depth look at equity securities, common stock, preferred stock, stock options and warrants. It first takes a look at how common stock is valued based on the cash flows that investors can expect to receive from their investment. The various growth models used to value common stock are examined in detail, and the special situation of valuing stocks that do not pay dividends is discussed. Corporate organization and the rights of stockholders is explained. The characteristics of preferred stock are discussed as well as the method of valuation. Then the chapter takes a look at the two approaches to securities analysis, and the efficient market hypothesis is defined and examined. Finally, the chapter discusses the function of stock options and warrants in financial markets. Basic definitions are provided, and the use of both put and call options are introduced.

CHAPTER REVIEW

COMMON STOCK

1. **Common stockholders** are the owners of corporations. They vote to elect directors who then appoint top managers to run the firm. The large number of shares and the large number of stockholders for most corporations means that individual stockholders have virtually no control over the activities of the corporation, so their ownership role is severely restricted. People purchase common stock as an investment, not because they expect to play an ownership role.

2. Stockholders receive two kinds of returns from their investment. Corporations may pay dividends, and the stock may be sold for a higher (or lower) price than the price paid to purchase it. The gain or loss on the sale of the stock is called a **capital gain or capital loss.** The formula used to value the return on common stock that is held for **one year** is:

    RETURN = [DIVIDEND + (SALE PRICE − PURCHASE PRICE)]/PURCHASE PRICE

    Or

    $$k = \frac{D_1 + (P_1 - P_0)}{P_0}$$

    If the stock is sold for less than the purchase price, the return may be negative.

    If you want to calculate the price of the stock today, rework the equation and solve for P_0:

    PRICE = DIVIDEND + SALE PRICE/(1 + INTEREST RATE)

    Or

    $$P_0 = \frac{D_1 + P_1}{(1 + k)}$$

3. There are important differences between the cash flows associated with bonds and the cash flows associated with common stocks. A bond's interest payments are similar to dividends paid to common stockholders, but the bond's interest payments are guaranteed and are a fixed amount. **Neither the payment of dividends nor the amount of those dividends to common stockholders is guaranteed.** Bondholders are guaranteed the receipt of the face value of the bond when it is held to maturity, but stockholders must sell at whatever price the market dictates in order to get a final payment for their investment. The return of the stockholder's investment doesn't come from the issuing company, but rather from another investor in the secondary market.

4. One method for valuing common stock is based on the present value of its expected cash flows, but its cash flows are much less certain than the cash flows from bonds. Because the amount of future dividends is not certain, estimates about these amounts must be made. The value of a stock based on its future cash flows is called its **intrinsic value.** The intrinsic value of a stock may differ from one investor to another because of differences of opinion as to the amount of future cash flows and the rate at which those future cash flows should be discounted. The market price is a consensus of investors' opinions of that stock's intrinsic value.

The Valuation and Characteristics of Stocks   83

GROWTH MODELS OF COMMON STOCK VALUATION

5. Growth models of common stock valuation are based on the idea that the dividends of many companies increase each year. The basis for these models is the idea of valuing **the future stream of dividends** and ignoring the final payment made when an investor sells the stock. The conceptual support for this model assumes that the selling price at any time in the future is the value of the expected future dividends, and so if an infinite stream of dividends is considered, the future selling price is already accounted for. Because the value of stock is based on the investment community setting the stock's price, the only value they place on the stock is its future stream of dividends.

6. The **Constant Growth Model** (also known as the Gordon model) assumes that a stock's dividend will grow at a constant rate forever. This model is often applied to stable, well established companies. If a stockholder receives a dividend of $1.00 this year and the predicted growth rate is 10%, the dividend for the next year will be $1.00 multiplied by 1.10, which is $1.10. If the growth rate is constant, the next year the dividend will be $1.10 times 1.10 or $1.21. The Gordon Model provides an equation to use to value a share of stock when the growth rate of dividends is expected to continue at a constant rate.

   PRICE = THE NEXT DIVIDEND /[INTEREST RATE − GROWTH RATE]

   Or

   $$P_0 = \frac{D_0(1+g)}{(k-g)} = \frac{D_1}{(k-g)}$$

   D_0 represents the most recent dividend paid (already paid so it's not a future cash flow) and D_1 represents the next dividend to be paid. "k" is the interest (or discount) rate, and "g" is the expected constant growth rate.

7. If a stock is expected to pay a constant dividend amount with no growth, the formula for valuation is:

   PRICE = DIVIDEND AMOUNT/INTEREST RATE

   Or $\qquad P_0 = D_1/k$

   This is the same formula that is used for the present value of a perpetuity. A constant stream of dividends from a no growth stock that continues forever meets the definition of a perpetuity.

8. The Gordon Model can be rearranged to calculate the expected return of a stock:

   EXPECTED RETURN $= \dfrac{\textit{DIVIDEND AMOUNT FOR NEXT PERIOD}}{\textit{PRICE}} + \textit{GROWTH RATE}$

   Or
   $\qquad k_e = D_1/P \;+\; g$

9. The **Two-Stage Growth Model** is often applied to companies that are introducing a new

product that is expected to affect the company's growth rates for a few years. After a short period of high (or low) growth, constant growth is expected. In order to calculate the value of a stock with this two-stage growth pattern, a combination of methods has to be employed. For the first stage, dividends have to be calculated individually. Once the constant growth period has begun, the Gordon model can be used to value all of the rest of the dividends. Be sure to apply the Gordon model to the **beginning of the constant growth period**.

10. Growth rate models for stocks work well in theory, but they should only be considered as **approximations** of stock prices and not as exact values. This is in contrast to bond valuations, where the future cash flows are guaranteed. Bond valuations are extremely accurate.

11. Some firms pay no dividends at all, and yet their stock still has considerable value. These firms are normally young and in rapid growth periods where their earnings are being reinvested to support this growth. Investors most likely expect that these companies will pay large dividends at some point in the future. Other stock valuation models have to be used to approximate the price of a common stock that pays no dividend.

SOME INSTITUTIONAL CHARACTERISTICS OF COMMON STOCK

12. Corporations are controlled by a **board of directors,** who are elected by the stockholders. The board selects the top management of the company, and they in turn select the middle and lower managers. Boards are made up of top managers, major stockholders, and some outside directors who otherwise have no direct role in managing the company.

13. Existing stockholders with **preemptive rights** have the right to maintain their existing proportion of corporate ownership. If new shares of stock are issued, they have the right to purchase the number of shares of new stock that will give them the same total percentage of ownership they had before the new stock was issued. Common stock usually comes with **voting rights** that give the stockholders the right to vote for the Board of Directors and for major changes in the company's charter. Different classes of stock may have different voting rights associated with each class.

14. Stockholders have a **residual claim** on both assets and incomes. Only after all other expenses and claims are paid do stockholders realize any return on their investment. In bad times, there may be nothing left; in good times, there may be huge amounts remaining for the payment of dividends or to reinvest in the business. Dividends result in immediate income for the stockholders. Reinvestment makes the company grow, which if invested effectively, will cause the stock price to increase.

PREFERRED STOCK

15. **Preferred stock** is a form of investment that has some characteristics of bonds and some characteristics of common stock. It pays a constant dividend, which is set when the stock is issued. The formula used to value preferred stock is:

PRICE = PREFERRED STOCK DIVIDEND/INTEREST RATE

Or

$$P_P = D_P/k$$

This is just another form of the formula for valuing a perpetuity, shown earlier. Preferred stock usually is issued with a **cumulative feature** that prohibits the payment of dividends to common stockholders until preferred stock dividends are paid. Should a company declare bankruptcy, preferred stockholders have a claim on corporate assets before common stockholders, but after bondholders. Unlike common stockholders, preferred stockholders typically do not have voting rights. Just as for common stockholders, dividends paid to preferred stockholders are not tax deductible.

16. Characteristics of preferred stock can be grouped as follows:

    Characteristics that are like bonds
    a. Payments to investors – constant
    b. Voting rights – usually none

    Characteristics that are between bonds and stocks
    a. Assurance of payment – the cumulative feature
    b. Priority in bankruptcy
    c. Riskiness as an investment

    Characteristics that are like common stock
    a. Maturity and return of principal – none and no obligation by the issuing company
    b. Tax deductibility of payments to investors – none
    c. Partial tax exemption for dividends received by corporations

SECURITIES ANALYSIS

17. **Securities analysis** is performed to help people select appropriate investments. There are two basic approaches to securities analysis.

    a.) **Fundamental analysis** involves learning everything one can about a business and using that knowledge to make estimates about its future cash flows.

    b.) **Technical analysis** relies on studying past market movements and price changes in order to detect patterns that technical analysts believe will repeat themselves. Because technical analysts prepare elaborate charts that are studied in an effort to detect patterns, they are also known as **chartists**.

18. **The efficient market hypothesis** (EMH) says that information moves so rapidly throughout financial markets that prices adjust almost instantaneously in response to that information. This hypothesis tends to refute the technical analysis school of thought about studying past patterns to predict movements, because stock prices already account for available information. It also refutes the fundamentalists, however, because the professionals who are always performing fundamental analyses will have already spread the information.

STOCK OPTIONS AND WARRANTS

19. An option is a contract that gives the option holder the right (for a limited period of time) to purchase (or sell) an asset to another party. In particular, stock options are financial assets that are purchased by investors who are interested in speculating on the movement of stock prices. An option to "buy" a stock at a fixed price is a **call option**. The option to "sell" stock at a fixed price is a **put option**.

    Call options are typically **written** by investors who believe the price of stock will not increase substantially. For example, a stock may be currently selling for $40. A call option could give the holder of the option the right to purchase that stock for $45 at any time during the next 90 days. Assume that the cost of the option is $2 per share. The writer of the option is working on the assumption that the stock price will not rise above $45 during that period, and therefore the option will not be exercised. In that case, the writer will simply earn $2 per share for the number of options written. On the other hand, the purchaser of the option assumes that the stock price will rise above $47 during that period so that the purchase of the stock at $45 and the subsequent resale at or above $47 will cover the cost of the option, and the remaining proceeds will result in a profit.

    In the example above, the $45 price is called the **strike price**, **striking price** or **exercise price**. When the market price of the stock is below the strike price, the option is **out of the money**. If the market price of the stock is above the strike price, the option is **in the money**.

20. One of the reasons investors buy and sell options is to leverage their investments. Leverage implies potential high returns and high risks. In the above example, if the stock price never reaches $45, the holder of the option will not exercise it and will experience a 100% loss in the investment in the option. On the other hand, if the stock price goes to $49, the holder will make $4 per share on the purchase and sale of the stock, based on a $2 investment in the option – a 100% return.

21. When a call option is written, it is either covered or naked. A covered option means that the writer owns the shares that the option refers to. A naked option means that the writer does not own the shares, and if the options are exercised, the writer will have to go to the market to purchase the shares to resell to the holder. Covered calls have no downside potential but limit upside potential based on stock price movements. Naked calls have large upside and downside potential and therefore are much riskier than covered calls.

22. Put options allow the holder to sell stocks at a specified price. Investors purchase put options if they think the price of the security is going to fall. If the stock price falls below the strike price, the holder can go to the marketplace, purchase stock below the strike price with a guaranteed sale at a higher price.

23. Valuing stock options is a complex process. A model that has received a high level of acceptance for valuing stock options is called the **Black-Scholes Option Pricing Model**. The following variables are included in this model:
    1) Underlying stock's current price
    2) Option's stock price
    3) Time remaining until the option's expiration
    4) Volatility of the market price of the underlying stock
    5) Risk-free interest rate

24. **Stock warrants** are similar to call options. They are often attached to other financial assets (e.g. bonds from the same corporation) to make the sale of the financial asset more attractive to potential investors. Warrants normally have a longer term than call options (e.g. several years), and they allow the holder to purchase stock at a fixed price, called the **exercise price**. They have value when the market price rises above the exercise price. Warrants can typically be detached from the financial asset with which they were issued, and they can be marketed on their own.

25. **Employee stock options** are often used to attract and retain employees without having to pay exorbitant salaries. Like warrants, employee stock options have an exercise price, normally well above the market price when the options are issued. Employee stock options are often given to top executives with the expectation that the executives will act in the best interests on the company to drive the stock price up. Recently, we have seen a number of examples of executives artificially driving up the stock price by issuing inaccurate financial statements. This potential conflict of interest is supposed to be managed through effective auditing, but this process has also broken down in a number of these examples.

TESTING YOUR UNDERSTANDING

TRUE-FALSE QUESTIONS

____1. Nearly all preferred stock comes with a cumulative feature.

____2. Stocks that pay a constant, unchanging dividend are valued by the present value of a perpetuity formula.

____3. The final payment for common stock comes from another investor.

____4. The efficient market hypothesis has been proven to be 100% correct.

____5. Growth rate models should be treated as approximations for real-world valuations.

____6. Common stock is usually expected to pay the same dividend forever.

____7. It is easy for stockholders in widely held corporations to organize against incumbent boards.

____8. When valuing common stock, future dividend cash flows are assumed to continue forever.

____9. Different classes of stock may have different voting rights.

____10. Preferred stock dividends automatically increase as a company grows.

____11. Stockholders in widely held corporations do not have any significant role in management, but instead are interested in the cash flows that come from stock ownership.

____12. A firm that has a long history of paying dividends must give stockholders a 12-month notice before it can stop paying dividends.

____13. Bond pricing models are even less accurate than stock pricing models.

____14. The "greater fool theory" says that people who buy non-dividend paying stocks depend upon finding a greater fool to sell the stock to for a higher price.

____15. Corporations are legally required to hold annual stockholders' meetings.

____16. Stockholders are first in line among all the claimants on a firm's resources.

____17. Preferred stock dividends are tax-deductible for the issuing firm while common stock dividends are not.

____18. If a firm does poorly or fails, preferred stock is preferable to common stock ownership.

MULTIPLE CHOICE QUESTIONS

1. Preferred stock:
   a. pays a constant dividend forever.
   b. has an initial specified selling price.
   c. usually has no voting rights.
   d. all of the above.

2. Dividend payments for common stock:
   a. are guaranteed.
   b. may be discontinued at any time.
   c. are seldom a constant amount over long periods of time.
   d. b and c only.

3. The efficient market hypothesis:
   a. refutes Fundamental and Technical Analysis.
   b. refers to information flows throughout US financial markets.
   c. says that stock prices adjust almost immediately to new information.
   d. all of the above.

4. The constant growth model:
   a. is also called the Gordon model.
   b. assumes that dividend amounts remain unchanged.
   c. assumes that dividends increase each year by a constant amount.
   d. b and c.

5. Bond valuation is:
   a. less accurate than common stock valuation.
   b. more accurate than common stock valuation.
   c. equally as exact as common stock valuation.
   d. dependent upon unpredictable cash flows.

6. A cumulative feature:
   a. comes with almost all preferred stock.
   b. comes with almost all common stock.
   c. enhances the safety of bonds.
   d. requires that common stock dividends be paid.

7. Stockholders:
   a. have a residual claim on assets and income.
   b. are first in line among all claimants on a firm's resources.
   c. are in the best position of all when business is bad.
   d. are in the worst position of all when business is good.

8. Stockholders benefit when:
   a. EAT are paid out as dividends.
   b. EAT are reinvested into business.
   c. both a and b.
   d. none of the above.

9. Investors will buy stock in companies that do not pay dividends because:
   a. these firms are typically young and experiencing rapid growth.
   b. they expect to get large dividends in the future.
   c. they may believe in the bigger fool theory.
   d. all of the above.

10. Common stock ownership:
    a. gives the owner a vote on day-to-day decisions.
    b. gives the owner a vote in electing the Board of Directors.
    c. allows the owner to vote on charter changes and mergers.
    d. b and c only.

11. Firms may not pay dividends because:
    a. they are growing rapidly and need the cash.
    b. they have no earnings from which to pay dividends.
    c. both a and b.
    d. none of the above; by law a firm must pay dividends.

12. A fundamental analysis involves:
    a. studying past movements of stocks.
    b. relying on predictable market phenomena to make investment decisions.
    c. doing research to study everything possible about a firm, its business, and its industry.
    d. preparing elaborate charts displaying the price and volumes of all stocks traded.

13. The one-year return on a stock will include
    a. the dividends received
    b. the increase in the stock price
    c. the stock price at the end of the year
    d. both a. and b. above

14. The intrinsic value of a stock is:
    a. the current market price
    b. a mathematical calculation of the stock price based on assumptions
    c. the same for every investor
    d. none of the above

15. The expected return of a stock is a function of:
    a. the growth rate of the stock
    b. the growth rate and the dividend of the stock
    c. the growth rate, the dividend and the current price of the stock
    d. none of the above

16. The two-stage growth model is often used for pricing stocks that:
    a. have had a temporary downturn but are expected to return to normal growth soon
    b. have introduced a new product
    c. are relatively new companies that have not reached their expected market share
    d. all of the above

17. Preemptive rights allow current stockholders to:
    a. sell their stock above the market price
    b. maintain their proportionate share of stock when new stock is issued
    c. purchase 100 shares of stock whenever the company issues new stock
    d. vote for the board of directors

18. The writer of a call option expects the price of the stock to:
    a. stay the same or go down
    b. go up
    c. stay the same or go up
    d. all of the above could be the writer's expectation

19. If the market price of a stock drops below the strike price, the holder of a put option will:
    a. exercise the option
    b. sell the option in the secondary market
    c. nothing, since the option is worthless
    d. both a. and b. above are true

20. When an investor writes a call option without owning the stock, it's called a:
    a. put option
    b. covered call
    c. naked call
    d. exercised call

FILL-IN THE BLANK QUESTIONS

1. When stock ownership is spread out among a large number of investors with no one person or group controlling a large percent, the company is said to be _____.

2. A stock's _____ is the present value of its future cash flows.

3. Stockholders have a _____ claim on the assets and income of the firm.

4. _____ allow existing stockholders to maintain their proportionate ownership in corporations.

5. Bonds are the least risky securities, followed by _____ stock, and then by _____ stock.

6. Technical analysts are also known as _____.

7. _____ give designated parties the right to vote shares.

8. _____ stock is a cross between common stock and bonds.

9. _____ become experts in a company and then use their expertise to predict future cash flows.

10. If a stock is sold for more than the price the stockholder paid for it, this is called a _____ gain.

11. The _____ growth model can value stocks expected to grow at an unusual rate for a limited time.

12. The _____ feature of preferred stock says that no common stock dividends can be paid until preferred dividends in arrears are caught up.

PROBLEMS

1. If a person buys a share of stock for $30, receives a $5 dividend, and one year later sells the stock for $32, what is her return?

2. What is the price of a share of stock today that will be sold in one year for $60, will pay a dividend of $4, and have a return of 10%?

3. A corporation pays a dividend of $2 this year and is expected to grow at 10% per year. What are its next two dividends?

4. Aurand Bikes is expecting a constant growth rate of 5% for its dividends. Its most recent dividend was $1.50 a share, and similar stocks are returning 9%. What should a share of Aurand sell for today?

5. What is the current price for a share of preferred stock that returns 9% and pays a dividend of $6.20?

6. Saira Hasham is interested in purchasing a stock that is expected to do well for the next 3 years, paying a dividend of $3 next year, $4 the following year, and $4.50 the third year, when Saira will sell her shares for an estimated price of $60 a share. Current stocks such as this one are earning 10%. What is the maximum the stock should sell for now?

7. McFadden Corporation is beginning a period of no projected growth. Its yearly dividend is $6.50, and this is expected to continue indefinitely. The yield on similar stocks is 9%. What should the stock sell for?

8. Gowen, Inc. just paid a dividend of $2.00. They have just released a new product that will cause the company (and dividends) to grow by 20% for the next two years, after which growth will return to 8% for the foreseeable future. Comparable stocks are offering a 12% return. What is the intrinsic value of Gowen's stock?

9. Millie purchased a call option on 100 shares of stock with a strike price of $43 for $2 per share. If Millie exercises the option when the market price reaches $48, what percent return did Millie receive on her investment? What is the greatest loss that Millie could have experienced on her investment?

10. See the previous problem. If instead, Millie had purchased the stock at $39 (which was the market price when the call options were written) and sold them when the market price reached $48, what percent return would Millie have received on her investment? What is the greatest loss Millie could have experienced on this investment?

ANSWERS TO QUESTIONS

TRUE-FALSE

1. t
2. t
3. t
4. f
5. t
6. f
7. f
8. t
9. t
10. f
11. t
12. f
13. f
14. t
15. t
16. f
17. f
18. t

FILL IN THE BLANKS

1. widely held
2. intrinsic value
3. residual
4. Preemptive rights
5. preferred, common
6. chartists
7. Proxies
8. Preferred
9. Fundamental analysts
10. capital
11. Two-stage
12. Cumulative

MULTIPLE CHOICE

1. d
2. d
3. d
4. a
5. b
6. a
7. a
8. c
9. d
10. d
11. c
12. c
13. d
14. b
15. c
16. d
17. b
18. a
19. d
20. c

ANSWERS TO PROBLEMS

1. $R = \dfrac{5+2}{30} = 23.33\%$

2. Future cash flow at the end of one year is $60 + $4 = $64
$P_0 = \$64\ [PVF_{10,1}] = 64\ (0.9091) = 58.18$

3. $D_0 = \$2.00$
$D_1 = \$2.00\ (1.10) = \$2.20$
$D_2 = \$2.20\ (1.10) = \$2.42$

4. $P_0 = \dfrac{D_0(1+g)}{k-g} = \dfrac{\$1.50(1.05)}{0.09-0.05} = \$39.38$

5. $P_P = \dfrac{D_P}{k_P} = \dfrac{\$6.20}{0.09} = \$68.89$

6. $P_0 = \$3\ [PVF_{10,1}] + \$4\ [PVF_{10,2}] + \$4.50\ [PVF_{10,3}] + \$60\ [PVF_{10,3}]$
   $= \$3(0.9091) + \$4(0.8264) + \$64.50(0.7513)$
   $= \$2.73 + \$3.31 + \$48.46$
   $= \$54.50$

7. $P_0 = \dfrac{D}{k} = \dfrac{\$6.50}{0.09} = \$72.22$

8. $D_0 = \$2.00$
   $D_1 = \$2.00(1.20) = \$2.40$
   $D_2 = \$2.40(1.20) = \$2.88$
   $D_3 = \$2.88(1.08) = \$3.11$

   Gordon Model = $D_3/(k-g) = \$3.11/(.12-.08) = \$77.75$

   $P_0 = \$2.40\ [PVF_{12,1}] + \$2.88\ [PVF_{12,2}] + \$77.75\ [PVF_{12,2}]$
   $= \$2.40(0.8929) + \$2.88(0.7972) + \$77.75(0.7972)$
   $= \$2.14 + \$2.30 + \$61.98$
   $= \$66.42$

9. Gain on stocks $\$48 - \$43 = \$5$
   Investment $\$2$ option price
   Percent return ($\$5 - \$2)/\$2 = 1.5$ or 150%

   If the market price of the stock never rises above $43, the call option will expire and become worthless. Millie will have lost 100% of her investment.

10. Gain on stock $48 - $39 = $9
    Return $9/$39 = .2307 or 23.07%

Theoretically, the stock price could drop to zero while she is holding the stock which would result in a 100% loss in her investment. More likely, the stock would remain in its recent trading range which would limit the amount of the loss if the stock price went down.

Problems 9 and 10 demonstrate the difference between investing in a stock and investing in an option. Options are leveraged investments and therefore have a much higher potential for high returns or huge losses.

CHAPTER EIGHT

RISK AND RETURN

LEARNING OBJECTIVES

After studying this chapter you should understand the following terms and concepts:

1. definitions of risk and return, why they are important to the study of finance, and their relationship to each other;
2. Portfolio Theory;
3. the definition of risk as variance;
4. why most investors prefer to avoid unnecessary risk;
5. systematic (market) risk and unsystematic (business specific) risk;
6. risk and return for portfolios and the effect of diversification on portfolio risk;
7. using beta to measure market risk and to project returns;
8. the components of the Capital Asset Pricing Model (CAPM).

CHAPTER SUMMARY

This chapter offers an in-depth examination of the concepts of risk and return. It begins with a discussion of why it is necessary to study and understand these two concepts, and then looks at the relationship between the two. The feelings that most investors have regarding risk are explained so that the student might then take a complete look at portfolio theory. Portfolio theory defines investment risk in a measurable way, and then relates that risk to the level of return on an investment. Systematic and unsystematic risk are examined, and a complete explanation of beta, what it does and how it is used, is undertaken. Finally the capital asset pricing model (CAPM) is illustrated, and the importance of the security market line (SML) is emphasized.

CHAPTER REVIEW

WHY STUDY RISK AND RETURN

1. In general, **equity investments** have a higher rate of return (around 10% over the past 75 years) than do debt investments (between 3% and 4% for the same period), but over the short term they are much more volatile or variable than debt investments.

2. Investing in a combination of stocks, called a **portfolio**, is one method to help control and manage the risk of equity investments while capturing the high average rate of return provided.

3. The general relationship between risk and return in the financial world is simple: the higher the possible rate of return, the higher the probability of losing the entire investment, and therefore the higher the risk. In other words, there is a direct relationship between risk and return; as one increases so does the other. While this concept is simple to express and to understand in concept, it is more difficult to accurately predict just how much risk is actually associated with a certain level of return.

4. **Portfolio theory** is one of a very few theoretical concepts that has had important consequences in the real world. It defines the risk of an investment in a way that can be measured and then relates that measurable risk to the expected level of return for the investment. What an investor expects to receive from the investment, such as the interest from a bank or the dividends and capital gains expected from investing in a stock, is called the **expected return**. No logical person makes an investment without the expectation of receiving something in return.

   What an investor thinks he or she should receive for making a particular investment is called the **required rate of return**. The required rate of return is related to the perceived riskiness of an investment. Investments that have a higher probability of resulting in the loss of all or part of the investment will have a higher required rate of return.

5. A simple definition of **risk** is the probability that the return on an investment will be less than the investor's expected rate of return when the investment was made. So if an investor's expected rate of return is 10%, the risk is the probability that the actual rate of return may be something less than 10%. The term **risk aversion** is used to describe investors who prefer to avoid risk. If investors are offered two investment opportunities that have the same expected rate of return, the will prefer the investment with the lower risk.

PORTFOLIO THEORY

6. **Portfolio theory** is a statistical model of the investment world. In this model, the return on an investment is treated as a **continuous random variable**, which means that the return can take on any numerical value within some range. Consider a group of 1,000 investors contemplating the return on a specific stock investment opportunity for the coming year. Remember that the return will be measured based on the dividend yield and the capital gains yield using the following formula:

$$k = \frac{D_1 + (P_1 - P_0)}{P_0}$$

Many factors will be considered by each investor in forecasting next year's return. The end result will be a range of forecasts, with the lowest possible return being negative 100% (if the entire investment is lost) and there is no practical limit to the highest possible return, although one-year returns rarely exceed 100%.

A graphic representation of the probability distribution of the expected return for this stock shows the likelihood that a return occurring within a certain range will result. The most likely outcome is the **mean** and is found under the highest point of the curve. The mean represents the average investor's **expected return**. According to portfolio theory, this probability distribution represents all the knowledge that investors have about the expected future performance of a stock. A probability distribution with steeply sloped sides and a high crest indicates that investors anticipate a small variance from the mean. For example, a mean of $5 with a small variance may indicate that returns are likely to vary only from $4.75 to $5.25. Clearly this investment carries a lower risk than an investment where the mean is also $5, but there is a much larger variance (demonstrated by a probability distribution with gently sloping sides and a low crest) where the range of returns is from $1.50 to $8.50.

In portfolio theory, **risk is defined as the variance of the probability distribution of its return**. Variance (or alternatively **standard deviation**) is calculated using normal statistical methods to measure the dispersion of possible outcomes around the mean. Low variability of returns means low risk, and high variability of returns means high risk. Because most investors are risk averse, low variability will be preferred to high variability in cases where expected returns are equal.

7. The return on an investment in a stock is subject to two kinds of risk. The first is **systematic (or market) risk** and results from certain stimuli such as a change in interest rates, political events or concerns about an economic downturn. These stimuli have a common effect on all stocks, and it is market risk that tends to make stocks move up and down at the same time. The second is **unsystematic (or business-specific) risk** and results from events that occur in a particular business or industry, such as a labor strike, a product recall or a major change in the management team. These stimuli tend to affect one company, or at most a group of companies in a similar industry.

8. Based on these two risk components, each stock has its own specific expected return and risk. However, very few investors hold only one stock. It is much more common for an investor to hold several stocks, called a **portfolio**. A portfolio also has an expected return and risk. The return for the portfolio is the weighted average return of the stocks it contains and can be easily calculated. The risk is the variance of the probability distribution of the portfolio's return, but this calculation is much more complex because of the interaction of the individual stocks in the portfolio.

    Portfolio theory assumes that investors are not concerned with the individual performance of stocks, but only with the performance of their portfolio as a whole. By investing in the stocks of different companies, investors can attempt to reach their goal of avoiding as much risk as possible while attaining the highest average rates of return.

9. **Diversification**—investing in the stocks of many different companies—can reduce risk, but cannot eliminate it entirely. If a portfolio consists of the stocks of companies in fundamentally different industries, **unsystematic or business risk** can be essentially diversified away.

Since stocks in the market tend to move up or down together, **systematic or market risk** cannot be entirely diversified away. However, given an existing portfolio, stocks can be added that can change the risk characteristics of the portfolio. If Stock A tends to move with changes in the portfolio (e.g. when the portfolio's returns are up, Stock A is way up), adding Stock A to the portfolio will increase risk. However, if Stock B has a different return pattern than the portfolio (e.g. when the portfolio's returns are up, Stock B is up sometimes and down sometimes), then adding Stock B to the portfolio will tend to reduce the portfolio's risk, maybe only by a little bit. It is this incremental reduction in the portfolio's risk that explains how diversification can help reduce market risk.

10. **Beta** is a measurement that describes how the variation in a particular stock's return relates to the variation in the overall market return. **It is a measure of the market risk of a stock held in a well diversified portfolio.** It is based on the analysis of the past performance of the individual stock versus the market, and it assumes that in the future the stock's returns will vary in the same way. This may not always hold true. If a stock has a beta of 1.0, this means that the stock's returns will move just as much as the market's returns. A 10% change in the market's return will tend to result in a 10% movement of the stock's returns. A beta of less than 1 means that this stock tends to move with the market but less. So a 10% market rate movement would result in something less than a 10% movement for the return of this stock. A beta of more than 1.0 means that when the market moves 10%, this stock's returns will move more than 10%. A beta of less than zero means that the stock tends to move in the opposite direction of the market. Stocks with negative betas are quite rare.

When the market is moving up, stocks with betas of more than 1.0 will generate greater increases in rates of returns for their investors. When the market is moving down, stocks with betas of more than 1.0 will produce even greater decreases in rates of returns for their investors than the overall market. This would suggest that in good times investors will be rewarded by investing in stocks with high betas, and in bad times they can minimize their downward movement by investing in stocks with low betas. **Beta for a portfolio** is the weighted average of the betas for the individual stocks in the portfolio.

11. The **capital asset pricing model (CAPM)** is a mathematical model that defines the required return of a particular stock, using the components of the required return of the market in general and the risk of the particular stock as defined by beta. CAPM divides the required return on the market (k_M) into two components: (1) the risk-free component (k_{RF}), and (2) the risk premium ($k_M - k_{RF}$). The rate of interest paid on 3-month treasuries is generally taken to be a good surrogate for the risk-free rate. The risk premium reflects the average tolerance investors have for taking on risk, a measure of risk aversion. The required return for any particular stock (e.g. Stock X) can be estimated by multiplying the market risk premium by that stock's beta and adding that factor to the risk-free rate, as shown in the following formula:

$$k_X = k_{RF} + (k_M - k_{RF})b_X$$

The **security market line** is the essence of the CAPM and is the generalized version of the equation shown above. For a given risk-free rate and market risk premium, the required return on any stock can be calculated using that stock's beta. The security market line is a graphical representation of this relationship, where the risk-free rate is the y-intercept and the market risk premium is the slope of the line. It assumes that business risk does not enter into the picture because it can be diversified away. Any stock's required rate of return can be found by locating its beta on the x-axis of the graph and finding the value of "y" on the security market line.

The SML represents an equilibrium situation where there are an equal number of buyers and sellers for a particular stock, and the expected rate of return equals the required rate of return. When the risk free rate of return changes, the SML will shift upward or downward, parallel to its previous position. When investors become more or less risk aversive, the SML will move to become more or less steep while maintaining the same y-intercept. The CAPM is a theoretical pricing model and cannot be assumed to be an accurate predictor of behavior in the real world. One major limitation is that it only considers market risk and not a stock's total risk.

TESTING YOUR UNDERSTANDING

TRUE-FALSE QUESTIONS

____1. Beta measures a stock's total volatility.

____2. Stocks with negative betas are rare.

____3. Diversification can eliminate all risk from a portfolio.

____4. Investors' required rates of return are related to the perceived risk of investments.

____5. The result of a coin toss is a continuous random variable.

____6. Generally, it easy to predict just how much risk is associated with a given level of return.

____7. The security market line accounts only for unsystematic risk.

____8. Beta assumes a stock's future return will vary as it has in the past.

____9. The majority of rational people make investments without expecting any return.

____10. A bank savings account has almost zero risk.

____11. The return on a stock investment can be thought of as a continuous random variable.

____12. On average, returns to debt investments are higher than returns to equity investments.

____13. A risky stock will have a smaller variance than a less risky stock.

____14. When choosing between two investments with the same expected return, most people will prefer to invest in the lower risk investment.

____15. Over the past 75 years, equity investments have achieved much higher average returns than debt investments.

____16. All investors have the same required return for a stock.

____17. Risk aversion means that risk is to be avoided at all costs.

____18. An investment with a small variance is more likely to have returns that are close to the mean than is an investment with a large variance.

____19. Most stock movements go up and down with no relationship to the movement of other stocks.

____20. Diversification can eliminate business-specific risk only when the portfolio contains stocks exclusively from companies in the same industry.

MULTIPLE CHOICE QUESTIONS

1. The SML:
   a. is the equation that defines the required rate of return for a stock in terms of its risk.
   b. says that required rates of return are determined by the risk free rate, market risk premium, and the beta coefficient.
   c. is the heart of the CAPM.
   d. all of the above.

2. A stock that reaches its highs and lows at exactly the same times as other stocks in the portfolio and whose highs are higher and lows are lower than the portfolio's:
   a. will add risk to the portfolio.
   b. is said to be positively correlated with portfolio returns.
   c. should be added to the portfolio to reduce risk.
   d. a and b only.

3. When investors construct diverse portfolios:
   a. they are trying to capture the high average return of equity.
   b. they are trying to avoid as much risk as possible.
   c. they care more about the performance of the portfolio as a whole rather than individual stock performance.
   d. all of the above.

4. Business-specific risk:
   a. results from chance or random events.
   b. can be diversified away in a portfolio.
   c. is the same as market risk.
   d. all of the above.
   e. a and b only.

5. The mean of a probability distribution:
   a. is also called the expected value.
   b. occurs under the highest point of the curve.
   c. is the weighted average of all possible outcomes where each outcome is weighted by its probability.
   d. all of the above.

6. Equity investment returns:
   a. on the average are lower than debt investment returns.
   b. are subject to huge swings during short periods.
   c. have relatively small swings during short periods.
   d. none of the above.

7. If a distribution has steeply sloping sides and a high peak:
   a. it has a small variance.
   b. it has a large variance.
   c. it has a high risk.
   d. b and c only.

8. When investors become more risk averse:
   a. SML gets flatter.
   b. SML gets steeper.
   c. SML remains unchanged.
   d. none of the above.

9. When the market is moving up, investors will benefit more than the average market return by:
   a. holding stocks with betas of greater than 1.
   b. holding stocks with betas of less than 1 but more than zero.
   c. holding stocks with betas of less than zero.
   d. none of the above.

10. Discrete random variables:
    a. can take on only specific values.
    b. can take on any value within a specific range.
    c. are the outcome of a chance process.
    d. a and c only.

11. Portfolio theory:
    a. comes from financial theory.
    b. has had a major practical impact.
    c. terminology is used all the time.
    d. all of the above.

12. A distribution with a large variance:
    a. is more likely to produce results close to the mean than is a distribution with a small variance.
    b. has less risk than a distribution with a small variance.
    c. is more likely to produce results that vary substantially from the mean than is a distribution with a small variance.
    d. none of the above.

13. Investment A has an expected return of 8% and a variance of 3%, and investment B has an expected return of 8% with a variance of 1%.
    a. Investors will tend to prefer A to B.
    b. Investors will tend to prefer B to A.
    c. B and A will be equally desirable.
    d. none of the above.

14. Equity investments over the past 70+ years:
    a. have achieved higher average returns than debt investments.
    b. have annually averaged about 10%.
    c. were subject to much greater swings during short periods than debt investments.
    d. all of the above.

15. A risk-averse investor will prefer:
    a. stocks with a small standard deviation.
    b. stocks with a large standard deviation.
    c. stocks whose returns differ widely from year to year.
    d. none of the above.

16. When the risk-free rate changes and all other things remain equal, the SML will:
    a. have a steeper slope.
    b. have a slope that is less steep.
    c. shift up or down parallel to itself.
    d. remain the same.

17. The "expected return" on a stock:
    a. will always be equal to the required return
    b. is based on the investor's estimate of dividends and stock price increase
    c. is a function of beta, the risk-free rate and the market risk premium
    d. all of the above are true

18. The standard deviation of a distribution of an investment opportunity:
    a. is equal to the square root of the variance
    b. is a measure of how far a typical observation will be from the mean
    c. is directly related to the risk of that investment
    d. all of the above are true

19. The "coefficient of variation" of a distribution of an investment opportunity:
    a. will not help the investor evaluate the risk of that investment
    b. is the variance divided by the mean
    c. might be helpful in evaluating risk in investments of different dollar amounts
    d. none of the above

20. Adding a stock with a beta of 0.0 to any existing portfolio will:
    a. increase the risk of the portfolio
    b. decrease the risk of the portfolio
    c. move the beta of the portfolio toward 1.0
    d. change the risk of the portfolio but could either increase or decrease it

FILL IN THE BLANK QUESTIONS

1. _____ is a measure of a stock's volatility in relation to market changes.

2. The movement of a stock that occurs along with the movement of the market is known as _____ risk.

3. The anticipated return from an investment is called the _____.

4. _____ means that most people prefer to avoid risk, but not at all costs.

5. The return on a stock investment is a _____ random variable.

6. Over time, _____ investments average higher returns than debt investments.

7. In portfolio theory, risk is thought of as _____.

8. The _____ attempts to explain how stock prices are set in the market.

9. The movement of a stock in response to stimuli that are particular to that industry or firm is known as _____ risk.

10. The expected value or _____ of a probability distribution is found under its highest point.

11. In financial dealings, _____ is thought of as losing all or part of an investment.

12. An investor's total stock holdings are known as his _____.

13. Investment opportunities with higher returns usually have _____ risks.

14. _____ theory defines risk in a measurable way and relates it to the level of return that can be expected from an investment.

15. Another name for systematic risk is _____ risk.

16. Another term for unsystematic risk is _____ risk.

17. Adding different stocks to a portfolio is known as _____.

18. The _____ is the heart of the CAPM.

PROBLEMS

1. Short term Treasury bills are yielding 5% and an average stock return is 9%. Dowen Corporation has a beta of 1.5, paid an annual dividend of $2, and its expected dividend growth is 6% a year. What should Dowen's stock sell for?

2. Barry Corporation has a beta of 1.4. The risk free rate is 5% and the market is returning 12%. What is Barry's required rate of return?

3. In Problem 2, what is Barry's new required rate of return if the risk free rate decreases to 4%? Increases to 6%?

4. What is the expected return of the following portfolio of stocks?

STOCK	CURRENT MARKET VALUE	RETURN
A	$200,000	7%
B	100,000	6%
C	300,000	10%
D	250,000	8%
E	350,000	9%
	$1,200,000	

5. The stocks in the above portfolio have the following betas. What is the beta of the portfolio?

STOCK	BETA	CURRENT $ VALUE	PORTION OF VALUE
A	1.0	$ 334,000	
B	.9	166,000	
C	1.2	500,000	
D	.8	416,000	
E	1.4	584,000	
		$2,000,000	

6. The Becher Corporation paid an annual dividend of $4 and is expected to grow indefinitely at 4%. Short term T-bills are yielding 5%, and an average stock yields 12%. Becher is currently selling for $36.17. What is Becher's beta?

7. Use the information from the previous problem. Becher is looking at taking on a project that will increase its growth rate to 5%. However, it is expected to increase its beta by 0.2. Should Becher take on the project?

8. An investor purchased a stock for $35. The investor expects to receive $1.50 in dividends and expects the stock to increase in price to $38.75, at which time the investor will sell the stock. What return will the investor realize on this investment?

9. The mean value of a distribution is 13.5 with a variance of 2.4. Calculate the coefficient of variation for the distribution.

10. The slope of the SML is 5.0%. A stock with a beta of 1.2 has a required return of 9.4%. What is the implied risk-free rate?

ANSWERS TO QUESTIONS

TRUE-FALSE

1. f
2. t
3. f
4. t
5. f
6. f
7. f
8. t
9. f
10. t
11. t
12. f
13. f
14. t
15. t
16. f
17. f
18. t
19. f
20. f

FILL IN THE BLANKS

1. Beta
2. systematic/market
3. expected return
4. Risk aversion
5. continuous
6. equity
7. variability
8. CAPM
9. unsystematic/business specific
10. mean
11. risk
12. portfolio
13. higher
14. Portfolio
15. market
16. business-specific
17. diversification
18. security market line, or SML

MULTIPLE CHOICE

1. d
2. d
3. d
4. e
5. d
6. b
7. a
8. b
9. a
10. d
11. d
12. c
13. b
14. d
15. a
16. c
17. b
18. d
19. c
20. b

ANSWERS TO PROBLEMS

1. $k_D = k_{RF} + (k_m - k_{RF}) b_D$
   $= 0.05 + (0.09 - 0.05) 1.5$
   $= 0.05 + 0.06$
   $= 0.11 = 11\%$

   $P_0 = D_0(1 + g)/(k - g) = \$2.00(1.06)/(.11 - .06) = \$42.40$

2. $k_B = 0.05 + (0.12 - 0.05) 1.4 = 0.05 + 0.098 = 0.148 = 14.8\%$

3. $k_B = 0.04 + (0.11 - 0.04) 1.4 = 0.04 + 0.098 = 0.138 = 13.8\%$
   $k_B = 0.06 + (0.13 - 0.06) 1.4 = 0.06 + 0.098 = 0.158 = 15.8\%$

4.
Stock	Mkt Value ($K)	Weight	Return	Wt.×Return
A	$200	.167	.07	.012
B	100	.083	.06	.005
C	300	.250	.10	.025
D	250	.208	.08	.017
E	350	.292	.09	.026
	$1,200	1.000		.085
			Portfolio Return =	8.5%

5.
Stock	Beta	Value ($K)	Portion of Value	Beta × Portion of Value
A	1.0	$ 334	.167	.167
B	0.9	166	.083	.075
C	1.2	500	.250	.300
D	0.8	416	.208	.166
E	1.4	584	.292	.401
		$2000	1.000	1.109
			Portfolio Beta =	1.1

6. $P_0 = D_0(1 + g)/(k - g)$
   $\$36.17 = \$4.00(1.04)/(k - .04)$
   $\$36.17k - \$1.4468 = \$4.16$
   $\$36.17k = \$5.6068$
   $k = .155$ or 15.5%

   $k_B = k_{RF} + (k_M - k_{RF}) b_B$
   $15.5\% = 5.0\% + (12.0\% - 5.0\%) b_B$
   $10.5\% = 7.0\% b_B$
   $b_B = 1.5$

7. Becher's new required return will be:

$$k_B = k_{RF} + (k_M - k_{RF}) b_B$$
$$= 5.0\% + (12.0\% - 5.0\%) 1.7$$
$$= 16.9\%$$

With a growth rate of 5%, the revised stock price will be:

$$P_0 = D_0(1 + g)/(k - g)$$
$$= \$4.00(1.05)/(.169 - .05)$$
$$= \$35.29$$

Based on these calculations, the project will decrease the stock price. Therefore, the project should not be undertaken.

8. $(38.75 - 35.00 + 1.50)/35.00 = .15$ or 15%

9. $(2.4)^{½} / 13.5 = .115$

10. $9.4\% = x + 5\% (1.2)$
    $x = 3.4\%$

CHAPTER NINE

CAPITAL BUDGETING

LEARNING OBJECTIVES

After studying this chapter you should understand the following terms and concepts:

1. the three types of capital budgeting projects: (1) replacement, (2) expansion, and (3) new venture, and the degree of risk associated with each project type;
2. the difference between stand-alone or mutually exclusive projects;
3. the definition of cost of capital and why it is important;
4. capital budgeting techniques including payback period, net present value, internal rate of return, and profitability index;
5. two methods for dealing with projects of unequal length: (1) the replacement chain method, and (2) the equivalent annual annuity;
6. capital rationing.

CHAPTER SUMMARY

This chapter explores the concepts associated with capital budgeting, the planning and use of dollars for long-term projects. A differentiation is made between stand-alone and mutually exclusive projects, and then the four evaluation methods used for capital budgeting projects are examined and illustrated, with the strengths and weaknesses of each technique being explained in detail. Decision rules are established for each of the techniques for both stand-alone and mutually exclusive projects. A discussion follows on the problem of using net present value (NPV) for projects with unequal lives. Two methods are illustrated for dealing with this problem. Lastly the concept of capital rationing is defined and visited.

CHAPTER REVIEW

CHARACTERISTICS OF BUSINESS PROJECTS

1. Money spent by businesses can be divided into two categories: (1) short-term spending to fund daily activities such as buying inventory and paying expenses, and (2) capital spending to fund long-term projects. **Capital budgeting** involves planning and justifying how capital dollars are spent on long-term projects.

2. Long-term projects can be separated into three general categories:

    a.) **Replacement projects** typically involve the replacement of worn out capital equipment. These are major expenditures, but they don't involve any new business activities, so they generally are low risk projects.

    b.) **Expansion projects** involve investing additional money in resources and equipment so that the firm can do more of whatever it is already doing. Often, expansion projects are driven by higher sales forecasts, and as a result, these projects are more risky than replacement projects.

    c.) **New ventures** represent new businesses requiring large start-up amounts, but allow the firm to move into new areas of opportunity. Since these projects involve new ventures, they are the most risky of the three categories.

3. Projects can also be classified as either stand-alone or mutually exclusive. **Stand-alone** projects are proposed without a competing alternative. Stand-alone projects are evaluated on their own merits, not in comparison with other projects. **Mutually exclusive** projects arise when there is a choice between two or more alternatives. When one alternative is chosen, the other alternatives are eliminated.

4. When projects are being evaluated, the cash inflows and outflows of each project must be estimated for the entire life of the project. **Cash outflows** are the costs of the project—such as the purchase and installation of equipment or the salary and wages of additional employees, while **cash inflows** are the money that the project will bring to the organization, such as revenues from additional sales. Reductions in expenses (e.g. cost savings) are also treated as cash inflows.

5. Because investments only make sense if they return more to the company than they cost, the idea of a firm's **cost of capital** is critical to the concept of capital budgeting. Since capital is typically provided through a mix of debt (bonds) and equity (stock), the cost of capital is the weighted average of the returns that these sources of capital provide to their investors. Because outflows and inflows will occur at various times in the future, the **time value of money** is central to capital budgeting, as the value of the outflows and inflows will be calculated at their present value with most capital budgeting evaluation methods, using the cost of capital as the discount rate.

CAPITAL BUDGETING TECHNIQUES

6. The **payback period** is the simplest of the four capital budgeting techniques. This technique

simply measures how long it takes for a project to repay with cash inflows the amount of the cash outflow that the project required. The whole idea of this technique is that firms will prefer to recover their investment sooner rather than later. Companies set a maximum time for their payback periods and then evaluate projects by comparing the policy maximum to the payback period for the project.

Stand-alone projects must have a payback period that is no longer than the maximum allowable.

$$PAYBACK\ PERIOD < POLICY\ MAXIMUM \longrightarrow ACCEPT$$
$$PAYBACK\ PERIOD > POLICY\ MAXIMUM \longrightarrow REJECT$$

Mutually exclusive projects are evaluated using the criteria that the project with the shortest payback period is best.

$$P/B_A < P/B_B \longrightarrow CHOOSE\ PROJECT\ A\ OVER\ PROJECT\ B$$

The payback period technique has two major drawbacks. First, it **ignores the time value of money**, and second, it **ignores cash flows received after the payback period.** However, the payback period is considered to be a quick and easy method that can be used as an initial screening method for projects. Projects that fail this method are disqualified, and projects that pass the payback criteria go on for further consideration and evaluation.

7. The second capital budgeting technique is very popular and is called the **net present value (NPV)** method. This method calculates the present value of all cash inflows for a project and subtracts from that number the present value of all cash outflows. If the resulting answer is positive, the project is contributing to the wealth of the business and, ultimately to its owners. The present value of the cash flows is calculated using the firm's cost of capital as the discount rate.

$$NPV = C_0 + \frac{C_1}{(1+k)} + \frac{C_2}{(1+k)^2} + \ldots + \frac{C_n}{(1+k)^n}$$

For stand-alone projects, a positive net present value will increase the value of the firm and should be accepted. A negative net present value will result in the rejection of a stand-alone project.

$$NPV > 0 \longrightarrow ACCEPT$$
$$NPV < 0 \longrightarrow REJECT$$

For mutually exclusive projects, the value of the firm will be most significantly increased by choosing projects with the highest net present values.

$$NPV_A > NPV_B \longrightarrow CHOOSE\ PROJECT\ A\ OVER\ PROJECT\ B$$

The net present value method is widely accepted as an effective capital budgeting technique because it takes into account the time value of money, and it produces an easily understandable selection criterion.

8. The third capital budgeting technique is called the **internal rate of return (IRR)** method. This method calculates the actual rate of return that a project brings to the firm. The IRR is the discount rate that makes the present value of the cash inflows equal to the present value of the cash outflows. It can also be thought of as the discount rate that makes the **net present value equal to zero**. In the following formula, the IRR is represented by "k" when the NPV = 0.

$$NPV = C_0 + \frac{C_1}{(1+k)} + \frac{C_2}{(1+k)^2} + \ldots + \frac{C_n}{(1+k)^n}$$

a.) When the IRR is greater than the cost of capital, the project is contributing in a positive way to the value of the firm. Therefore, stand-alone projects are evaluated according to whether or not their IRRs exceed the firm's cost of capital.

IRR > k $\longrightarrow$ ACCEPT
IRR < k $\longrightarrow$ REJECT

b.) The selection among mutually exclusive projects is based on which project has the largest IRR, as long as the IRR exceeds the firm's cost of capital.

IRR$_A$ > IRR$_B$ $\longrightarrow$ CHOOSE PROJECT A OVER PROJECT B

NPV and IRR will usually result in the same acceptance decision among mutually exclusive projects. Occasionally, NPV and IRR will pick different projects when selecting among mutually exclusive projects. This occurs because of the reinvestment assumptions that are used by each method. NPV assumes that cash will be reinvested at the cost of capital; IRR assumes that cash will be reinvested at the IRR. When they result in different decisions, **NPV is the preferred method.**

9. While NPV and IRR are the most popular capital budgeting methods, there is a fourth technique called **profitability index** that is sometimes used. This method compares the present value of a project's cash inflows with the initial cash outflow needed to begin the project. The cash inflows are considered as benefits while the cash outflows are viewed as costs.

$$PI = \frac{\frac{C_1}{(1+k)} + \frac{C_2}{(1+k)^2} + \ldots + \frac{C_n}{(1+k)^n}}{C_0}$$

Or $\quad PI = \dfrac{\text{present value of inflows}}{\text{present value of outflows}}$

When the PI is greater than 1.0, a project is accepted. When the PI is less than 1.0, the project is rejected.

PI > 1.0 $\longrightarrow$ ACCEPT
PI < 1.0 $\longrightarrow$ REJECT

For mutually exclusive projects, the project with the higher PI is preferable.

PI$_A$ > PI$_B$ CHOOSE PROJECT A OVER PROJECT B

10. Sometimes, direct comparisons of mutually exclusive projects are difficult because the projects are of different lengths. This is particularly acute when using the NPV method, because a longer project has more time to generate positive cash flows. Two methods are available to address this problem. Both methods put the projects on a comparable time basis.

    a) The **replacement chain** method repeats the shorter project so that the repeated projects are the same length as the longer project. For example, if Project A is two years long and Project B is four years long, then the replacement chain method assumes that another Project A will be initiated when the first Project A is over. Those additional cash flows are included in the Project A NPV, and that revised NPV can then be directly compared to the NPV of Project B.

    b) The **equivalent annual annuity** method constructs an annuity for each project with a payment for the length of the project that generates the same NPV as the project itself. The annuities can then be compared directly, and the one with the largest payment is the preferred project.

11. A firm's **capital budget** is the total amount of money it has allocated for spending on capital projects. In theory, this amount should be large enough to allow the firm to undertake every project that has a positive NPV, because these projects will increase the value of the firm. In reality, most firms do not have such unlimited capital funds available and practice a policy called **capital rationing**. Capital rationing limits the amount of funds available for capital projects and necessitates that firms select the best combination of projects that fit into their capital constraints. The combination of projects that does not exceed budget limitations but does produce the highest combined NPV is the best choice.

TESTING YOUR UNDERSTANDING

TRUE-FALSE QUESTIONS

____1. An investment makes sense only if it returns at least 10% more than its cost of capital.

____2. A stand-alone project with a positive NPV should be accepted.

____3. Cash flows in the near future are easier to predict than are cash flows in the distant future.

____4. A replacement capital project is the least risky of the three capital project categories.

____5. The cost of capital is a single rate that reflects the weighted average of the cost of equity and debt.

____6. Cash inflows from a project are seen as benefits and cash outflows as costs when the profitability index is used.

116   Chapter 9

____7. The initial outlay for projects is always discounted by the cost of capital when using the NPV method.

____8. Capital dollars are used to pay expenses, compensate employees, and to purchase inventory.

____9. Trying to choose between purchasing a Pontiac or a Toyota is an example of a stand-alone project.

____10. The profitability index works best when the initial outlay is the only negative cash flow.

____11. The same rate of return is usually paid to both equity and debt investors.

____12. Decision rules for the payback period technique are founded on the idea that it is better to recover invested money sooner than later.

____13. The present value payback method is rarely used because it still ignores cash flows received after the payback period.

____14. Present value calculations use a firm's cost of capital as the interest rate.

____15. Two firms evaluating the same project using NPV could come up with different decisions if their cost of capital is different.

____16. If a project's total inflows exceeds its outflows, it will always have a positive NPV.

____17. The IRR is the interest rate at which the present value of a project's cash inflows equals the present value of the project's cash outflows.

____18. There can be more than one IRR when a project has negative cash flows interspersed among the positive cash flows.

____19. NPV and IRR methods always give the same solutions to capital budgeting evaluations.

MULTIPLE CHOICE QUESTIONS

1. Capital rationing:
    a. is usually practiced in the real world.
    b. places a limit on the capital budget.
    c. results in all projects with positive NPVs being accepted.
    d. a and b only.

2. If a company was only using the Payback Period method of evaluation for a stand-alone project and its maximum acceptable time was four years:
    a. a payback period of 3 years would be accepted.
    b. a payback period of 5 years would be accepted.
    c. there is not enough information in a or b to decide.
    d. none of the above.

3. The NPV method:
   a. considers the time value of money.
   b. uses the firm's cost of capital as the interest rate to discount inflows and outflows.
   c. results in accepting projects that increase shareholder wealth.
   d. all of the above.

4. If a project has a positive NPV, the odds favor the project:
   a. having an IRR that exceeds the cost of capital.
   b. having an IRR that is less than the cost of capital.
   c. also having an acceptable IRR.
   d. both a and c.

5. The payback period:
   a. is the simplest capital budgeting technique.
   b. is flawed because it does not consider the time value of money.
   c. does not consider cash flows that occur after the payback period.
   d. all of the above.

6. If the NPV method selects Project A, and the IRR selects Project B, two mutually exclusive projects:
   a. Project A should be accepted.
   b. Project B should be accepted.
   c. both Project A and Project B should be accepted.
   d. neither Project A nor Project B should be accepted.

7. For two mutually exclusive projects where A had a payback of 2 years, B had a payback of 3 years, and the firm's policy was a maximum acceptable 4-year payback period:
   a. both projects would be accepted.
   b. project A but not B would be accepted.
   c. project B but not A would be accepted.
   d. neither project would be accepted.

8. The profitability index:
   a. discounts cash inflows.
   b. compares inflows and outflows in terms of a ratio.
   c. is a variation of NPV.
   d. all of the above.

9. If a firm could use only one capital budgeting technique to evaluate projects, which one should it choose?
   a. Profitability index
   b. Internal rate of return
   c. Net present value
   d. Payback period

10. Projects A and B are stand-alone projects. A has a PI of .5 and B has a PI of .7.
    a. Project B but not A should be accepted.
    b. Project A but not B should be accepted.
    c. Both projects should be accepted.
    d. Both projects should be rejected.

11. The most difficult part of capital budgeting is:
    a. estimating the initial investment.
    b. estimating the project's cash inflows.
    c. both a and b.
    d. none of the above.

12. A primary reason why companies use the payback method is:
    a. it is quick and easy.
    b. it considers the time value of money.
    c. it serves as a rough screening device.
    d. both a and c.

13. If a firm is using the IRR, an acceptable project will have:
    a. an IRR equal to the cost of capital.
    b. an IRR more than the cost of capital.
    c. an IRR less than the cost of capital.
    d. the cost of capital has no relevance to the IRR decision.

14. Project cash flows:
    a. are always positive in the second year of the project
    b. can be negative in any given year of the project including the last year
    c. is always positive for more years of the project than it's negative
    d. none of the above

15. If a company has an 8% cost of debt and a 12% cost of equity, then the cost of capital will be:
    a. less than 8%
    b. greater than 12 %
    c. between 8% and 12%
    d. cannot be determined without knowing the weights of debt and equity

16. A project has an initial cash outlay of $200,000, a cash inflow of $50,000 in the first year and inflows of $40,000 each year for the next five years. The payback period for this project is:
    a. less than 5 years
    b. between 5 and 6 years
    c. more than 6 years
    d. cannot be determined without knowing the cost of capital

17. Which of the following best describes the relationship between NPV and shareholder wealth?
    a. a project with a positive NPV will always increase shareholder wealth
    b. a project with a negative NPV will always decrease shareholder wealth
    c. the relationship between NPV and shareholder wealth depends on the specific project
    d. both a. and b. are true

18. A project with an IRR greater than the cost of capital will:
    a. always be accepted
    b. will always be accepted if it is a stand alone project
    c. will always be accepted if it is a mutually exclusive project
    d. none of the above

Capital Budgeting 119

19. The reinvestment assumption is the same for the following capital budgeting techniques:
    a. IRR and NPV
    b. IRR and PI
    c. PI and NPV
    d. all of the above

20. Project A is five years in length and Project B is seven years in length. These two projects are mutually exclusive. What is the best capital budgeting technique to use to compare these projects?
    a. EAA
    b. NPV
    c. Replacement Chain
    d. IRR

FILL-IN THE BLANK QUESTIONS

1. The total amount of money a firm has allocated to spend on capital projects over a period of time is its _____.

2. If a stand-alone project has a PI of 2, it should be _____.

3. _____ is the difference between the present value of the cash inflows and cash outflows for a project.

4. The _____ technique gives a project's return on invested funds.

5. A _____ NPV is better than a smaller NPV.

6. The initial outlay for a project is a cash _____.

7. If selecting Project A means that you cannot select Project B, you are dealing with _____ projects.

8. Replacement, _____, and new ventures are categories of capital projects.

9. The IRR is the interest rate that makes a project's NPV equal _____.

10. When comparing two projects of unequal lives, the NPV is usually _____ for the project with the shorter life.

11. Two projects with different lives can be compared using the _____ method until a common time period is achieved.

PROBLEMS

1. Projects A and B are mutually exclusive. The cost of capital is 8%. Using the Payback Period technique, calculate the payback period for each project. Which project(s) should be accepted?

	Project A	Project B
Year 0	($5,000)	($4,000)
Year 1	$1,000	$ 500
Year 2	$2,000	$2,000
Year 3	$1,000	$1,500
Year 4	$1,000	$1,000
Year 5	$4,000	$1,000

2. Use the information from problem 1. Calculate the NPV for each project.

3. Use the information from problem 1. Calculate the IRR for each project.

4. Use the information from problem 1. Calculate the PI for each project.

5. Use the information from problem 1. Calculate the EAA for each project.

6. Omega Corporation is evaluating three stand-alone projects. Its cost of capital is 10%. Calculate the NPV of each project, and determine which of the three projects should be accepted?

	Project A	Project B	Project C
Year 0	($5,000)	($4,000)	($6,000)
Year 1	1,000	500	500
Year 2	3,000	3,000	2,000
Year 3	4,000	3,000	5,000

7. If the projects in Problem 6 were mutually exclusive, which project(s) would be accepted?

8. Compute the Profitability Index for the following project with a cost of capital of 10%. Will this project be accepted if it is a stand-alone project?

Year 0	($4,500)
Year 1	1,000
Year 2	2,000
Year 3	2,000
Year 4	1,000

9. Your firm has a capital budget of $180,000 and has the following projects available. What combination of projects should the firm choose?

	Initial Outlay	NPV
Project A	($90,000)	4,200
Project B	($40,000)	2,000
Project C	($50,000)	2,300
Project D	($70,000)	1,900
Project E	($60,000)	3,000
Project F	($15,000)	1,000
Project G	($45,000)	1,400
Project H	($10,000)	500
Project I	($ 5,000)	400

10. Calculate the NPV for a project with a cost of $20,000, followed by cash inflows of $10,000 for the first 4 years with a cost of capital of 8%.

11. A firm has a capital budget of $600,000. Which set of projects should it select?

	Project Cost	NPV
A	$200,000	+ 200
B	200,000	+ 400
C	400,000	+1000
D	600,000	+1350
E	300,000	+ 700
F	100,000	+ 420

ANSWERS TO QUESTIONS

TRUE-FALSE

1. f
2. t
3. t
4. t
5. t
6. t
7. f
8. f
9. f
10. t
11. f
12. t
13. t
14. t
15. t
16. f
17. t
18. t
19. f

FILL IN THE BLANKS

1. capital budget
2. accepted
3. Net present value
4. internal rate of return
5. bigger
6. outflow
7. mutually exclusive
8. expansion
9. zero
10. lower
11. replacement chain

MULTIPLE CHOICE

1. d
2. a
3. d
4. d
5. d
6. a
7. b
8. d
9. c
10. d
11. b
12. d
13. b
14. b
15. c
16. a
17. d
18. d
19. c
20. a

ANSWERS TO PROBLEMS

1. Project A has a payback of four years, and Project B has a payback of three years. Project B is preferable to Project A and should be accepted if three years is less than the policy maximum.

2.
	Project A	Project B
CF0	($5,000)	($4,000)
CF1	$1,000	$ 500
CF2	$2,000	$2,000
CF3	$1,000	$1,500
CF4	$1,000	$1,000
CF5	$4,000	$1,000

   I = 8%
   NPV Project A = $1,891.80
   NPV Project B = $704.00

3. Use the information from problem 2.

   IRR Project A = 19.15%
   IRR Project B = 15.02%

4. ($1,891.80 + $5,000.00)/$5,000 = 1.38
   ($704.00 + $4,000.00)/$4,000 = 1.18

5.
   Project A   Project B
   n = 5   n = 5
   I/Y = 8   I/Y = 8
   PV = $1,891.80   PV = $704.00
   FV = 0   FV = 0
   PMT = ? = $473.81   PMT = ? = $176.32

6. Project A
   1000 × .9091 = 909.10
   3000 × .8265 = 2479.50
   4000 × .7513 = 3005.20
   $6393.80 − $5000 = $1393.80

   Project B
   500 × .9091 = 454.55
   3000 × .8265 = 2479.50
   3000 × .7513 = 2253.90
   $5187.95 − $4000 = $1187.95

   Project C
   500 × .9091 = 454.55
   2000 × .8265 = 1653.00
   5000 × .7513 = 3756.50
   $5864.05 − 6000 = −$135.95

124 Chapter 9

Accept Projects A and B, because they have a positive NPV.

7. If the projects are mutually exclusive, Project A only would be accepted, because it has the highest NPV.

8. $1000 \times .9091 = 909.10$
     $2000 \times .8265 = 1653.00$ $\dfrac{4747.70}{4500} = 1.055 =$ Profitability Index
     $2000 \times .7513 = 1502.60$
     $1000 \times .6830 = \underline{683.00}$
     $\$4747.70$

Project would be accepted, because PI is more than 1.

9. Rank the projects in descending order of NPV and cumulate the initial outlays.

$(000)

RANK	PROJECT	NPV	I/O	CUM I/O
1	A	$ 4,200	90	90
2	B	3,000	60	150
3	C	2,300	50	200
4	D	2,000	40	240
5	E	1,900	70	310
6	F	1,400	45	355
7	G	1,000	15	370
8	H	500	10	380
9	I	400	5	385

Projects A and E should be accepted. This leaves $30,000 in the budget. Projects C, B, D, and G all require more than $30,000, so they cannot be accepted within the budget. Projects F, H, and I require a total of $30,000, so they can all be done.

10. NPV $= C_0 + C[PVFA_{8,4}]$
         $= -20,000 + 10,000(3.3121)$
         $= \$13,121$

11. Try combinations of projects that fit within the capital budget and choose the combination with the highest NPV.

Project Combination	Cost (I/O)	NPV
D	$600,000	$1,350
B + C	$600,000	$1,400
B + E + F	$600,000	$1,520

Projects B, E, and F should be accepted.

10

CHAPTER TEN

CASH FLOW ESTIMATION

LEARNING OBJECTIVES

After studying this chapter you should understand the following terms and concepts:

1. the importance of cash flow estimating in the capital budgeting process;
2. a general approach to cash flow estimating;
3. the definition of incremental cash flows;
4. estimating cash flows for new venture projects;
5. estimating cash flows for replacement projects;
6. understanding the limitations of cash flow estimates and how this affects evaluation techniques.

CHAPTER SUMMARY

This chapter is a continuation of the capital budgeting discussion that was begun in Chapter 9. In Chapter 9, we assumed that the cash outflows and inflows were known amounts to which we could apply various capital budgeting techniques. This chapter illustrates some of the techniques that are used to arrive at these cash flows. Two projects are analyzed – a new venture and a replacement project. The techniques for estimating the cash flows for each of these projects are thoroughly developed. Concern for the accuracy of these cash flow estimates is discussed, and this chapter introduces the concept of risk in capital budgeting which is more thoroughly developed in Chapter 12.

CHAPTER REVIEW

CASH FLOW ESTIMATION

1. **Capital budgeting** consists of two distinct processes. The first process requires estimating the **incremental cash flows associated with the projects under consideration**. The second process involves **applying capital budgeting techniques to the estimated cash flows to evaluate projects**.

126   Chapter 10

2. All of the capital budgeting evaluation techniques depend on the accuracy of the cash flow estimates. If the estimates are inaccurate, the evaluation will also be inaccurate. It is much easier to evaluate projects using NPV or IRR than it is to develop accurate cash flow figures.

PROJECT CASH FLOWS

3. Developing cash flow estimates for **new venture projects** is the most difficult because the business doesn't have past experience on which to base its estimates.
   - a.) Prior to the project startup there are almost always initial costs (e.g. purchasing equipment and installing it). All of these expenses are part of the **initial outlay** and are treated as a cash flow that takes place at time zero (C_0), the beginning of the project.
   - b.) The incremental sales in terms of units and dollars (a cash inflow) must be estimated. If this project introduces a new product that may reduce sales of existing products, that loss of revenue must be subtracted from the new sales to calculate incremental revenues.
   - c.) Costs and expenses (cash outflows) associated with this project must be estimated
   - d.) Depreciation associated with new asset acquisitions must be estimated even though depreciation is a noncash expense. Depreciation expense will affect taxable income which, in turn will impact tax expense, the next cash outflow.
   - e.) Finally the inflows and outflows discussed above must be combined to arrive at a net cash flow estimate for each period.
   - f.) **Expansion projects** involve the same elements as new ventures but with fewer new facilities and equipment.
   - g.) **Replacement projects** are easier to calculate because they involve known costs and usually don't impact revenue. Replacement projects often include the sale of old equipment, which must be included in the analysis, both because the sale represents a cash inflow, and because the sale may have tax implications.

4. The **typical pattern** for most projects is **early outflows, followed by later inflows** throughout the life of the project.

5. The only cash flows that are considered for evaluating capital projects are **incremental cash flow.** They must be in addition to any revenue that the firm is currently generating or any expenditure that the firm is currently incurring. The cash flows to be considered are the **difference** between costs and revenue including the project as opposed to without the project.

6. **Opportunity costs** should be included as cash flow estimates, even though opportunity costs are not recorded on the firm's accounting records. Opportunity costs are the cash flows lost related to the next best use of the asset. For example, if a vacant building is going to be used for a project, the opportunity cost might be the rent that is forgone because the building isn't available for its next best use. In this regard, no resource is used free of charge.

7. **Sunk costs**, costs that have already been incurred, **are not included**. The reason for this is that the decision either to do a project or not do a project will not change the fact that the sunk cost has already been incurred. Sunk costs do not qualify as incremental costs.

8. **Projects often require additional working capital**. For example, when a new product is under consideration, build-ups in accounts receivable and inventory are anticipated. Working capital requirements usually increase (a cash outflow) at the beginning of the project, and may continue to change (up or down) during the life of the project.

9. **Financing costs** (e.g. the interest paid on bonds sold to raise enough cash to begin the project) **are not included** in the cash flow analysis. Capital budgeting decisions should be made independent of the specific source of funding for the project, and therefore only operating cash flows are considered.

10. The cash flows that are included in capital budgeting analysis can be categorized as follows:

    a.) **Initial cash flows** – These cash flows typically occur only once at the beginning of the project. Included would be:
    - The purchase of a fixed asset (e.g. equipment)
    - The sale of an old fixed asset
    - An initial build-up of net working capital

    b.) **Operating cash flows** – These cash flows typically occur every year during the life of the project, but not necessarily the same amount each year. Included would be:
    - Incremental revenues from the sale of product
    - Incremental cost of goods sold
    - Other operating expenses
    - Opportunity costs (e.g. building rent)
    - Changes in working capital
    - Taxes
    - Depreciation (noncash, but affects taxes)

    c.) **Terminal cash flows** – These cash flows typically occur only at the end of the project. Included would be:
    - Sale of the equipment at the end of the project
    - Final change in net working capital
    - Tax implications of any of the terminal cash flows
    - For projects that are assumed to go on forever, the terminal value represents the present value of a perpetuity with an annual payment equal to the annual cash inflow.

TESTING YOUR UNDERSTANDING

TRUE-FALSE QUESTIONS

____1. The purchase of a fixed asset is not included in the cash flow estimating of a capital project because the asset purchase doesn't initially affect the Income Statement.

____2. Capital budgeting consists of one process: estimating incremental cash flows of all projects under consideration.

____3. The approximate cost of a resource is whatever has to be given up to use it.

____4. Depreciation is a noncash expense and can be ignored in capital budgeting.

____5. Many projects require an increase in working capital, which should be treated as a cash outflow.

____6. Almost anyone can be taught to use NPV and IRR to make correct capital budgeting decisions; it is estimating the correct incremental cash flows that causes the most difficulty.

____7. Unintentional biases are not a problem associated with estimating incremental cash flows because the people doing the estimating have no vested interest in the project's approval.

____8. Additional personnel and taxes should be reflected in a project's projected cash flows.

____9. There is a typical pattern for most capital projects consisting of early outflows followed by later cash inflows.

____10. Using a perpetuity is one way to estimate cash flows for a project that is expected to continue forever.

____11. Once cash flows and the cost of capital have been determined, calculating NPV or IRR involves making judgments.

____12. When calculating the initial outlay for a project, any tax implications are ignored.

____13. The estimating process for new projects tends to be less elaborate than for other projects.

____14. A piece of land would be a zero cost item only if it had no market value and no other use by the company.

____15. Interest expense for a project is not included, because the time cost of money has already accounted for it.

____16. Incremental cash flows are more difficult to estimate for new ventures.

MULTIPLE CHOICE QUESTIONS

1. Which of the following cash flows should be included in a capital budgeting analysis:
   a. incremental revenues and expenses.
   b. financing costs.
   c. sunk costs.
   d. a and b only.

2. Early cash inflows for a project that are lower than estimated:
   a. make it likely that later cash inflows will be higher than estimated.
   b. have no impact on later cash inflows.
   c. make it likely that later cash inflows will be lower also.
   d. none of the above.

3. Depreciation expense should be:
   a. excluded from a capital budgeting analysis because it is a noncash expense.
   b. included and treated like every other incremental expense.
   c. included because of its impact on tax expense.
   d. none of the above.

4. A project that steals business from other existing projects:
   a. must reflect this loss of income as a negative cash flow.
   b. need not make any allowances for this loss of business.
   c. must declare this loss of business as a positive cash flow.
   d. must declare 50% of the lost income as a negative cash flow.

5. Estimating incremental cash flows associated with capital projects is:
   a. easy and produces exact answers.
   b. difficult and arbitrary.
   c. requires a great deal of judgment about what to include and to exclude.
   d. both b and c.

6. Opportunity costs are:
   a. rarely included in a capital budgeting analysis.
   b. only included if they will improve the NPV of the project.
   c. only included if they are recorded in the firm's accounting system.
   d. none of the above.

7. New venture projects:
   a. tend to be a great deal riskier than current business.
   b. are the most difficult ones to estimate cash flows.
   c. do not involve new revenues.
   d. both a and b.

8. Changes in working capital are:
   a. not included as an estimated cash flow in capital budgeting.
   b. always included as a cash flow in capital budgeting.
   c. can create cash flows in more than one year of a project
   d. both b and c.

9. An Environmental Protection Agency requirement that requires strip coal mining companies to restore the land to its original condition:
   a. will probably make the last cash flow of a project negative.
   b. will probably make the last cash flow of a project positive.
   c. will increase the NPV of a project.
   d. none of the above.

10. A company owns an idle factory and is considering using it for a project. The factory's opportunity cost is:
    a. zero because the company already owns the resource.
    b. the amount of the factory's next best use.
    c. the cost of revamping the factory.
    d. the cost of building a new factory.

11. Replacement projects:
    a. are riskier than current operations.
    b. are less risky than current operations.
    c. carry the same risk as existing operations.
    d. none of the above.

12. Sunk costs:
    a. should be included in capital budgeting cash flows.
    b. can be changed by decisions about the project.
    c. have already been spent at the time of the analysis and should not be included.
    d. both a and b.

13. Capital budgeting requires _____ and _____ .
    a. computing NPV; computing IRR
    b. projecting cash flows; applying capital budgeting techniques
    c. projecting cash flows; computing NPV
    d. projecting cash flows; excluding depreciation

14. Which of the following cash flows is not incremental for the purposes of applying capital budgeting techniques?
    a. revenues from a new product
    b. taxes from new profits
    c. the cost of studying the new project last year
    d. the sale of an old piece of equipment in a replacement project

15. Which of the following best describes the treatment of the purchase of fixed assets and business expenses as cash flows?
    a. fixed assets are initial cash flows and business expenses are operating cash flows
    b. fixed assets are operating cash flows and business expenses are initial cash flows
    c. fixed assets can only be initial cash flows, but business expenses could be either initial or operating cash flows
    d. both fixed assets and business expenses could be either initial cash flows or operating cash flows

16. Which of the following cash flows is most likely to occur in a replacement project?
    a. the sale of an old piece of equipment
    b. incremental revenues
    c. incremental cost of goods sold
    d. additional working capital

17. If a project requires incremental borrowed money, the interest on the borrowed money should:
    a. be treated as an initial cash outflow in the capital budgeting analysis
    b. be included each year as an operating cash flow
    c. be based on when the actual cash payments are made
    d. not be included in the capital budgeting analysis

18. Working capital requirements:
    a. will always increase at the beginning of a project
    b. may or may not change during the life of a project
    c. will be less in the first year of a project than in the last year
    d. none of the above

19. Terminal values:
    a. should be calculated when projects are expected to continue forever
    b. may be the most significant cash flow of the project
    c. can sometimes be calculated using the constant growth model
    d. all of the above

20. MACRS:
    a. generates more depreciation expense over the life of the project than straight line
    b. is always depreciated over 3-, 5- or 7-years
    c. will recognize more depreciation expense in the first year than straight line
    d. all of the above

FILL-IN THE BLANK QUESTIONS

1. The two distinct processes involved in capital budgeting are _____ and _____.

2. Everything that must be spent before a project is started makes up the project's _____.

3. Replacement projects, where an old piece of equipment is sold, must consider this income as a cash _____.

4. The value of a resource in its best alternative use is its _____.

5. Projected cash flows should be _____, or in addition to, the company's normal business.

6. Since capital budgeting is based on operating cash flows, _____ costs are not included in the analysis.

7. Sunk costs should _____ be included in capital budgeting cash flows.

8. If a project is expected to continue forever, its _____ can be estimated using a perpetuity.

9. _____ projects are generally expected to save costs without generating new revenue.

10. Capital budgeting deals with _____ -tax cash flows.

11. _____ biases are one of the biggest problems in capital budgeting.

12. The Modified Accelerated Cost Recovery System (MACRS) allows a firm to recognize the cost of a fixed asset _____ than straight line depreciation.

PROBLEMS

1. Which of the following cash flows would be considered in evaluating a replacement project for a new machine?
   a. Cost of a new machine
   b. Cost of the old machine
   c. Salvage value of the old machine
   d. Salvage value of the new machine
   e. Annual maintenance of old machine
   f. Annual maintenance of new machine
   g. Existing operator's salary (he will also be running the new machine)
   h. Training cost for existing operator to learn new machine

2. What is the opportunity cost of a building that cost $1,000,000 five years ago and that today could be sold for $2,000,000 or could be converted into loft apartments for a cost of $1,500,000? (Assume that the conversion to loft apartments is the project under consideration.)

3. A replacement project involves the purchase of a new machine for $100,000 that will be depreciated over 10 years. The old machine was purchased six years ago for $60,000 and was depreciated using a 15-year life. Both machines use straight-line depreciation, including the half-year convention. What will the incremental depreciation expense be in the first year of the project if the old machine is sold and the new machine is purchased? What will it be in the second year of the project?

4. Refer to problem 3 (above). If the old machine is sold for $28,000, what is the after-tax cash flow associated with the sale of the machine that will be included in the initial cash outlay? Assume a 40% tax rate.

5. A new business venture capital project is expected to produce a $90,000 annual cash flow, beginning in Year 5 of the project and continuing indefinitely. If this company's cost of capital is 11%, what is this project's terminal value at the end of Year 6?

6. Referring back to problem 5, suppose that the cash flow of $90,000 is forecasted to grow at an annual rate of 2.5% beginning in Year 6. What is now the terminal value at the end of Year 6?

7. Calculate the cash flows associated with the following 8 year project:
   a. required purchase of a $100,000 machine to be depreciated using the straight line method of depreciation over 10 years (no half-year convention).
   b. before tax net inflows of $22,000 a year.
   c. a marginal tax rate of 32%.

8. Fezwick, Inc. just purchased a machine for $120,000 that will be depreciated using the 7-year MACRS table. If the tax rate is 40%, how much will Fezwick's tax be reduced each year as a result of recognizing the depreciation expense associated with the new machine?

9. Use the information from problem 8. If the purchase of the machine will reduce expenses by $40,000 each year, what is the operating cash flow for the project in Year 3?

10. Capital Corp. is introducing a new product that is estimated to generate the following revenues for the first three years of the project: $400,000; $750,000; $1,200,000. Cost of goods sold is forecast to be 45% of revenues. Accounts receivable are expected to increase by 8% of the increase in revenues; inventory is expected to increase by 14% of the increase in cost of goods sold, and accounts payable are expected to increase by 11% of the increase in cost of goods sold. Assuming no other factors will impact current assets and liabilities, what cash flow should be included in Year 3 related to changes in working capital?

ANSWERS TO QUESTIONS

TRUE-FALSE

1. f
2. f
3. t
4. f
5. t
6. t
7. f
8. t
9. t
10. t
11. f
12. f
13. f
14. t
15. t
16. t

FILL IN THE BLANKS

1. cash flow estimating; evaluation
2. initial outlay
3. inflow
4. opportunity cost
5. incremental
6. financing
7. never
8. terminal value
9. replacement
10. after
11. unintentional
12. more quickly

MULTIPLE CHOICE

1. a
2. c
3. c
4. a
5. d
6. d
7. d
8. d
9. a
10. b
11. c
12. c
13. b
14. c
15. d
16. a
17. d
18. b
19. d
20. c

ANSWERS TO PROBLEMS

1. a, c, d, e, f, h

2. $2,000,000

3.
	Year 1	Year 2
Depreciation on the new machine	$5,000	$10,000
Depreciation on the old machine	$4,000	$ 4,000
Difference	$1,000 Incr.	$ 6,000 Incr.

4.
Sale price of the old machine	$28,000
Book value of the old machine	$38,000 (purchase price- accum. depr.)
	($60,000 - $2,000 – 5x$4,000)
Loss on sale	$10,000
Times the tax rate	40%
Tax Reduction	$ 4,000

Cash flow related to sale = $28,000 sale + $4,000 tax savings = $32,000

5. $TV = \dfrac{\$90,000}{0.11} = \$8,181,818$

6. $TV = \dfrac{\$90,000(1.025)}{0.11 - 0.025} = \dfrac{\$92,250}{0.085} = \$1,085,294$

7. $C_0 = (\$100,000)$ to buy machine.
   In years 1 through 8
1) Inflows	$ 22,000
2) Depreciation	10,000
3) Incremental EBT	$ 12,000
4) Tax on Incremental EBT	3,840
Net Cash Flow [(1) – (4)]	$ 18,160

8.
Year 1 $120,000 x 40% x .143 =	$6,864
Year 2 $120,000 x 40% x .245 =	$11,760
Year 3 $120,000 x 40% x .175 =	$8,400
Year 4 $120,000 x 40% x .125 =	$6,000
Year 5 $120,000 x 40% x .089 =	$4,272
Year 6 $120,000 x 40% x .089 =	$4,272
Year 7 $120,000 x 40% x .089 =	$4,272
Year 8 $120,000 x 40% x .045 =	$2,160

9.
Expense reduction	$40,000
Additional depreciation	8,400
Increase in op. revenues	31,600
Tax (.4)	12,640
Operating income	18,960

Add depreciation	<u>8,400</u>
Operating cash flow	$27,360

10. ($1,200,000 - $750,000) x [.08 + (.14 - .11)(.45)] = $42,075

CHAPTER ELEVEN

RISK TOPICS AND REAL OPTIONS IN CAPITAL BUDGETING

LEARNING OBJECTIVES

After studying this chapter you should understand the following terms and concepts:

1. the importance of factoring in risk for cash flow estimates and capital budgeting techniques;
2. using scenario/sensitivity analysis and Monte Carlo simulations to evaluate NPV and IRR calculations;
3. using a decision tree to explore various capital budgeting outcomes;
4. the definition of real options and how they can impact capital budgeting decisions;
5. incorporating risk into capital budgeting through the theoretical approach of risk adjusted rates of return;
6. the difficulty associated with building risk into any capital budgeting analysis.

CHAPTER SUMMARY

This chapter illustrates that while capital budgeting techniques treat cash flow estimates as precise, in fact they are just estimates. If they turn out to be different than the estimates, the capital budgeting decisions that were based on the estimates will be wrong. Managers need to consider techniques for evaluating the risk that is introduced into the capital budgeting process by the uncertainty associated with cash flow estimating. This chapter examines several of these techniques, including the concepts of scenario/sensitivity analysis and Monte Carlo simulation, which attempt to incorporate risk into the capital budgeting situation through the use of numerical methods. The use of a decision tree, which allows a capital project to be evaluated considering several possible outcomes, is also discussed. The concept of introducing real options into the capital budgeting process is reviewed. Finally, we take a look at a theoretical attempt to incorporate risk into the process by using risk-adjusted rates of return.

CHAPTER REVIEW

RISK IN CAPITAL BUDGETING

1. Cash flow estimates are not exact simply because they are estimates of the future. The estimates may be off by a little or off by a lot. This potential variability of estimated cash flows fits the risk scenario that we have been dealing with in earlier chapters. **The more our cash flows vary, the more risk we introduce to our evaluation techniques' results.**

2. Every cash flow estimate can be viewed as having a most likely value (the expected value) and a range of other possible values dispersed around the most likely value. In this sense, every cash flow estimate can be thought of as a distribution of a random variable with a probability distribution centered on the expected value.

3. Risk aversion applies to capital budgeting just as it does to investing. Any new capital project that a company takes on will have the potential of affecting the way the investors view the riskiness of the entire company. Taking on projects that are riskier than normal will increase the riskiness of the entire organization, which can result in investors demanding a higher required rate of return.

INCORPORATING RISK INTO CAPITAL BUDGETING – NUMERICAL AND COMPUTATIONAL METHODS

4. **Scenario analysis** attempts to incorporate risk into the capital budgeting analysis by developing a range of values that the cash flows may actually take on based on a worst, most likely, and best case scenario. By calculating the NPV for the cash flows for each of these scenarios we develop a good estimate of the range of possible NPVs along with the most likely NPV. Clearly if the worst case scenario still results in a positive NPV, the project is not very risky.

5. **Computer simulations,** such as the **Monte Carlo** simulation, can consider a great number of possibilities for NPV using randomly selected values for each cash flow estimate and can calculate the probability distribution for a project based on the probability distributions of all the individual cash flows. There are several drawbacks to this approach: (1) estimating the probability distributions for cash flows can be difficult; (2) cash flows in a capital project are related, not random events, so the random selection of cash flows may not be realistic, and (3) even with a range of possible results, it is difficult to select among competing projects.

6. A **decision tree analysis** is a method for evaluating capital projects by incorporating several different possible outcomes into a single analysis. For example, this technique would allow a firm to evaluate the introduction of a new product and incorporate a range of consumer responses from extremely popular to very unpopular. Each scenario would be assigned an estimated probability, and the expected value of the decision tree (e.g. the NPV of the project) would be the weighted average of each possible outcome, using the probabilities as weights.

REAL OPTIONS

7. A **real option** in a business setting is the ability to take a course of action different than the original plan that has the potential to lead to a more financially favorable result. The term "real"

is used to distinguish it from a financial option like a "call option." A real option is the business equivalent for "keeping your options open." Consider a company that is planning to introduce a new product. Once the product is introduced, subsequent business decisions may depend on the success of the product. If it is unsuccessful, plans may be made to phase it out early. If it is successful, plans may be made to introduce complimentary product lines. However, financial commitments may have to be made at the beginning of the project just to keep these two possible real options open, whether or not either of them actually occurs. The up-front cost of a real option must be considered in relation to the possible financial improvement that can result if the option is exercised.

8. Real options can be valued based on their expected impact on a project's profitability (e.g. NPV), but the concept of risk must also be addressed. Having real options can reduce the overall risk of a project, and one way to incorporate that reduced risk is to evaluate the project (e.g. using NPV) including the real option using an interest rate lower than the cost of capital. This technique is theoretically pleasing, but it is also subjective and difficult to do with precision.

9. Following are several types of real options that are used in business:

   a.) **Abandonment option** – incurring a cost to maintain the ability to discontinue a project before its planned completion (normally used if the project isn't going well).
   b.) **Expansion option** – incurring a cost to expand a project beyond its original scope (normally used if a project is doing better than expected).
   c.) **Investment timing option** – incurring a cost to keep an option open because the correct decision on the option isn't known at the beginning of the project.
   d.) **Flexibility options** – incurring a cost to maintain flexibility in a project (e.g. buying from two suppliers at a higher price to protect against one supplier failing).

INCORPORATING RISK INTO CAPITAL BUDGETING – THE THEORETICAL APPROACH AND RISK-ADJUSTED RATES OF RETURN

10. The theoretical approach to incorporating risk into capital budgeting involves using an interest rate (discount rate) other than the cost of capital based on the individual project's risk. Projects with risks higher than the average project undertaken by the firm would use a discount rate higher than the cost of capital, and vice versa. Using a higher discount rate to calculate the present value of the cash flows will result in a lower NPV, making it more difficult for a project to be accepted. The required IRR will be higher because of the higher percent used for the discount rate.

11. **Replacement projects** are usually evaluated at the cost of capital, because they generally have the same level of risk as current projects. **Expansion projects** are a little riskier and are usually evaluated by adding one to three percentage points to the cost of capital for their risk premium. **New venture** projects are the riskiest, but just how risky and how much to add for risk can be difficult to estimate.

12. If we look at a company as simply being a portfolio of the capital projects that it has undertaken since it began business, then it makes sense to look at portfolio theory in order to incorporate risk into capital budgeting for new ventures. Taking on a new venture project can be viewed as a form of diversification, and so the measure of risk could be considered to be the beta of the project.

One way to determine the **beta** of that project would be to find an outside firm that is solely in the line of business of the new venture. The beta of that firm can be used as a surrogate for the beta of the project. This is known as the **pure play** method of selecting a beta for a capital project. This approach sounds simple, but it can be very difficult to find the pure play betas of many types of new ventures. We are often forced to estimate betas based on similar types of businesses, and again estimates reduce the certainty of the conclusions.

Also, plugging beta into the CAPM does not account for all risk, only systematic risk. For these reasons, the CAPM is used to adjust for risk in theoretical situations more often than actual situations. Risk is most often accounted for in business decisions by the judgments of the business managers who are making the final decisions.

TESTING YOUR UNDERSTANDING

TRUE-FALSE QUESTIONS

_____1. Better decision making concerning capital projects means that decision makers must at least recognize and consider the risk of each different project.

_____2. Capital budgeters are risk averse.

_____3. A higher cost of capital means a higher IRR will be required for a project to be accepted.

_____4. Risky cash flow estimates can result in incorrect decisions using NPV or IRR.

_____5. Every capital budgeting project affects the total risk of a company.

_____6. The cost of capital plus 5 percentage points is usually the appropriate discount rate for replacement projects.

_____7. Almost every estimated cash flow has an expected value and a range of other possible values.

_____8. Scenario analysis allows the capital budgeter to predict cash flows with total accuracy.

_____9. One of the drawbacks to the Monte Carlo simulation is that individual cash flows are not usually independent.

_____10. A decision tree is limited to looking at five possible outcomes for a capital project.

_____11. Decision trees assign probabilities to possible outcomes for capital projects.

_____12. Real options provide important additional considerations for capital budgeting decisions.

____13. The cost of abandoning a project might be treated as a real option.

____14. The effect of a real option on a capital project should include an adjustment for any change in the risk of the project that the real option might introduce.

____15. The pure play method can be used to risk adjust almost any capital project.

MULTIPLE CHOICE QUESTIONS

1. Capital projects that have the same risk of current projects:
   a. will be evaluated using the firm's cost of capital.
   b. will increase the total risk of the firm.
   c. will keep the firm's total risk the same.
   d. a and c only.

2. Which of the following is not a type of real option?
   a. Abandonment option
   b. Expansion option
   c. Financial call option
   d. Investment timing option

3. When using scenario analysis, if the best case scenario results in a negative NPV:
   a. no analysis of most likely or worst case needs to be done.
   b. the project will be rejected.
   c. both a and b.
   d. none of the above.

4. A Monte Carlo simulation
   a. only uses the most likely values in estimating a project's risk.
   b. is a computer simulation that creates thousands of scenarios.
   c. provides a range of NPVs for a project to help assess risk.
   d. all of the above
   e. b and c only.

5. The decision tree analysis method
   a. incorporates several different possible outcomes for a capital project.
   b. assigns probabilities to outcomes
   c. uses a weighted average of the possible outcomes to evaluate the project.
   d. all of the above.

6. Using a higher cost of capital for riskier projects:
   a. will decrease a project's chance of acceptance.
   b. will increase a project's NPV.
   c. will decrease a project's required IRR.
   d. all of the above.

142   Chapter 11

7. New venture projects:
    a. tend to be a great deal riskier than current business.
    b. can be discounted with the help of the CAPM.
    c. diversify a company's portfolio of projects.
    d. all of the above

8. Using the CAPM to estimate risk adjusted rates:
    a. works well all the time in the real world.
    b. works best in theory because it is hard to get an appropriate beta.
    c. ignores systematic risk.
    d. none of the above.

9. A real option
    a. always provides an improved financial return for a project.
    b. may involve an up-front payment that will end up having no value to the firm.
    c. would never consider the abandonment of a project.
    d. both a and b.

10. Which of the following methods is/are used to risk adjust rates of return?
    a. the pure play method.
    b. the accounting beta method.
    c. management judgment.
    d. all of the above.
    e. only a and b.

11. Replacement projects:
    a. are riskier than current operations.
    b. are less risky than current operations.
    c. carry the same risk as existing operations.
    d. none of the above.

12. Risk in cash flow estimates implies that:
    a. they cannot be predicted with assurance
    b. they could be described as random variables
    c. the expected value is the mean of the distribution
    d. all of the above

13. A company can be viewed as:
    a. a portfolio of all of its projects since the company's inception
    b. a portfolio of all of the current year's projects
    c. a portfolio of all of the current year's projects that are riskier than the company's average project.
    d. none of the above

14. Scenario analysis:
    a. only calculates best case, worst case and most likely scenarios
    b. always uses the most likely scenario as the appropriate evaluation of the project
    c. only applies to NPV calculations, not IRR calculations
    d. none of the above

15. Which of the following is not a drawback to using Monte Carlo simulations?
    a. project cash flows are negatively correlated
    b. it is difficult to interpret simulated probability distributions
    c. probability distributions of cash flows have to be estimated subjectively
    d. all of the above are drawbacks

16. The decision tree technique will:
    a. always result in the same decision as the scenario analysis approach
    b. consider only the best and worst possible scenarios
    c. have a branch representing each possible series of cash flows
    d. will always generate both positive and negative NPVs

17. Which of the following would not be included in a real option analysis?
    a. a land option contract
    b. the cost of escaping from a contract early
    c. the cost of reserving a space in a production line
    d. all of the above would be included in a real option analysis

18. Which of the following is a real option?
    a. a call option
    b. a put option
    c. an option to borrow money
    d. all of the above

19. The abandonment option:
    a. will prevent a project from losing money if it is not successful
    b. should lower the cost of abandoning a project
    c. always has an upfront cost
    d. both a. and b. above

20. Real options can:
    a. increase the perceived risk of a project
    b. lower the perceived risk of a project
    c. increase the potential profit of a project
    d. both b. and c. above

FILL-IN THE BLANK QUESTIONS

1. If a capital budgeting project is viewed as a business in a particular field, a _____ common to that field and the SML can be used to estimate a risk-adjusted rate for project analysis.

2. When a project can turn out more than one way, a _____ can be used to help evaluate the project.

3. The ability or right to take a certain course of action, which will generally lead to a favorable financial result is known as a _____.

144   Chapter 11

4. _____ uses a worst case, most likely, and best case analysis.

5. Regressing a division's historical return on equity against the return on the S&P 500 in order to assess risk is known as the _____.

6. Firms that take on riskier projects can cause investors to require a _____ required rate of return.

7. _____ makes assumptions that specify the shapes of probability distributions for each future cash flow in a capital budgeting project.

8. Using a higher discount rate for riskier projects results in a _____ NPV.

9. Another name for scenario analysis is _____.

10. Scenario analysis estimates the _____, _____, and _____ values for each cash flow.

11. _____ projects are somewhat risky and are discounted at 1 to 3 percentage points above the cost of capital.

12. The most likely value of each cash flow is called the _____.

PROBLEMS

1. The initial cost of a project is $10,000. There is a 30% chance that the project will be highly successful, in which case cash flows of $4,500 are expected for the next four years. There is a 70% chance that the project will only be marginally successful, in which case the cash flows are expected to be $3,200 for the next four years. Using the decision tree method and a 12% cost of capital, what is the expected NPV of this project?

2. Use the information from the previous problem. What is the range of NPVs for this project?

3. A project has an initial outlay of $2,800 and 3 variable cash inflow scenarios. Assume the cost of capital is 12%. What is the NPV for each scenario?

	YEAR 1	YEAR 2	YEAR 3
WORST	1,200	1,000	800
MOST LIKELY	1,400	1,300	1,200
BEST	1,600	1,400	1,300

4. Average stocks are paying 7.0%, and short term treasuries are paying 3.0%. Marshall, Inc. has a beta of 1.3 and is considering a risky project in an industry with direct competitors who have betas that average 1.8. What discount rate should Marshall use in evaluating the cash flows from this project?

5. Use the information from the previous problem. If the project will have an initial cost of $1.8 million with expected cash inflows of $450,000 for the next five years, should Marshall accept the project?

6. An abandonment option will have an upfront cost of $1.0 million. There is a 40% chance that the abandonment option would be used, in which case cash outflows of $800,000 in Year 4, $1,400,000 in Year 5 and $1,200,000 in Year 6 will be avoided. If the discount rate is 7.0%, should the abandonment option be exercised?

ANSWERS TO QUESTIONS

TRUE-FALSE

1. t
2. t
3. t
4. t
5. t
6. f
7. t
8. f
9. t
10. f
11. t
12. t
13. t
14. t
15. f

FILL IN THE BLANKS

1. beta
2. decision tree
3. real option
4. Scenario analysis
5. accounting beta method
6. higher
7. Monte Carlo simulation
8. lower
9. sensitivity analysis
10. worst case, most likely, best case
11. Expansion
12. point estimate

MULTIPLE CHOICE

1. d
2. c
3. c
4. e
5. d
6. a
7. d
8. b
9. b
10. d
11. c
12. d
13. a
14. d
15. a
16. c
17. d
18. c
19. b
20. d

ANSWERS TO PROBLEMS

1. NPV (successful) = ($10,000) + ($4,500)(3.0373) = $3,668
   NPV (marginal) = ($10,000) + ($3,200)(3.0373) = ($281)

   NPV (project) = .3(3,668) + .7(-281) = $904

2. Highly successful: (10,000) + 3.0373 x 4,500 = 3,667.86

   Marginally successful: (10,000) + 3.0373 x 3,200 = (280.64)

3. WORST = NPV = −2800 + 1200(.8929) + 1000(.7972) + 800(.7118) =
   −2800 + 1071.48 + 797.20 + 569.44 = −$361.88

   MOST = NPV = −2800 + 1400(.8929) + 1300(.7972) + 1200(.7118) =
   LIKELY −2800 + 1250.06 + 1036.36 + 854.16 = +$340.58

   BEST = NPV = −2800 + 1600(.8929) + 1400(.7972) + 1300(.7118) =
   −2800 + 1428.64 + 1116.08 + 925.34 = +$670.06

4. 3.0% + (7.0% - 3.0%) x 1.8 = 10.2%

5. PV of cash inflows:
   n = 5
   PMT = 450,000
   FV = 0
   I/Y = 10.2
   PV = ? = $1,697,173.93

   Since the PV of the cash inflows is less than the initial cost, the project should be rejected.

6. Cost of abandonment option = $1.0 million

   Potential savings: .4 x [(800,000 x .7629) + (1,400,000 x .713) + (1,200,000 x .6663)]
   = $963,232

   In this case, the potential savings is less than the cost, so the abandonment option should not be exercised.

CHAPTER TWELVE

THE COST OF CAPITAL

LEARNING OBJECTIVES

After studying this chapter you should understand the following terms and concepts:

1. the three basic components of capital and the determinants of capital structure;
2. the relationship between the return received by an investor and the cost of capital to the firm;
3. how the weighted average cost of capital (WACC) is calculated;
4. three ways to look at capital structure: book value, market value and target capital structure;
5. calculating the component costs of capital for debt, preferred stock, and equity (both retained earnings and new equity);
6. three different ways to calculate the cost of retained earnings: CAPM, the dividend growth approach, and the risk premium approach;
7. the marginal cost of capital (MCC) and the investment opportunity schedule (IOS);
8. how to handle projects that are to be funded with a single source of capital.

CHAPTER SUMMARY

This chapter begins with a reminder that no company should invest in any project that does not return at least the firm's cost of capital. Capital is defined and the three components of capital are discussed. Three different concepts of capital structure are discussed (book value, market value and target), as are the practical limitations of maintaining an exact capital structure at all times. The weighted average cost of capital (WACC) is defined, and its calculation is illustrated.

The appropriate methods for calculating the individual component costs for capital (debt, preferred stock, retained earnings and new equity) are explained. The marginal cost of capital (MCC) and the investment opportunity schedule (IOS) are illustrated, demonstrating the importance of the MCC as part of the capital budgeting process. The chapter concludes with a comprehensive problem that details all of the calculations needed to develop a company's WACC and the marginal cost of capital.

CHAPTER REVIEW

THE PURPOSE OF THE COST OF CAPITAL

1. A company's **cost of capital** is the average rate it pays for the use of its capital funds. No company should invest in any project unless it returns more than the cost of capital. In practical terms, this means that any acceptable project must have a positive NPV when the cost of capital is used as the discount rate or an IRR that exceeds the cost of capital.

COST OF CAPITAL CONCEPTS

2. The two primary **capital components** are debt and common equity. Preferred stock shares some of the characteristics of both debt and equity, but for cost of capital development, it is considered to be a third component that is treated separately.
    a.) The mix of capital components used by a company at any moment in time is known as its **capital structure.**
    b.) A firm's most desirable mix of capital components is called its **target capital structure**. Although firms do not maintain the exact same capital structure every time additional capital is raised, the assumption is made that all new funds are raised in the same proportions as the existing capital structure.

3. Each capital component has a different rate of return and a different cost. Debt tends to have the lowest return (consistent with the concept that debt investors take on the lowest risk) and cost, followed by preferred stock, and then common stock, which represents the highest risk to investors.

4. A firm's overall **cost of capital** is the weighted average cost of the separate sources of capital used. This is called the **weighted average cost of capital (WACC)**. The dollar amount of each capital component is calculated and computed as a percent of the total dollar amount of capital. These percentages are used as the weights in the WACC calculation. Then the cost of each component is multiplied by its percentage, and the separate calculations are added to get the WACC.

5. Three different approaches can be used to calculate the weights that are used in the development of the WACC.
    a.) A **target capital structure** can be selected. This is usually based on management judgment as to what capital structure seems to best fit the individual company.
    b.) The **book value** approach reflects the prices at which the securities were originally sold. Book value accurately reflects the cost of capital for capital projects that the company has already undertaken.
    c.) **Market value** approach reflects the current market price of those same securities. Market value should be used to calculate the cost of capital for projects being considered, because it reflects the cost of capital under current conditions that will prevail for the new projects. Very often, the market based capital structure will closely resemble the target capital structure that the firm has established.

CALCULATING THE WACC

6. Calculating the WACC involves three steps: developing a market-value-based capital structure, adjusting the market returns to reflect the component costs of capital, and putting these two factors together to calculate a WACC.

   a.) Taxes affect only the debt component of capital structure because interest payments are tax deductible to the firm paying the interest (while dividends paid on preferred and common stock are not deductible). The after-tax cost of debt is the interest rate paid on debt multiplied by (1 - the tax rate), or

   Cost of debt (after tax) = $k_d(1 - T)$

   Since debt was already the lowest cost of capital (on a before-tax basis), computing the cost on an after-tax basis reduces the cost of debt even further and helps to explain why debt is a real bargain.

   b.) **Flotation costs** are the administrative fees and expenses that add to the cost of issuing and selling securities. These costs are relatively small when debt is issued and are often ignored, but they must be factored in when considering the cost issuing preferred or common stock.

   c.) **Preferred stock** has no tax considerations, but flotation costs must be considered. The cost of preferred stock is the preferred dividend divided by the return on the investment multiplied by one minus the flotation costs percentage (f) expressed as a decimal, or

   Cost of preferred stock = $D_P/(1 - f)P_P$

   d.) The **equity component** has two sources: retained earnings and the sale of new stock. These two sources must be treated individually because retained earnings are internally generated and are not affected by floatation costs, while the sale of new stock must include the effect of floatation costs.

   e.) Three different approaches can be used to compute the **cost of retained earnings**.
   (1) The CAPM may be used to estimate the required rate of return for retained earnings for a particular stock.
   (2) The Gordon Model can also be used to price a stock that is expected to grow at a constant rate for the indefinite future.

   $$P_0 = D_0(1 + g)/(k_e - g)$$

   By solving the Gordon Model for k_e, we get

   $$k_e = [D_0(1 + g)/P_0] + g$$

   (3) Finally, a risk premium of from 3% to 5 % can be added to the before-tax cost of debt to allow for the greater riskiness of the equity component.

   f.) The **cost of new stock** will be the same as the cost of retained earnings **except** for the flotation costs associated with the sale of new shares of stock.

   $$k_e = [D_0(1 + g)/P_0(1 - f)] + g$$

152   Chapter 12

THE MARGINAL COST OF CAPITAL (MCC)

7. The **marginal cost of capital (MCC)** is defined as the cost of raising the next dollar of capital. The WACC for a firm will depend to some extent on the amount of capital that is being raised because the cost of capital increases as funding requirements increase. These increases are illustrated in the marginal cost of capital schedule, a graph that plots the size of the capital program on the horizontal axis (x-axis) and the cost of capital on the vertical axis (y-axis).

   a.) The first increase typically occurs when the firm runs out of retained earnings and must sell new shares of stock. At this time, the cost of equity will increase as a component of the WACC because of the floatation costs associated with issuing new stock.
   b.) Another increase typically occurs when a firm is attempting to raise a large amount of funds that will increase the riskiness of the firm, so that investors will demand a higher required rate of return on both debt and equity investments.
   c.) The breakpoints (places where the cost of WACC changes) on the graph can be calculated as follows. Suppose equity is 40% of the capital structure. If $1 million of retained earnings is expected to be available, then $.40 of every dollar of capital will be provided by retained earnings until ($1 million/40%) or $2.5 million has been spent. At that time, all of the $1 million in retained earnings will have been used, and any additional capital requirements will have to be satisfied using new common stock as the equity component. Therefore, $2.5 million would represent a breakpoint on the MCC schedule.
   d.) **The investment opportunity schedule (IOS)** rank orders capital projects from high to low (based on IRR) and plots them on the MCC schedule as rectangles, with the width of the base representing the size of the project in dollars and the height representing the IRR. By combining the MCC and the IOS, a firm can identify which projects should be funded based on the expected return. To avoid confusion as to the appropriate WACC to use based on the MCC schedule, **the intersection of the MCC and the IOS should define the WACC for the planning period.**

HANDLING SEPARATELY FUNDED PROJECTS

8. Even when an individual capital project will be funded by a single component of funding (e.g. funded totally through the issuance of debt), the project must be evaluated as part of the total capital budgeting picture. All capital projects should be evaluated using the WACC, not the cost of a single source of financing.

TESTING YOUR UNDERSTANDING

TRUE-FALSE QUESTIONS

____1. Book value most accurately reflects the current state of capital markets.

____2. A firm's capital structure can be based on either book or market value.

____3. Retained earnings are a free source of funding for a firm.

____4. An exact capital structure is maintained continuously by most firms.

___5. The first break point in the MCC usually occurs when the firm runs out of retained earnings.

___6. The cost of each capital component is related to the returns required by the investors who provide that component.

___7. No company should invest in any project that returns less than the company's cost of capital.

___8. Incorrectly estimating a firm's cost of capital can cause a firm to make incorrect investment decisions.

___9. Calculating a book value based capital structure is easier than calculating a market value based capital structure.

___10. The need to raise large amounts of capital has no effect on the MCC.

MULTIPLE CHOICE QUESTIONS

1. The cost of retained earnings can be estimated by using:
   a. the CAPM.
   b. the Gordon Model.
   c. a risk premium.
   d. all of the above.
   e. none of the above.

2. If a capital project is to be funded by a single source of capital:
   a. only the cost of that source should be used to evaluate the project.
   b. the project should be evaluated using the firm's WACC.
   c. a close matching of the funding source and use should be made.
   d. none of the above.

3. MCC refers to:
   a. the cost of the last dollar of capital raised.
   b. the cost of the next dollar of capital raised.
   c. the average cost of all previously raised capital.
   d. none of the above.

4. Capital refers to:
   a. money used to get businesses started.
   b. money used to acquire long term assets.
   c. money acquired for new venture projects.
   d. all of the above.

5. The tax effect on individual capital structure components applies:
   a. to debt and preferred stock.
   b. to preferred stock and common stock.
   c. to debt only.
   d. none of the above.

6. The three components of capital structure listed from highest to lowest cost are:
   a. common stock, preferred stock, debt.
   b. debt, preferred stock, common stock.
   c. preferred stock, debt, common stock.
   d. debt, common stock, preferred stock.

7. The WACC:
   a. can remain constant after retained earnings are exhausted when moderate levels of capital are raised.
   b. tends to jump when large capital projects must be funded.
   c. both a and b.
   d. none of the above.

8. It is more expensive to sell new shares of common stock than to:
   a. use retained earnings.
   b. issue debt.
   c. issue preferred stock.
   d. all of the above.

9. In order to calculate a firm's WACC, a person must have:
   a. the dollar amounts of the capital components in use.
   b. the cost of each capital component.
   c. both a and b.
   d. none of the above.

10. The cost of debt can be considered a bargain because:
    a. it does not increase the risk of the firm.
    b. of the tax deductibility of interest payments.
    c. there are no significant flotation costs to issue debt.
    d. all of the above.
    e. both b and c.

11. The market return on an equity investment:
    a. is easier to calculate than the market return on debt.
    b. is harder to calculate than the return on debt.
    c. is harder to calculate than the return on preferred stock.
    d. both b and c.

12. The cost of capital:
    a. depends on the risk of the project relative to the overall risk of the company
    b. is critical for the company to make correct investment decisions
    c. determines whether or not a project contributes to increasing shareholder wealth
    d. all of the above
    e. only b. and c. above

13. The target capital structure is:
    a. always the same as the market based capital structure
    b. always the same as the book value based capital structure
    c. is largely based on management experience and judgment
    d. none of the above

14. If the percent debt in the market based capital structure is below the target percent debt, then management will:
    a. raise capital based on the best judgment of management
    b. always issue debt as the way to raise additional capital
    c. raise capital using the all of the capital components in the target capital structure percentages
    d. raise capital using the all of the capital components in the market capital structure percentages

15. The return received by an investor on debt or equity is:
    a. equal to the after-tax cost of that source of capital to the company
    b. based on the risk that the investor is taking by making the investment
    c. equal to the company's WACC
    d. none of the above

16. The weights used to calculate the market based WACC:
    a. can be determined from the company's balance sheet
    b. require an analysis of the market based values of the equity components
    c. require an analysis of the market based values of the debt components
    d. both b. and c. are correct

17. Floatation costs:
    a. are part of the cost of capital calculation for all debt and equity components
    b. are normally ignored for debt
    c. are normally ignored for retained earnings
    d. all of the above are true

18. The risk premium approach to calculating the cost of retained earnings:
    a. uses the before-tax cost of debt as a basis
    b. uses the after-tax cost of debt as a basis
    c. uses the average coupon rate for all outstanding debt as a basis
    d. none of the above is true

19. The IOS:
    a. rank orders capital projects from highest to lowest NPV
    b. determines the size of the capital program for the coming year
    c. rank orders capital projects from highest to lowest IRR
    d. rank orders capital projects from highest to lowest capital requirement

20. The WACC for the planning period is:
    a. the highest WACC shown on the MCC
    b. the intersection of the MCC and the IOS
    c. the project with the lowest IRR that is accepted in the capital program
    d. none of the above

FILL-IN THE BLANK QUESTIONS

1. The _____ value basis for capital structure is appropriate for calculating WACC.

2. _____ are the only internally generated capital source.

3. _____ value is when a firm's capital structure is valued at the prices at which the securities were originally sold.

4. Administrative fees and expenses incurred with issuing and selling securities are known as _____ costs.

5. The mix of capital components in use by a company at a point in time is known as its _____.

6. A firm's cost of debt tends to be the cheapest of the capital components because debt is the least _____ of the components.

7. Using the _____ approach, between 3% and 5% is added to the cost of debt in order to estimate the cost of equity investments.

8. The mix of capital components that management considers most desirable is known as a firm's _____.

9. _____ is a cross between debt and equity.

10. To compute the WACC, management must know the _____ and the _____ of the capital components..

PROBLEMS

1. Calculate the WACC for the following firm given this information about its capital structure (assume a 40% tax rate):

Capital Components	Value	Cost
Debt	$ 75,000	8% (before tax)
Preferred Stock	50,000	10%
Common Stock	100,000	13%

2. What is the after tax cost of debt for a firm issuing 11% coupon rate bonds which yield 10% to investors buying them now when the firm's marginal tax rate is 34%?

3. What is a corporation's cost of preferred capital if the interest rate on similar stocks today is 8% and flotation costs are expected to average 9%?

4. Estimate a firm's cost of retained earnings using the CAPM when its beta is 1.5, the return on the S & P 500 is 11.5% and is expected to remain at that level, and the risk free rate is 6%.

5. Using the Gordon Model, estimate the cost of retained earnings for a firm whose stock is currently selling for $40, who paid a dividend of $.75 last year, and whose growth is expected to be 6% indefinitely.

6. Use the following information to determine (1) how much the WACC will change as it uses up retained earnings and moves into new equity, and (2) at what dollar amount will the WACC increase. Assume a 40% tax rate.

		Component Cost
Debt	30%	9% (before tax)
Equity	70%	11% from retained earnings
		13% from new stock

Expected Retained Earnings $ 5m
Total Capital Requirements $12 m

7. Rand Corp. has issued 200,000 shares of stock at an average issue price of $24. They also have $1,000,000 in outstanding 7% coupon bonds and $800,000 in 8% coupon bonds. Both bond issues are semiannual and have eight years to maturity. What is Rand's capital structure based on book values?

8. Use the information from the previous problem. If Rand stock is currently selling for $21.50, and bonds comparable to Rand's are currently yielding 6.0%, what is Rand's capital structure based on market values?

9. Harrigan Corp's only outstanding bond issue was issued 20 years ago. They were 30-year, semiannual bonds with an 11% coupon, and they are currently selling for $1,371.94. Based on this information, determine the range for the cost of retained earnings using the risk premium approach.

10. Yandell, Inc. is reviewing the following projects for next year's capital program:

Project	IRR	Capital Required
A	10.5%	$1.2 million
B	10.0%	$0.6 million
C	9.5%	$0.6 million
D	9.0%	$0.5 million
E	8.5%	$0.5 million
F	8.0%	$0.8 million

Yandell's cost of capital is 8.5%. They will have $0.9 million available from net income to help fund the capital program. Requirements beyond that will require the issuance of new stock which will raise the cost of capital to 9.3%. They can borrow $1.0 million at their current borrowing rate, but additional borrowing will cause the cost of capital to rise to 9.7%. Yandell's capital structure is 40% debt and 60% equity. Which of the above projects should be accepted for next year's capital program?

158 Chapter 12

ANSWERS TO QUESTIONS

TRUE-FALSE

1. f
2. t
3. f
4. f
5. t
6. t
7. t
8. t
9. t
10. f

MULTIPLE CHOICE

1. d
2. b
3. b
4. d
5. c
6. a
7. c
8. d
9. c
10. e
11. d
12. d
13. c
14. a
15. b
16. d
17. b
18. a
19. c
20. b

FILL IN THE BLANKS

1. market
2. Retained earnings
3. Book
4. flotation
5. capital structure
6. risky
7. risk premium
8. target capital structure
9. Preferred stock
10. mix, cost

ANSWERS TO PROBLEMS

1. $75000/225000 = .3333 \times .08(1 - .4) = .0160$

    $50000/225000 = .2222 \times .10 = .0222$

    $100000/225000 = .4444 \times .13 = .0578$ .0960 or 9.60%

2. $.10(1 - .34) = 6.6\%$

3. $8\% / 1 - .09 = .08 / .91 = .0879$ or 8.79%

4. $k_x = 6\% + (11.5\% - 6\%)1.5$
    $= 6\% + 8.25\% = 14.25\%$

5. $.75(1.06) / 40 + .06 = .07988$ or 7.99%

6. With equity from retained earnings
Debt	$.3 \times .09(1 - .4) = .0162$
Equity	$.7 \times .11 = .077$
WACC	$= .0932 = 9.32\%$

    With equity from new stock
Debt	$.3 \times .09(1 - .4) = .0162$
Equity	$.7 \times .13 = .091$
WACC	$= .1072 = 10.72\%$

    The increase in the WACC is 10.72% - 9.32% = 1.4%

    The break point will occur when retained earnings are used up $5/.7 = $7,142,857

7. Book value of stock: 200,000 x $24 = $4,800,000
    Book value of bonds: $1,800,000

    Capital structure: Stock   4.8/6.6 = 72.7%
                                Bonds   1.8/6.6 = 27.3%

160 Chapter 12

8.   Market value of stock: 200,000 x $21.50 = $4,300,000

Market value of 7% bonds: n = 16
                            I/Y = 3
                            PMT = 35
                            FV = 1,000
                            PV = ? = 1,062.81 x 1,000 = $1,062,810

Market value of 8% bonds: n = 16
                            I/Y = 3
                            PMT = 40
                            FV = 1,000
                            PV = ? = 1,125.61 x 800 = $900,488

Total market value = $4,300,000 + $1,062,810 + $900,488 = $6,263,298

Capital structure: Stocks 4,300,000/6,263,298 = 68.7%
                     Bonds   1,963,298/6,263,298 = 31.3%

9.   The current return on Harrigan's bonds is:

n = 20
PV = (1,371.94)
PMT = 55
FV = 1,000
I/Y = ? = 3.0 x 2 = 6.0%

Therefore, the risk premium approach would indicate that retained earnings should have a cost of between 9.0% and 11.0% (with a 3% to 5% risk premium).

10. Breakpoint for retained earnings: $900,000/.6 = $1,500,000
     Breakpoint for debt: $1,000,000/.4 = $2,500,000

Projects A and B will be accepted because they exceed even the highest MCC. Those two projects require $1.8 million and Project C will require an additional $0.6 million, totaling $2.4 million. The cost of capital at this level is 9.3%, so Project C will be accepted. Project D requires an additional $0.5 million, increasing the total to $2.9 million, which has a MCC of 9.7%. Since Project D only returns 9.0%, it will be rejected. Therefore, the capital program for the next year will include Projects A, B and C.

CHAPTER THIRTEEN

CAPITAL STRUCTURE AND LEVERAGE

LEARNING OBJECTIVES

After studying this chapter you should understand the following terms and concepts:

1. the difference between business risk and financial risk;
2. financial leverage and how it impacts return on equity (ROE) and earnings per share (EPS);
3. the relationship between financial leverage and return on capital employed (ROCE);
4. the impact of financial leverage on financial risk;
5. how to calculate the degree of financial leverage (DFL) and what it means;
6. operating leverage and how it impacts EBIT;
7. definitions of breakeven and contribution margin and how to calculate each;
8. how to calculate the degree of operating leverage (DOL) and what it means;
9. the compound effect of DFL and DOL;
10. the Modigliani and Miller capital structure theory, including some modifications;
11. how financial leverage relates to mergers and acquisitions.

CHAPTER SUMMARY

This chapter examines capital structure and the impact that it can have on the performance of the firm. The question of financial leverage, using borrowed funds to increase or decrease the effectiveness of equity, or the value of the firm as reflected by the price of the stock, are illustrated in detail. The various measures of performance are discussed, as is the factoring in of risk to the area of capital structure. Financial leverage and operating leverage are individually discussed and then combined for the examination of total leverage. An introductory discussion of capital structure theory is provided, using the work done by Modigliani and Miller as a baseline. Information is provided on the assumptions that were included in that work, and how modifications to those assumptions help define the relationship between the use of financial leverage and the impact financial leverage has on the price of a stock.

CHAPTER REVIEW

BACKGROUND

1. For this chapter the definition of **capital structure** has been modified to include just two components, debt and equity. Preferred stock is considered as a form of debt.

2. **Leverage** refers to the ability to enhance the effect of some effort. **Financial leverage** refers to the use of borrowed money or debt to enhance or increase the effectiveness of the equity that has been invested in a firm. If a firm has borrowed money, it is leveraged. The higher the percent of debt to total capital, the more highly leveraged the firm is considered to be. When a firm has a capital structure that consists of 15% debt and 85% equity, we say that it has 15% financial leverage. If a firm operates with only equity capital, it is considered to be **unleveraged.**

3. **Capital restructuring** involves exchanging some equity for debt, or some debt for equity, so that the percentages of equity and debt that make up the capital structure are changed. Exchanging equity for debt often increases the price of the remaining shares and thus the value of the firm. Sometimes, however, increasing debt decreases the price of the stock and the value of the firm. Management is looking for an **optimal capital structure** that will maximize the price of the stock and the value of the firm.

4. **Earnings before interest and taxes (EBIT)** is also called **operating income** and reflects the lowest line on the income statement before any financing expense (interest) is considered. Financial leverage has no effect on EBIT.

    a.) **Return on equity (ROE)** is earnings after taxes (also called **net income**) divided by equity.

    $$ROE = \frac{EAT}{equity}$$

    The more highly a firm is financially leveraged, the less equity there will be, so ROE will increase as financial leverage increases.

    b.) **Earnings per share (EPS)** is earnings after taxes divided by the total number of outstanding shares of common stock.

    $$EPS = \frac{EAT}{number\ of\ shares}$$

    The fewer shares that a firm has outstanding (reflecting higher financial leverage), the higher EPS will be.

5. In this chapter we will think of **risk** as a variation in financial performance as measured by ROE and EPS.

    a.) **Business risk** is defined as a variation in a firm's operating performance as measured by EBIT. This occurs when there are changes in revenue, costs, and expenses.

    b.) **Financial risk** is the additional variation (over and above business risk) in ROE and EPS that comes from including debt as part of the capital structure. Firms that have no debt have identical variations in ROE and EPS to the variation in EBIT, so when EBIT varies 10%, ROE and EPS will also vary 10%. Financial leverage causes financial risk.

FINANCIAL LEVERAGE

6. Financial leverage can have a positive effect on stock prices when it improves financial performance, and it can have a negative effect when it decreases financial performance. Because it increases the variability of financial performance, **financial leverage always increases risk**.

    When the basic profitability for a firm is good, a dollar for dollar replacement of debt for equity will result in higher interest charges but lower equity and a lower number of shares of stock. This combination of changes will result in improved financial performance as measured by ROE and EPS and will tend to drive stock prices up. When basic profitability for a firm is weak, the opposite occurs. Under these conditions, ROE and EPS decrease with increasing leverage, which will tend to drive stock prices down.

    Return on capital employed (ROCE) is a ratio that calculates the after tax cost of capital. ROCE is calculated as follows:

    $$\text{ROCE} = \frac{\text{EBIT}(1-T)}{\text{debt} + \text{equity}}$$

    EBIT(1 – T) is called after-tax operating income. The comparison of ROCE and the after-tax cost of debt will indicate whether additional debt will improve or degrade a stock's performance, as measured by ROE and EPS. Whenever the ROCE is more than the after tax cost of debt, the firm should use as much debt as possible because financial leverage will make operating results better. When the ROCE is less than the after-tax cost of debt, financial leverage will make operating results worse. This comparison would appear to make the decision of whether or not to take on more debt quite simple. However, increasing levels of debt means that a firm is taking on more risk, and the other implications of more risk have not been considered at this point. When we studied risk and return (Chapter 8), we determined that higher risk resulted in a higher return which, among other effects, can drive a stock price down, the exact opposite effect of an increasing ROE or EPS. These factors must be considered in the overall picture of financial leverage.

    In the real world operating figures can change almost instantly, while changing capital structure usually takes some time. So unless one can accurately predict future results and events, any firm can be surprised by unexpected downturns, which may be caused by lower than expected EBIT.

    Financial leverage positively enhances good results, but it negatively magnifies bad results. Because financial leverage causes more variations in results, it increases risk. The more financial leverage, the greater the possible variations and the greater the risk.

7. When leverage is low to moderate, investors tend to view it positively and to ignore the increased risk, especially when the economic outlook is positive. This causes the stock price to increase. When leverage is high or when economic prospects are negative, leverage is viewed negatively by investors, and stock prices of highly leveraged firms tend to drop. A firm will want to use the amount of leverage that maximizes the value of the price of its stock and thus the value of the firm. At this level of debt, the firm has its **optimal capital structure**.

8. As with many theoretical concepts, the optimal capital structure works better on paper than in the real world. We can summarize the concept with general guidelines that state firms with good profit potential and little or no debt should use more borrowed money when interest rates are reasonable. A capital structure with debt of between 30% and 50% is normally optimal for most businesses, and firms should typically avoid a debt level that exceeds 60%.

9. We know that financial leverage magnifies changes in EBIT into larger changes in ROE and EPS. But just how large are the impacts of these changes at various levels of leverage? A concept called **degree of financial leverage (DFL)** expresses the relative changes that occur in EPS and EBIT at a specific level of leverage.

$$DFL = \frac{EBIT}{EBIT - INTEREST}$$

When a percent change in EBIT is multiplied by the DFL, you get the actual percent change that will occur in EPS. The higher the DFL, the greater a small change in EBIT will be magnified into a larger change in EPS.

$$\%\Delta EPS = DFL \times \%\Delta EBIT$$

For example, when a firm has a DFL of 1 (which will occur when a firm has no debt), a 10% change in EBIT will result in only a 10% change in EPS (10% change in EBIT × 1 = 10% change in EPS). When the DFL increases to 2, a 10% change in EBIT will result in a 20% change in EPS (10% change in EBIT × 2 = 20% change in EPS). This is great when EBIT is increasing, but terrible when EBIT is decreasing.

OPERATING LEVERAGE

10. There is another kind of leverage called **operating leverage**.
    a.) Operating leverage is related to a company's **cost structure**. Cost structure is determined by the mix of fixed costs and variable costs. **Fixed costs** are costs that do not change at differing levels of production or sales. Typical fixed costs include things like management salaries and rent expense. **Variable costs** are costs that are incurred with each unit of product that is produced or sold. Typical fixed costs would include raw materials, labor and sales commissions.
    b.) Operating leverage has a similar effect on business risk as does financial leverage on financial risk. Operating leverage increases as the cost structure moves more toward using fixed costs rather than variable costs. For example, a company that uses a lot of machines (depreciation expense on machines is considered a fixed cost in this reference) as opposed to using a large workforce (labor is considered a variable cost) would have high fixed costs and a high operating leverage.
    c.) When a firm operates above **breakeven (defined as zero operating income),** operating leverage will enhance financial performance. When a firm operates below breakeven, operating leverage will increase the negative impact on the firm's financial performance.

11. **Breakeven analysis** is used to determine the level of sales that a firm must achieve in order to operate at a zero profit—and a zero loss—level. At this point, revenues exactly equal costs and expenses.

a.) **Contribution** is the amount that a unit's sale price exceeds its variable cost. This extra amount can then contribute to the payment of fixed costs, and when fixed costs are covered, contribute to profit. The **contribution margin** is the percent of the sale price that the contribution equals. The contribution margin can be calculated as follows:

$$\text{CONTRIBUTION MARGIN} = \frac{\text{PRICE - VARIABLE COST PER UNIT}}{\text{PRICE}}$$

Or $\quad C_M = \dfrac{P - V}{P}$

b.) **Breakeven quantity** is the number of units that a firm must sell in order to reach a zero operating income or a zero EBIT. Breakeven expressed in units is calculated as follows:

$$\text{BREAKEVEN QUANTITY} = \frac{\text{FIXED COSTS}}{\text{PRICE - VARIABLE COST PER UNIT}}$$

Or $\quad Q_{B/E} = \dfrac{F_C}{P - V}$

Breakeven sales level is the breakeven point stated in terms of dollar sales instead of units.

$$\text{BREAKEVEN SALES} = \frac{\text{FIXED COSTS}}{\text{CONTRIBUTION MARGIN}}$$

Or $\quad S_{B/E} = \dfrac{F_C}{(P - V)/P} = \dfrac{F_C}{C_M}$

Operating leverage magnifies the change in EBIT that occurs from a change in sales volume. **Increased operating leverage increases business risk, just as increased financial leverage increases financial risk.** Firms that have higher operating leverage (a higher percent of fixed costs) receive a larger contribution from each sale and also have more fixed costs to cover before they can begin to make a profit. Once fixed costs have been covered (at breakeven), then there is more contribution for each unit sold to increase profits because there are proportionately lower per unit variable costs. Firms with high operating leverage will have better operating results when sales levels are high. Firms with low operating leverage will have better operating results when sales are low, especially if they are below the breakeven point.

12. A concept called **degree of operating leverage (DOL)** measures the extent to which operating leverage magnifies changes in sales volume into larger changes in EBIT.

$$\text{DOL} = \frac{\text{QUANTITY (CONTRIBUTION PER UNIT)}}{\text{QUANTITY (CONTRIBUTION PER UNIT) - FIXED COSTS}}$$

Or, $\quad \text{DOL} = \dfrac{Q(P - V)}{Q(P - V) - F_C}$

166   Chapter 13

13. Similarities between financial leverage and operating leverage include the idea that both share fixed and variable charges. Debt is a fixed cost method of financing because it has set interest charges, while equity is a variable cost method of financing because dividends paid to stockholders may be changed or even eliminated. Increasing both kinds of leverage involve substituting fixed charges for variable charges.

Another similarity is that both types of leverage increase risk. It should be noted that although financial leverage is totally responsible for financial risk, some business risk will exist even with no operating leverage. All firms have some fixed costs, so there is no way to totally eliminate operating leverage. Some firms do operate with no debt, in which case they have no financial leverage.

14. For firms who operate with both kinds of leverage, the effects are compounded. This can result in small changes in sales levels leading to large changes in ROE and EPS. The combined effect of the two kinds of leverage is called **degree of total leverage (DTL)**, and is calculated as follows:

$$DTL = DOL \times DFL$$

CAPITAL STRUCTURE THEORY

15. Modigliani and Miller, two financial scholars referred to as MM, devised a mathematical model that explains the effects of capital structure on the value of a firm. Their original theory included some assumptions that are not applicable to the real world: no income taxes, no transaction costs for securities, no costs associated with bankruptcy and the idea that interest rates remain the same no matter how much money a firm chooses to borrow. In spite of these simplifying and largely unrealistic assumptions, the work of MM demonstrated that a firm's total value is **not affected by its capital structure**. They showed that a firm's value is the present value of its expected operating income stream, and that this value will be constant no matter what changes are made to the capital structure.

Although a complicated theory, in essence it says that the value of the firm will remain constant because of upward pressure put on the price of *unleveraged* firms' stock by investors selling their shares of *leveraged* firms' stock whose price has increased because of leverage. Investors' actions are not responsible for the effects of leverage, but this does not mean that leverage has no effect. It means, instead, that the effect of leverage on the value of the firm comes from the effects of taxes, transaction costs, and higher interest rates when borrowing levels increase.

16. In many mergers one company purchases the stock of another company called the **target**. In order to make such large purchases of stock in a short time, the acquiring firm offers a deal to all stockholders to buy their shares at market value plus a premium. The corporate buyer is paying considerably more for the stock than the market value. This is often done because the stock of target firms is undervalued, due to the firm's low financial leverage (low use of debt). This makes good sense only if the purchasing company can borrow money at a reasonable enough rate to change the capital structure of the new organization and increase the value of the firm more than the cost of the purchase.

TESTING YOUR UNDERSTANDING

TRUE-FALSE QUESTIONS

____1. Our US tax system favors debt over equity financing.

____2. A firm with high levels of fixed costs has high operating leverage.

____3. EBIT is not affected by financial leverage.

____4. Stock prices reach their highest levels when firms use 100% leverage.

____5. Firms that are unsure of their output level should trade variable costs for fixed costs.

____6. For the purposes of analyzing capital structure, preferred stock is treated as a form of equity.

____7. The three original assumptions made by the MM model were unrealistic and made this model worthless.

____8. All firms have some financial leverage, but not all firms have operating leverage.

____9. EPS will increase when financial leverage increases if ROCE exceeds the after tax cost of debt.

____10. The cost of increased financial leverage can be increased risk.

____11. Both financing and operating leverage involve substituting variable cash outflows for fixed cash outflows.

____12. The more leverage a firm uses, the larger the variation in EPS and ROE in relationship to variation in EBIT.

____13. A firm should increase its use of leverage during bad times in order to make poor results look more positive.

____14. An unleveraged (focusing on financial leverage) firm operates with only equity capital.

____15. Leverage influences stock price, because it changes the risk-return relationship in an equity investment.

____16. EPS is a major determinant of a stock's market price.

____17. Financial leverage sometimes improves performance and sometimes makes it worse, but it never increases risk.

____18. The nature of a company's business and the economic climate both affect the appropriate level of leverage for that company.

____19. When a firm's cost structure consists primarily of fixed costs, it has a great deal of operating leverage.

168   Chapter 13

____20. A labor-intensive plant will have more operating leverage than will an automated plant.

____21. Debt is a fixed cost method of financing and equity is a variable cost method.

____22. To a large extent, technology determines operating leverage while management determines financial leverage.

MULTIPLE CHOICE QUESTIONS

1. The degree of total leverage is equal to:
    a. DFL + DOL.
    b. DFL – DOL.
    c. DOL – DFL.
    d. DFL × DOL.

2. Increased operating leverage:
    a. increases business risk.
    b. magnifies the change in EBIT that results from a change in sales.
    c. expands profits more quickly above breakeven and expands losses more quickly below breakeven.
    d. all of the above.

3. A firm with 12% financial leverage:
    a. has a capital structure of 12% debt and 88% equity.
    b. has borrowed money for an average 12% interest rate.
    c. has a capital structure of 12% equity and 88% debt.
    d. none of the above.

4. At low to moderate levels of debt:
    a. the risks outweigh the benefits in investors' eyes.
    b. the benefits outweigh the risks in investors' eyes.
    c. investors view this level of leverage negatively.
    d. both a and c.

5. EPS:
    a. is not affected by financial leverage.
    b. has no impact on a stock's market price.
    c. is an indication of a firm's future earning power.
    d. none of the above.

6. Modigliani and Miller's theory explains:
    a. why changing the capital structure will increase or decrease the value of the firm.
    b. why investment value changes as leverage changes.
    c. explains that the reason why leverage appears to affect value actually comes from market imperfections.
    d. none of the above.

7. When a firm's DFL is 2:
    a. a 10% decrease in EBIT will result in a 2% change in EPS.
    b. a 10% decrease in EBIT will result in a 10% decrease in EPS.
    c. a 10% decrease in EBIT will result in a 20% decrease in EPS.
    d. a 10% decrease in EBIT will result in a 20% increase in EPS.

8. A firm with high leverage:
    a. tends to have better performance results when basic profitability is good than does an unleveraged firm.
    b. tends to have worse results than an unleveraged firm when ROCE is less than the after-tax cost of debt.
    c. both a and b.
    d. none of the above.

9. Firms with good profit potential and very little debt should:
    a. maintain their current capital structure.
    b. use more borrowed money when interest rates are reasonable.
    c. increase their debt level to 70% or more.
    d. increase equity and decrease debt even further.

10. Adding financial leverage:
    a. increases risk.
    b. often increases the price of the remaining shares up to a point.
    c. sometimes decreases the stock price and the value of the firm.
    d. all of the above.

11. Operating and financial leverage:
    a. compound one another.
    b. involve increasing variable costs and reducing fixed costs.
    c. when combined have an additive effect.
    d. none of the above.

12. Target companies:
    a. are often undervalued.
    b. tend to have low leverage.
    c. tend to have high leverage.
    d. both a and b.

13. As financial leverage increases from nothing to very high levels:
    a. stock prices decrease, bottom out, and then increase.
    b. stock prices increase, peak, and then decrease.
    c. stock prices remain the same.
    d. none of the above.

14. Optimal capital structure for most firms has debt at:
    a. less than 10%.
    b. between 10 and 30%.
    c. between 30 and 50%.
    d. between 50 and 70%.

170   Chapter 13

15. EBIT may vary over time due to:
   a. changes in costs.
   b. management effectiveness.
   c. variations in sales.
   d. all of the above.

16. At breakeven:
   a. revenue equals costs.
   b. profit is zero.
   c. losses are zero.
   d. all of the above.

17. Greater operating leverage:
   a. can be achieved through the use of more variable costs
   b. will always increase EBIT
   c. implies greater risk
   d. all of the above

18. An increase in operating leverage and a decrease in financial leverage will:
   a. increase EBIT but reduce EPS
   b. increase EBIT and increase ROE
   c. decrease EBIT but increase EPS
   d. cannot be determined without more information

19. Which of the following describes the market value of the firm?
   a. the market value of the firm's equity
   b. the market value of the firm's debt and equity
   c. operating income divided by the average cost of capital
   d. both b. and c.

20. Which of the following is not an assumption of the original MM model?
   a. the firm's total value is unaffected by capital structure
   b. there are no income taxes
   c. there are no costs of bankruptcy
   d. investors can borrow as much as they want at the same rate

FILL-IN THE BLANK QUESTIONS

1. _____ means making a profit by buying and selling the same thing at the same time in two different markets.

2. _____ costs remain unchanged when sales levels vary.

3. _____ risk means variation in EBIT.

4. _____ leverage is defined as using borrowed money to multiply the effectiveness of the equity invested in a firm.

5. The probability of a business failing _____ as debt increases.

6. _____ leverage is related to a firm's cost structure, which describes the amounts of fixed and variable costs the firm uses.

7. At breakeven, profits are _____ and losses are zero.

8. _____ is the amount by which a unit's price exceeds its variable cost.

9. A company that operates with no debt and all equity is _____.

10. When contribution is expressed as a percent of revenue, it is called the _____.

11. 15% financial leverage implies a capital financing structure that is _____ debt and _____ equity.

12. Operating income is also called _____.

13. Investors are _____ sensitive to risk when the economic outlook is poor than when it is good.

14. A firm's mix of fixed and variable costs is known as its _____.

15. The higher the fixed cost, the _____ the profit at a given point above breakeven.

PROBLEMS

1. What is the DTL for a firm with a DOL or 2.1 and a DFL or 1.7? What change is EPS would a 10% increase in EBIT produce?

2. A company has EBIT of $2,400,000 and interest expense of $300,000. What is its DFL?

3. Use the information from the previous problem. Assume a 40% tax rate and 600,000 shares of outstanding stock with a current market value of $35 and a book value of $24. Calculate EPS and ROE.

4. What is the contribution for a unit that sells for $8 and has variable costs of $3? What is its contribution margin?

5. What is the breakeven sales level in units and dollars for the company in Problem 3 that has fixed costs of $2,500 per month?

6. What will happen to the contribution, contribution margin, and breakeven for the company in Problems 4 and 5 if it increases its fixed costs to $3,000 and its variable costs per unit decline to $2.50?

7. If a company has fixed costs of $40,000, a unit selling price of $12, and variable costs of $4 per unit, how many units will it have to sell to make a profit of $20,000?

8. If a company sells its products for an average price of $16, has variable costs of $10 per unit, and fixed costs of $1500 per month, what is its DOL when sales are 10% above breakeven?

9. Mercer, Inc. has an EBIT of $400. Its capital structure is made up of $1,000 debt and $4,000 equity (400 shares currently selling at the book value of $10). The interest rate is 10% (before tax) and the tax rate is 40%.
   a. What is Mercer's current EPS?
   b. What is Mercer's ROCE?
   c. If Mercer decided to borrow an additional $1,000 and repurchase 100 shares of stock, what would Mercer's new capital structure be?
   d. After the repurchase, what would Mercer's EPS be?
   e. Is this change in EPS consistent with your understanding of ROCE? Why?

10. Hatfield, Inc. sells its product for $14.00. Variable costs are $9.00 per unit, and Hatfield has $800,000 in fixed costs. Assume that Hatfield has $1.0 million in total debt and equity and a 40% tax rate. What is Hatfield's ROCE when sales are (1) at 10% above breakeven? (2) at 20% above breakeven?

ANSWERS TO QUESTIONS

TRUE-FALSE

1. t
2. t
3. t
4. f
5. f
6. f
7. f
8. f
9. t
10. t
11. f
12. t
13. f
14. t
15. t
16. t
17. f
18. t
19. t
20. f
21. t
22. t

20. a

FILL IN THE BLANKS

1. Arbitrage
2. Fixed
3. Business
4. Financial
5. increases
6. Operating
7. zero
8. Contribution
9. unleveraged
10. contribution margin
11. 15%, 85%
12. EBIT
13. more
14. cost structure
15. higher

MULTIPLE CHOICE

1. d
2. d
3. a
4. b
5. c
6. c
7. c
8. c
9. b
10. d
11. a
12. d
13. b
14. c
15. d
16. d
17. c
18. d
19. d

174   Chapter 13

ANSWERS TO PROBLEMS

1. DTL = DOL × DFL
   DTL = 2.1 × 1.7
   DTL = 3.57
   10% × 3.57 = 35.7% increase in EPS

2. $\dfrac{2,400,000}{2,400,000 - 300,000} = 1.1429$

3.
EBIT	2,400,000
Interest	300,000
EBT	2,100,000
Tax (.4)	840,000
EAT	1,260,000

   EPS = 1,260,000/600,000 = $2.10 per share
   ROE = $2.10/$24.00 = 8.75%

4. Contribution = $8 - $3 = $5

   Contribution margin = $5/$8 = 62.5%

5. $\dfrac{2500}{8-3} = 500$ units, 500 × $8 = $4,000

6. 8 − 2.50 = 5.50, $\dfrac{8-2.50}{8} = 68.75\%$

   B/E = $\dfrac{\$3,000}{\$5.50}$ = 545 units

   545 × $8 = $4,360 in sales

7. Breakeven = $\dfrac{40,000}{12-4}$ = 5,000 units
   Profit = $\dfrac{20,000}{8}$ = 2,500 units
   2500 + 5000 = 7500 units

8. Breakeven = $\dfrac{1500}{16-10}$ = 250 units
   Breakeven + 10% = 275 units

   $\dfrac{275(16-10)}{275(6)-1500} = \dfrac{1650}{150} = 11$

9.   INT EXP   100
      EBT   300
      TAX   120
      EAT   180   EPS = 180/400 = $.45

   b. ROCE = 400 (1 - .4)/5000 = 240/5000 = 4.8%

   c. Debt = $2,000 = 40%
      Equity = $3,000 = 60%

   d. EBIT   400
      INT EXP   200
      EBT   200
      TAX   80
      EAT   120   EPS = 120/300 = $.40

   e. Since ROCE (4.8%) was lower than the after tax cost of debt 10% (1 - .4) = 6%, increasing financial leverage by purchasing additional debt would lower EPS, which is exactly what happened, with EPS going from $.45 to $.40.

10.   Breakeven (in units) = 800,000/(14 – 9) = 160,000 units

   At 176,000 units (10% above breakeven)

Contribution Margin	880,000	(14 – 9) x 176,000
Fixed Costs	800,000	
Operating Income	80,000	

   ROCE = 80,000 x (1 - .4)/1,000,000 = .48 or 4.8%

   At 192,000 units (20% above breakeven)

Contribution Margin	960,000	(14 – 9) x 192,000
Fixed Costs	800,000	
Operating Income	160,000	

   ROCE = 160,000 x (1 - .4)/1,000,000 = .96 or 9.6%

14

CHAPTER FOURTEEN

DIVIDENDS

LEARNING OBJECTIVES

After studying this chapter you should understand the following terms and concepts:

1. the relationship between dividends and value from the perspective of the individual investor and the from market as a whole;
2. the implications involved in the dividend payout decision;
3. the controversy over the effects on stock price of paying or not paying dividends, and paying large or small dividends;
4. the indifference theory and the effect of transaction costs and income taxes on it;
5. the dividend preference and the dividend aversion theories;
6. the clientele effect, the residual dividend theory, and the implications associated with the payment and nonpayment of dividends;
7. legal and contractual restrictions on dividend payments;
8. alternative dividend policies;
9. the mechanics of dividend payments;
10. stock splits and stock dividends and their effect on stock price and value;
11. stock repurchasing issues.

CHAPTER SUMMARY

This chapter looks at all aspects associated with the payment of common stock dividends. The payment of dividends appears to be a fairly straightforward issue—common stock investors expect and deserve a dividend payment as a return on their investment, but there are a number of complicating factors that all organizations must consider when determining whether or not to pay out dividends and what amount to pay. Even when the decision has been made to pay a dividend, the mechanics of the payout must be addressed, and the student should carefully study the definitions of the various terms discussed in this section. Lastly the chapter examines stock splits and stock repurchasing issues.

CHAPTER REVIEW

BACKGROUND

1. This chapter is concerned only with the payment of **common stock dividends**. In earlier chapters, the typical common stock was valued on its future expected dividend flows.

    a.) As a review, remember that for an **individual investor** the price of a share of stock was calculated using the present value of the future dividends discounted at the appropriate rate for an equity investment in that particular company plus the price to be received when the stock was sold.

    $$P_0 = \frac{D_1}{(1+k)} + \frac{D_2}{(1+k)^2} + \ldots + \frac{D_n}{(1+k)^n} + \frac{P_n}{(1+k)^n}$$

    b.) The **market view** of the value of the stock was based on an infinite stream of dividends with no final selling price. For this chapter, we will use the concept of stock value based on a stream of dividends for a certain number of years culminating in a final payment when the stock is sold.

2. Companies are not required to pay dividends; the payment of dividends is **legally discretionary**. A company's board of directors decides whether or not dividends will be paid and how much will be paid. The receipt of dividends by stockholders is never guaranteed.

3. **Earnings can either be paid out as dividends or retained for reinvestment in the company.** Both of these alternatives benefit the stockholders but in very different ways.

    a.) The payment of dividends rewards stockholders with an immediate cash payment; they do not have to wait for deferred gratification. Investors who want or need immediate income will prefer stocks that pay dividends.

    b.) Reinvesting earnings into the firm should increase the value of the firm as reflected by an increase in the market value of the firm's stock. This defers immediate gratification because only by selling the stock will the investor receive a cash reward. Investors who prefer to defer their income will choose to invest in firms that retain more of their earnings to use for reinvestment to increase the price of the stock.

THE DIVIDEND CONTROVERSY

4. A number of different theories have been developed to explain how companies decided whether or not to pay dividends and how large the dividend payments ought to be. The **dividend irrelevance theory** states that the payment of dividends matters little or not at all with respect to the market price of the stock. If early dividends are reduced or eliminated, retained earnings increase, the company becomes more profitable, the stock price goes up, and dividends go up. The negative impact of reducing or eliminating dividends is offset by the positive effect of a higher selling price and later dividends. Either way, the investor benefits to the same extent — sooner with dividends or later with an increase in the market value of the stock. This theory is only completely valid if there are no transaction costs associated with the buying and selling of shares of stock, which is not the case.

This theory seems to ignore those investors who invest in particular stocks for current income supplied by dividends. However, as an alternative they can sell some of their shares to provide for current needs and realize greater gains on future sales when the retained earnings cause the value of the stock to increase. This only works when the transaction cost of selling shares is relatively inexpensive. The higher the transaction costs become, the less likely that this theory will hold true for persons who need current income.

Another factor to be considered in this theory is the tax consequences of receiving dividends as opposed to selling shares of stock. Dividend income is taxed as ordinary income, typically at a higher tax rate than are capital gains that are received from the sale of stock. This means that it takes a smaller increase in the market value of the stock to offset the value of short-term dividend reductions or omissions than would be the case if both dividend and capital gains were taxed at the same rate.

From the viewpoint of the corporation, dividends represent a cash outflow that could be used instead as retained earnings for capital budgeting projects. When the firm runs out of retained earnings to use for capital projects, it may sell new shares of stock that will also require a dividend payment. If there were no flotation costs associated with issuing the new shares of stock, firms would be indifferent about issuing new shares. But we know there are flotation costs that increase the costs associated with issuing the new stock and paying the dividends. Firms, therefore, have an internal preference for not paying dividends and using retained earnings to fund projects rather than issue new stock.

5. The **dividend preference theory** says that stockholders would prefer to receive dividends as opposed to not receiving them, because dividends paid today are a certainty while future gains in market value of the stock are not. Of course, if investors do not trust the firm's management to increase the value of the firm, why have they chosen to invest in this company anyway?

6. The **dividend aversion theory** states that investors would prefer that dividends not be paid so that they can receive enhanced prices for their shares of stock in the future. This argument is based almost totally on the fact that capital gains are taxed at a lower rate than are dividends. Currently, the capital gains associated with the profits from the sale of stock enjoy a substantial tax advantage over dividend income which is taxed as ordinary income.

7. The **clientele effect** says that individual investors have individual preferences in favor of or against the payment of dividends based upon their needs for more or less current income. According to this theory, investors will choose to invest in firms that meet their particular needs. The clientele effect stresses that once a firm has a clientele of investors whose needs match the company's dividend policy, it is unwise to change that policy. A change in dividend policy (e.g. decreasing or eliminating dividends for a period of time) could result in the alienation of the current stockholders and could mean a large sell-off of shares by these individuals.

8. The **residual dividend theory** says that all earnings should be first used to fund viable capital projects. Only when the firm has run out of capital projects should any leftover funds be paid out as dividends. This sounds reasonable in theory, but is not normally practiced by many firms because there is usually no shortage of capital projects that appear to be profitable.

9. **Financial markets** read a great deal into the payment or non-payment of dividends. This is called the **signaling effect of dividends**. The money paid out by management in the form of

dividends tends to have more of an effect on the market (and the price of the stock) than do any words that management might use to influence investors as to the health of the company. Temporary decreases in earnings could signal a panic if they are accompanied by a decrease in dividends, so most firms continue to follow a normal pattern of paying dividends rather than respond to temporary changes in earnings. Firms who want to send a highly positive message about the health of the organization often elect to increase dividends.

10. The **expectations theory** states that investors have certain expectations regarding the amount of the company's next dividend, and any negative deviation by the company can cause great alarm. There can be no conclusive statements regarding the payment or non-payment of dividends. Most firms choose to pay dividends, and paying 50% of earnings seems to be the average policy.

PRACTICAL CONSIDERATIONS

11. Certain legal and contractual restrictions may be placed on the payment of dividends. Dividends must be paid out of **retained earnings**; they cannot be paid out of other sources of capital. Also, firms are prohibited from paying dividends if they are insolvent. The definition of **insolvency** is when liabilities exceed assets.

    Bond issues and loans often place restrictions on the payment of dividends to protect the creditors (e.g. bondholders) of the company. **Indentures** are bond restrictions, and **covenants** are loan restrictions. Another common restriction on the payment of common stock dividends comes from preferred stock restrictions. The **cumulative feature** on preferred stock says that no common stock dividends may be paid if preferred dividends have been passed until the preferred dividends have been cumulatively paid.

12. The **dividend payout ratio** is the ratio of dividends paid to earnings.

    $$\textit{DIVIDEND PAYOUT RATIO} = \frac{\textit{DIVIDENDS}}{\textit{EARNINGS}} = \frac{\textit{DIVIDEND PER SHARE}}{\textit{EPS}}$$

    A 30% dividend payout ratio means that the company pays a cash dividend of thirty cents out of every dollar it earns. **Stability** refers to how constant the payout of dividends is over time. A **stable growth rate** is a fairly constant percentage of increase over time. This is the most common practice used by companies to address a number of the concerns raised above.

13. There are three very common dividend policies that are used by many firms.

    a.) The **target payout ratio** is a policy that a firm uses when it selects a long-term payout ratio with which it is comfortable. This ratio is not guaranteed, and most firms try to allow for variations in earnings without varying dividends.
    b.) A **stable dividend per share** means that a firm pays a constant amount per share regardless of how badly the firm is doing, until the firm does so poorly that no money is available. If the firm does extremely well, the dividend will be raised from time to time. This is the most common dividend policy.
    c.) A **small regular dividend** with a year-end extra if earnings permit allows management the flexibility of paying more in good years and less in bad years, yet also assures stockholders of a certain minimum amount.

14. Dividends are typically paid quarterly and have four dates associated with each quarterly payment.
   a.) The **declaration date** is the date on which the board of directors authorizes the dividend.
   b.) The **date of record** is the date that determines that the owners of record, as of this date, will receive the dividend.
   c.) The **payment date** is the date when the dividend checks will actually be mailed.
   d.) The **ex-dividend date** is two days prior to the date of record when all stock sales for dividend purposes will be discontinued to allow ownership records to be updated.

15. **Dividend reinvestment plans** offer stockholders the option of having their dividends reinvested in additional shares of stock instead of being paid out. Reinvested dividends are treated as **taxable income** by the IRS, even though the stockholders do not actually receive the cash.

16. **Stock splits** occur when firms issue new shares to existing stockholders in numbers proportionate to the shares already outstanding. A 2 for 1 split, for example, means that stockholders will receive an additional share for each share they already own. There will then be twice as many shares outstanding, with each share worth half of the previous market value. The par value of each share will also be cut in half, and, at least initially, the dividend per share will also be half of the former dividend.

    Reverse splits call in all the shares and reissue fewer new shares for previously owned shares. A 1 for 2 reverse split means that a stockholder would then own half as many shares with each share worth twice its previous price. Under stock splits and reverse stock splits, each stockholder retains his/her proportionate share of ownership of the company.

   a.) With **stock dividends,** additional shares of stock are issued, but in order to be considered a stock dividend rather that a stock split, the number of new shares must be less than or equal to twenty percent of the original number of shares.
   b.) Stock splits and stock dividends are used when the trading price of a share of stock is seen as prohibitively high, limiting the number of potential investors. Splitting the stock keeps the price in a more reasonable trading range, usually thought to be $30 - $80. Stock splits and stock dividends are also viewed by investors as a positive signaling device by the company, which costs it nothing.

STOCK REPURCHASES

17. Some firms choose to use their cash to **repurchase shares of their own stock** instead of paying a dividend. This reduces the number of outstanding shares of stock and results in an increase in EPS. If the market attaches the same P/E ratio to the stock, this will result in an increase in price of the remaining shares. Stocks can be repurchased by buying the shares on the open market or by making a **tender offer** to buy shares from interested stockholders at a set price, usually a little above the current market price. A third method of repurchase involves dealing with a large investor—such as a mutual fund—and agreeing to purchase the shares from this investor at a premium above market price. When a company's stock is undervalued, repurchasing shares can be of great benefit to remaining stockholders. Firms that temporarily have large amounts of cash may elect to use this cash to repurchase stock instead of paying a one-time large dividend. This enriches remaining stockholders without the signaling effect that a large dividend might send. The restructuring of capital is a common reason for many companies to repurchase their shares.

TESTING YOUR UNDERSTANDING

TRUE-FALSE QUESTIONS

____1. Firms have an internal preference against paying dividends.

____2. Very favorable tax treatment of capital gains creates an investors' preference in favor of dividends.

____3. No one knows for sure whether paying more or less in dividends generally increases or decreases stock prices.

____4. Dividends may be paid from retained earnings or any other source of a firm's capital.

____5. Dividends are required by law to be paid.

____6. Equity received from the sale of new shares of stock is more expensive than retained earnings.

____7. The cumulative feature of preferred stock dividends is a restraint on the payment of common stock dividends.

____8. Reinvesting retained earnings should increase the value of the firm.

____9. Stocks usually increase in price after the ex-dividend date to an amount that is 20% to 30% more than the dividend amount.

____10. A two for one stock split doubles the value of an investor's holdings.

____11. Dividends that are reinvested are taxed as current ordinary income.

____12. Retained earnings produce deferred income for stockholders.

____13. Discontinuing dividends and requiring investors to sell shares to generate current income can be costly and could drive investors away.

____14. Paying a dividend increases earnings retained.

____15. Most companies pay dividends based on the residual dividend concept.

____16. Management will usually try to keep dividends from declining.

____17. When a company uses a target payout ratio dividend policy, that ratio is automatically applied each year.

____18. It is common for a stock's price to increase immediately after the ex-dividend date.

____19. In a dividend reinvestment plan, the proportional ownership of the company doesn't change.

____20. When a company repurchases its own stock, the EPS of the remaining stock increases.

____21. A stock repurchase can distribute money to stockholders without the signaling effect of a one-time dividend.

____22. Regular and predictable stock repurchases cause no taxation uncertainties or difficulty with the IRS.

MULTIPLE CHOICE QUESTIONS

1. Current tax laws:
    a. have a high bias in favor of capital gains.
    b. have a modest bias in favor of capital gains.
    c. have a high bias in favor of dividends.
    d. none of the above.

2. Dividends are:
    a. paid out by most corporations.
    b. subject to certain legal and contractual restrictions.
    c. paid out, on the average, to an amount equal to about 50% of earnings.
    d. all of the above.

3. A company that increases its dividends by about 2% each year is following a:
    a. stable dividend per share policy.
    b. stable growth rate dividend policy.
    c. small regular dividend with year end extra policy.
    d. fixed target payout ratio policy.

4. The signaling effect of dividends:
    a. can be used by management to send a message to stockholders.
    b. can be reassuring when earnings are down if the dividend remains the same.
    c. may cause investors to sell their stock when the dividend is decreased.
    d. all of the above.

5. If a person currently owns 10,000 shares of stock and the company issues that person 1,000 additional shares of stock:
    a. the company has declared a stock split.
    b. the company has issued a stock dividend.
    c. the company may be trying to send a positive message even though it has no available cash.
    d. both b and c.

6. the dividend preference theory states that:
    a. stockholders prefer current income from dividends rather than possible future capital gains.
    b. firms have an internal preference for paying dividends.
    c. stockholders prefer dividends to capital gains because dividends are taxed at a lower rate than are capital gains.
    d. both a and c.

7. After a two for one stock split:
   a. an investor will own twice as many shares of stock with each share worth half as much as before the split.
   b. an investor will own three shares of stock for each one share previously owned.
   c. an investor will own twice as many shares with the total value of the shares being twice as much as before the split.
   d. an investor will have the increased value of the holdings caused by the stock split taxed as ordinary income.

8. A company may declare a stock split:
   a. to immediately increase the total value of an investor's stockholdings.
   b. to keep stock prices within an acceptable trading range.
   c. in increase the economic value of the firm.
   d. all of the above.

9. The clientele effect:
   a. says that people tend to invest in companies that meet their needs.
   b. encourages companies to modify their dividend policies on a regular basis.
   c. says that individual investors have definite dividend preferences.
   d. both a and c.

10. A dividend payout ratio of 50% means that:
    a. 50% of revenue is paid out as dividends each year.
    b. the firm is legally obligated to pay out 50% of earnings as dividends each year.
    c. the firm pays a cash dividend of 50 cents for every dollar it earns.
    d. none of the above.

11. The dividend decision involves a choice between:
    a. no income or deferred income.
    b. current and future dividends.
    c. a dividend or nothing.
    d. none of the above.

12. If capital markets were perfectly efficient:
    a. securities could be traded without incurring costs.
    b. people would be indifferent to the payment of dividends.
    c. both a and b.
    d. none of the above.

13. Restrictions on dividend payments may include:
    a. dividends cannot be paid from capital sources other than retained earnings.
    b. an insolvent firm cannot pay dividends.
    c. bond indentures and loan covenants.
    d. all of the above.

14. Companies may repurchase stock by:
    a. buying shares on the open market.
    b. making a tender offer to stockholders.
    c. making a negotiated deal with an investor who holds a large block of stock.
    d. all of the above.

15. Which of the following best describes a company's requirements with respect to paying dividends?
    a. once a company begins to pay dividends, they must continue to pay them each year
    b. dividends are paid based on the vote of the stockholders
    c. dividends are paid based on the vote of the board of directors
    d. none of the above

16. The dividend irrelevance hypothesis states that:
    a. stockholders don't care if they received dividends now or later
    b. the payment or nonpayment of dividends should have very little effect on the stock price
    c. dividends are irrelevant if businesses have growth opportunities in which to invest earnings
    d. stockholders don't care if they receive large or small dividends as long as they receive a certain percent of the company's earnings

17. If a company has been paying regular dividends and then stops:
    a. the company may lose some of its stockholders who were counting on a steady stream of income
    b. stockholders can recreate the steady stream of income by selling a portion of the stock each year, however transaction costs will affect this action.
    c. both a and b are true
    d. none of the above

18. The appropriateness of the dividend aversion hypothesis depends on:
    a. the health of the economy
    b. the relationship of capital gains tax to ordinary income tax
    c. the company's dividend policy
    d. all of the above

19. The residual dividend theory:
    a. is based on a company's internal need for capital
    b. is used by a large number of major corporations
    c. is preferred by stockholders over other dividend payment approaches
    d. all of the above

20. The date on which brokers agree to cut off stock sales for dividend purposes is called the:
    a. declaration date
    b. date of record
    c. payment date
    d. ex-dividend date

FILL-IN THE BLANK QUESTIONS

1. A company is using a _____ concept if all viable capital budgeting projects are fully funded before any dividends are paid.

2. Dividends are taxed as ordinary income while stock appreciation is taxed as a _____.

186   Chapter 14

3. A _____ issues new shares of stock in proportionate numbers to those shares already outstanding.

4. Calling in all shares of stock and reissuing one share for every two shares previously owned is called a _____.

5. A dividend is payable to owners of record as of the _____.

6. When a firm makes an offer to buy shares of stock at a set amount that is somewhat higher than current market price, this is called a(n) _____ offer.

7. The _____ theory says that dividends matter little or not at all to stock price.

8. The date that the board of directors authorizes the dividend is called the _____.

9. A company whose liabilities exceeds its assets is said to be _____.

10. The _____ theory says that investors would prefer not to receive dividends so that stock prices will increase over time.

11. Dividends are an important part of the financial system because they help to determine the value of _____.

12. A firm with a 45% payout ratio would pay a cash dividend of _____ cents for each dollar it earns.

13. The date on which the dividend check is to be mailed is the _____ date.

PROBLEMS

1. A person has much of his savings invested in 15,000 shares of stock of a major corporation, currently selling for $12 a share and paying a yearly dividend of seventy-five cents a share. The corporation discontinues its dividend but begins to grow at 7% a year. Assuming no costs are involved to buy or sell securities, how can this person maintain his income and his position in the firm?

2. A company has 3 million outstanding share of stock with a $6 par value. It declares a 3 for 1 stock split. What will be the new par value of one share of common stock? If the company has total common equity of $27 million, what was the old book value of one share of stock? What is the new book value of one share of stock?

3. A firm has 4 million common shares outstanding and expects earnings of $20 million next year. If it has a dividend payout ratio of 40%, what will be the yearly dividend for next year?

4. If the company in problem 3 declares a 2 for 1 stock split and maintains a 40% payout ratio, what will the yearly dividend be?

5. An investor had 10,000 shares of stock valued at $5 a share. The firm declared a reverse stock split of 1 for 4. How many shares of stock would the investor now own and what would be the value per share?

6. A firm has after-tax earnings of $9 million and 3 million shares of common stock outstanding, trading at a P/E ratio of 15. Calculate its EPS and market price.

7. A firm has after-tax earnings of $3,150,000 and 3 million shares of common stock outstanding, trading at a P/E ratio of 15. How many shares can it repurchase and retire with the current year's earnings?

8. If earnings remain the same for the firm in problem 7, what will the new EPS be? What will the new market price be?

9. Use the information from problem 7 prior to the repurchase activity. If the firm has retained earnings of $7,410,000 prior to this year's earnings, what is the largest dividend per share that they could legally pay if they decided not to repurchase and retire outstanding shares?

10. Below is the equity section of Jackson Corp's balance sheet:

Common Stock (1.5 million shares outstanding, $0.50 par)	$ 750,000
Paid in Excess	14,250,000
Retained Earnings	10,357,000

    Jackson decides to declare a 2 for 1 stock split. What will this section of the balance sheet look like after the split?

11. Use the balance sheet from problem 10. If Jackson decided to declare a 10% stock dividend when the stock is selling for $47.00 per share, what would the balance sheet look like after the stock dividend is recorded?

ANSWERS TO QUESTIONS

TRUE-FALSE

1. t
2. f
3. t
4. f
5. f
6. t
7. t
8. t
9. f
10. f
11. t
12. t
13. t
14. f
15. f
16. t
17. f
18. f
19. f
20. t
21. t
22. f

MULTIPLE CHOICE

1. a
2. d
3. b
4. d
5. d
6. a
7. a
8. b
9. d
10. c
11. b
12. c
13. d
14. d
15. c
16. b
17. c
18. b
19. a
20. d

FILL IN THE BLANKS

1. residual dividend
2. capital gain
3. stock split
4. reverse split
5. date of record
6. tender
7. dividend irrelevance
8. declaration date
9. insolvent
10. dividend aversion
11. stocks
12. forty-five (45)
13. payment

ANSWERS TO PROBLEMS

1. 15,000 × 12 = $180,000 value of shares

    15,000 × $.75 = $11,250 dividend income

    12 × 1.07 = $12.84 stock value after 1 year

    $\frac{\$11{,}250}{12.84}$ = 876 shares sold

    15,000 − 876 = 14,124 remaining shares × $12.84 = $181,352

2. $6 / 3 = $2, 9 million shares

    $27 m / 3m = $9 previous book value

    $27 m / 9m = $3 new book value

3. $20 m × .40 = $8m / 4m = $2 a share dividend

4. 4 million shares × 2 = 8 million shares
    $8m / 8m = $1 a share dividend after stock split

5. 2500 shares @ $20 a share

6. EPS = $\frac{9{,}000{,}000}{3{,}000{,}000}$ = $3 a share

    Market price = $3 x 15 = $45

7. $\frac{3{,}150{,}000}{45}$ = 70,000

8. $\frac{9{,}000{,}000}{2{,}930{,}000}$ = $3.07

    Market price = 3.07 x 15 = $46.05

9. Theoretically, the firm can pay out all of its current and retained earnings, so the maximum payout would be:
    (3,150,000 + 7,410,000)/3,000,000 = $3.52 per share

10. The only change would be to the parenthetical phrase next to common stock which would read: (3.0 million shares outstanding, $0.25 par)

11. Common Stock (1.65 million shares outstanding, $0.50 par) $ 825,000
    Paid in Excess (old number plus 150,000 x $46.50)   21,225,000
    Retained Earnings (adjust to keep total equity the same)   3,307,000

CHAPTER FIFTEEN

THE MANAGEMENT OF WORKING CAPITAL

LEARNING OBJECTIVES

After studying this chapter you should understand the following terms and concepts:

1. the definition of working capital and the importance of working capital management;
2. spontaneous financing arising from operating activities;
3. the objective of working capital management and the elements included in working capital;
4. how the cash conversion cycle works;
5. permanent and temporary working capital needs and the options firms have for financing these needs;
6. the sources for short-term financing including spontaneous financing, unsecured bank loans, secured loans, commercial paper, and receivables and inventory financing;
7. the basics of cash management and the check clearing cycle;
8. the management of accounts receivable through credit and collections policies;
9. the management of inventory and the economic order quantity model.

CHAPTER SUMMARY

This chapter begins by looking at the definition of working capital and its components. The funding alternatives for working capital are examined, and the benefits and costs of choosing long and/or short-term financing are discussed. The individual components of working capital are reviewed, and the various steps of the cash conversion cycle are illustrated. The importance of working capital for all firms is stressed, including the amount and types of financing options available. The choice of the types of financing used and the amount of each type can have major impact on the profitability of the firm. Firms that do not understand the importance of managing all the aspects of working capital may find themselves facing much larger costs than firms that do a good job of managing this area. Working capital management almost always requires a trade-off between reductions in costs (e.g. driving accounts receivable levels down) and lower levels of sales and/or customer service. These trade-offs require the day-to-day management of these issues and significant cooperation between the financial and marketing managers of the business.

CHAPTER REVIEW

WORKING CAPITAL BASICS

1. **Working capital** refers to the assets and liabilities required by all businesses in order to operate on a daily basis. The assets include cash, accounts receivable, and inventories, and the liabilities include accounts payable and accruals. All of these items are short term in nature and, because they turn over constantly, they are held for very short periods.

    GROSS WORKING CAPITAL = CASH + ACCOUNTS RECEIVABLE + INVENTORY

    Or

    GROSS WORKING CAPITAL = CURRENT ASSETS

2. Even though working capital is constantly turning over (e.g. individual accounts receivable balances are paid by customers and are replaced by new credit sales), there is a permanent level that always exists, and that requires a permanent investment of funds. There is also a permanent level of liabilities (e.g. accounts payable and accruals) that is created by operating activities and partially offsets the funding requirements needed for permanent short-term asset levels. The automatic nature of the liabilities that come from operating activities, and the fact that they arise spontaneously from daily operations, explains why they are referred to as **spontaneous financing**.

    NET WORKING CAPITAL = GROSS WORKING CAPITAL – SPONTANEOUS FINANCING

    Or

    NET WORKING CAPITAL = CURRENT ASSETS – CURRENT LIABILITIES

3. **Working capital management** requires businesses to find the levels of current assets and liabilities that best address the costs and benefits of working capital. It is easier to run a business with more, rather than less, current assets. Cash is available to deal with emergencies, customers aren't pushed to pay their invoices, and inventory is available to satisfy customers' orders. However, there is a cost related to carrying high levels of current assets. In general, these assets are not earning anything for the business (in the form of a return). They are not productive assets, so any extra current assets that are carried preclude the purchase of fixed assets which are productive.

    It is less costly to maintain smaller levels of inventory, but customers may have to wait longer for their orders, and the firm may risk production delays caused by a shortage of needed materials. Firms with large accounts receivables have happy customers because they grant credit easily and give customers a long time to pay, but the firm risks large bad debt losses and big interest charges to finance the receivables. So the dilemma faced by all businesses is that using more working capital increases sales and makes customers and vendors happy, while costing the firm extra money.

4. The **cash conversion cycle** refers to the process that current assets go through as cash is transformed into inventory and labor, which then combine to become the product. Once the product is sold on credit, a receivable is created which in turn becomes cash when the invoice is

paid, and the cycle begins anew. The period of time that elapses between the disbursement of cash for materials and labor and the receipt of cash from the payment of an account receivable is the duration of the cash conversion cycle. The **operating cycle** of a business is the time period from the acquisition of inventory to the receipt of cash from the payment of an account. The operating cycle is slightly longer than the cash conversion cycle because it starts with the acquisition of inventory, not the payment for inventory.

5. Firms have a requirement for more or less working capital depending upon their sales level. More sales typically means more working capital needs, usually because more sales will require more inventory and will generate a higher level of accounts receivable. Firms that operate at fairly constant sales levels throughout the year will have fairly constant working capital requirements. Seasonal businesses with varying sales levels will require varying levels of working capital.

   a.) **Permanent working capital** is the amount needed to support a constant or minimum sales level.
   b.) **Temporary working capital** is the extra amount that is required for peak periods during the year, often associated with seasonal businesses.

6. **The requirement for working capital, particularly temporary working capital, lends itself to short-term financing**, because the loan (or other source of short-term financing) can be paid off as soon as the merchandise is sold and/or the receivables are collected. Both the inventory and the accounts receivable can be pledged as security for the loan, which makes it more attractive to the lender and is usually an easier kind of loan for even small businesses to receive.

7. The **maturity matching** concept means the maturity date of financing should be matched to the duration of the asset or project being financed. Short-term projects should be funded with short-term financing, while long-term projects should be funded with long-term financing.

8. The maturity matching concept offers good general guidelines, but clearly there is a problem with working capital. The assets are short term, but there are permanent minimum levels that must always be maintained. Because a significant portion of working capital assets is permanent, each business has to decide whether to use long-term or short-term financing to fund its working capital requirements.

   a.) Long-term financing is safe because it provides for long-term needs in amounts that assure that the firm will not be caught short. However, it is also expensive because long term rates are usually higher than short-term rates, and long term financing incurs flotation costs.
   b.) Short-term financing is cheaper, but riskier. Short-term rates are lower and the transaction costs are minimal, but every time a new loan is needed, market conditions may have changed and financing costs may be significantly higher or not available at all.

9. A **conservative working capital policy** consists of using mostly long-term financing for working capital, with a small amount of short-term financing used to cover only the peak requirements of temporary working capital.

10. An **aggressive working capital policy** is defined as using short-term funds to cover all temporary and much of the firm's permanent working capital needs. This reduces costs, but a sudden short-term market rise in interest rates could cause serious problems.

SOURCES OF SHORT-TERM FINANCING

11. There are four categories of short-term financing.

    a.) **Spontaneous financing** consists of accruals and accounts payable. Accruals occur from services that have been received but not yet paid for. The most common of these is accrued salary and wages. This form of financing has minimal benefit to a company because of the regular requirement to pay employees (e.g. weekly or monthly), which reduces the spontaneous financing to zero. Accounts payable represent the **trade credit** that the seller has informally extended to its customers in the form of products that have been received but not yet paid for. This is an attractive, free source of financing, but it is only extended for short periods of time. The **terms of sale** spell out the number of days after delivery when the payment is expected, and there is often a discount for early payment. Unlike accruals, this form of financing is available on a continuous basis because new purchases are always being made, and a balance is always maintained in accounts payable. Delaying payment beyond the due date is called **stretching payables** or **leaning on the trade**.

    b.) **Bank loans** are another source for financing for working capital.

        1.) A **promissory loan** is the traditional method of bank lending. The borrower signs a legal document that specifies the amount borrowed, the interest rate, and the date when the maturity value is due.
        2.) A **line of credit** is an informal, non-binding agreement that specifies the maximum amount that the firm can borrow during any period of time. If the bank chooses to do so, it can reduce the line of credit during this period.
        3.) A **revolving credit agreement** is much like a line of credit except that the bank guarantees that the maximum amount of money will be available to the borrower. However, the borrower will be required to pay a **commitment fee** on the unborrowed portion of the maximum amount.
        4.) A **compensating balance requirement** often accompanies short-term bank loans. This represents a percentage of the loan amount that must remain in the borrower's account, and increases the effective interest rate on the loan, because although the money has been borrowed, it is not available to be used.
        5.) **Clean up requirements** are imposed by banks to prevent companies from using a series of short-term loans to fund long-term projects. This requirement forces borrowers to pay off all unsecured short-term debt on a periodic basis and to remain out of debt for a certain amount of time, usually 30 - 45 days.

    c.) Another category of short-term funding is **commercial paper** and is only available to large, strong companies. The paper is a promise by the corporation to repay the money borrowed at a specified date and is backed only by the company's promise to repay.

    d.) The final category of short-term working capital financing is the use of **short-term assets to secure a loan**. Borrowing against accounts receivables and inventories is more common in some industries than in others and is very common in seasonal industries where there are substantial, temporary, working capital needs. The primary criterion used to determine the value of receivables is the creditworthiness of the customers that owe the money.

        1.) **Pledging receivables** involves using their cash value as security for the loan, and the borrower promises that the money collected will be used to repay the lender.

2.) **Factoring receivables** does not really involve borrowing, but instead involves selling the receivables, at a discount, to a financial organization. This financial organization, called a **factor**, becomes the owner of the debt and takes responsibility for its collection. Factors review the accounts and choose which receivables they wish to purchase.

3.) **Inventory financing** involves using inventory as security for short-term loans. Inventory financing is expensive and difficult to administer, because inventory does not automatically turn to cash as receivables do, but instead must be sold.

    a. A **blanket lien** gives the lender a lien against all inventories that are held by the borrower, but the borrower remains in complete control of the inventory.

    b. A **trust receipt or chattel mortgage agreement** identifies all inventory by serial number and prohibits the borrower from selling it without the lender's permission.

    c. A **warehousing agreement** places the financed inventory in a warehouse under the control of a third party who controls the borrower's access. A **secured warehouse agreement** places the inventory in a secured area within the borrower's own facility. A **public warehouse agreement** places the inventory in a warehouse that is physically removed from the borrower's facility.

These are secure arrangements for the lenders, but the administrative costs make this method of borrowing very expensive.

CASH MANAGEMENT

12. **Cash management** does not make a weak company strong, but can definitely improve financial results. Bad cash management can weaken even the strongest firm. A firm that does not have enough cash to pay its bills and meet its payroll will go out of business, no matter how optimistic the future looks. **Cash** is the money a firm has on hand in currency and in checking accounts. Firms may hold cash for three economic and one administrative reason.

    a.) One economic reason for cash is called the **transactions demand**. This is the cash needed for firms to pay bills for the goods and services they use.

    b.) The second economic reason for holding cash is the **precautionary demand**. This demand requires holding some cash for emergency situations that may require immediate expenditure of dollars.

    c.) The final economic reason for holding cash is called the **speculative demand**. This is the need that firms may have for cash in order to take advantage of unexpected opportunities.

    d.) The administrative reason for holding cash has to do with **compensating balances** associated with loan agreements with banks, discussed above.

13. Although firms need cash, cash that is deposited in commercial checking accounts does not earn interest. **Cash management** involves maintaining a balance between a firm's cash needs and the costs of maintaining cash to meet these needs. Precautionary and speculative needs for cash do not occur on a daily basis and can be satisfied by assets that are slightly less liquid than cash, known as **marketable securities**. Marketable securities are short-term obligations of very secure organizations that include treasury bills and commercial paper, and can be sold almost instantly; they are referred to as **near cash** or **cash equivalents**.

196   Chapter 15

14. Another aspect of cash management is the check clearing process. This cash management issue arises because of the time that elapses between when a check is written and when it is actually recorded as a reduction to the payer's checking account. Money tied up in this process is called **float**. During check clearing, the payee does not have use of the money even though the payer has written and mailed the check. Speeding up the collection of checks after they have been mailed will get funds into the payee's hands more quickly. Slowing down the collection of checks after they have been mailed will allow the payer to retain the use of the funds longer.

Several methods are used to accelerate the collection of cash after checks have been mailed.

- a.) **Lock box systems** help to accelerate the collection of cash after a check has been mailed by eliminating a check's stop at the payee's office and sending it immediately to the bank; this usually eliminates two to three days of the clearing process.
- b.) **Electronic wire transfers** are the fastest ways to move money from bank to bank, but are too expensive to use for transferring small amounts.
- c.) **Pre-authorized checks** can eliminate mail float and allow a vendor to deposit a preauthorized check in his account when the product is shipped to the customer.

15. In the management of cash outflows from the viewpoint of the payer, the two goals are to maintain control of disbursements and to slow down checks in the clearing process.

- a.) Decentralized organizations with physically scattered operating divisions have numerous cash disbursement facilities that all can have cash on hand, resulting in an undesirable total amount of available cash. **Zero balance accounts** are empty accounts that the divisions can write checks on, but the funds actually come from a master account at the concentration bank of the firm. This helps to control cash but maintains the benefits of decentralization.
- b.) **Remote disbursing** is a way to keep checks in the bank clearing process for a longer time. A check written on a bank in a remote city that is not the site of a federal reserve branch will take a day or two longer to leave that bank and return to it, thereby increasing float and keeping the money in the payee's account longer.

16. The acceleration of cash receipts can reduce the amount of funds that a firm has to have tied up in their cash accounts, meaning that less money must be borrowed, and less interest paid. These savings must be measured against the costs of the cost management system to be sure that all the efforts are worthwhile.

MANAGING ACCOUNTS RECEIVABLES

17. Managing accounts receivables has as its primary objective the reduction of the accounts receivable balance. Carrying fewer receivables will reduce the interest cost of supporting this asset and will also minimize bad debt losses. However, customers are usually happier when accounts receivable are allowed to increase, and this can lead to more sales and improved customer relations. Accounts receivable management has to strike a balance between these two opposing views. The following three issues have to be addressed in establishing policy for managing accounts receivable.

- a.) When a firm establishes its **credit policy**, it makes a decision as to which of its customers it will extend credit. This decision is usually made on the financial strength of the individual

customer. For a current customer, this decision can be made using payment history. For a new customer, a firm may need to get a credit history from an external service known as a **credit agency (or credit bureau)**.
  1.) A **tighter credit policy** means that there are higher requirements for credit customers and has the effect of reducing sales.
  2.) A **looser credit policy** means that more customers of lower credit quality will be extended credit, which may result in higher sales, but more bad debt losses. The best policy is one that maximizes profits.

b.) The **terms of sale** can also affect receivables. A typical term of sale might be **2/10, net 30**, which means that a customer will receive a 2% discount if the invoice is paid within ten days. Otherwise, the net amount of the bill is due in 30 days. The prompt payment discount (2/10) is an effective but expensive way to reduce receivables. Shortening or lengthening the net period tends to affect the maximum length of time a paying customer will take to pay. However, most companies must use at least the net period that is common to the industry and therefore have little control over this aspect.

c.) The implementation of the **collections policy** of the firm is a major function of its credit department and involves how quickly and aggressively a firm follows up on customers who are overdue in paying their bills. Being too aggressive can permanently damage customer relations, so a close working relationship between the collections department and the sales department can help to minimize problems with customers who have a legitimate reason for not paying.

INVENTORY MANAGEMENT

18. **Inventory** is product held for sale to customers. It is almost always an expensive and critical item for retail and manufacturing businesses, but plays a minor role for service businesses. It is easier, but much more costly, for firms to operate with higher rather than lower levels of inventory.

    a.) Carrying more inventory reduces stock-outs and backorders, both of which are expensive, and makes operations run more smoothly, makes customers happy, and tends to increase sales.
    b.) The negative effects of higher inventory levels are higher interest costs, higher storage and security costs, additional insurance costs, and higher tax amounts levied by many state and local governments on inventory levels.
    c.) Another cost of carrying higher levels of inventory is the potential loss in value of the inventory caused by shrinkage, spoilage, breakage, and obsolescence. These costs and losses are called the **carrying costs of inventory**.
    d.) Other costs associated with inventory are called **ordering costs** and include the expenses of placing orders, receiving shipments, and processing materials into inventory.

19. **Inventory management** refers to the overall management of a firm's inventory and the way it manages the benefits and controls the costs of carrying inventory. The **economic order quantity (EOQ)** minimizes the total cost of inventory by calculating the optimum order size that will minimize total costs, which are the sum of carrying costs plus ordering costs.

$$EOQ = \left[\frac{2FD}{C}\right]^{1/2}$$

In the above equation:

F = the cost of placing an order
D = the annual demand for the product, and
C = the carrying cost per unit of product.

Another factor involved in inventory management is how much **safety stock** to hold. Safety stock is additional inventory that is held in case normal working stock runs out. It increases the overall cost of carrying inventory, but it also improves service levels. Two other concepts that are associated with inventory management are lead times and reorder points. **Lead time** is the period of time that elapses between the placing of an order for inventory and the actual receipt of that order. A **reorder point** is the inventory level at which an order for additional inventory is placed. Understanding how to set safety stock levels, reorder points and lead times are all parts of effective inventory management.

The amount of time and effort devoted to inventory management has to do with how critical inventory is to the business and how much of an investment the firm has in inventory. The **ABC system** assigns different priorities to different items of inventory and spends more time and effort on items that are critical (the A items) than on items that can be easily attained or have ready substitutes. The **just-in-time (JIT)** inventory system almost eliminates factory inventory by carefully estimating demand and trusting suppliers to make regular deliveries consistently. JIT is most practical for large firms that have a great deal of control over their suppliers.

TESTING YOUR UNDERSTANDING

TRUE-FALSE QUESTIONS

____1. A firm's cash conversion cycle is shorter than its operating cycle.

____2. Seasonal businesses experience constant working capital needs throughout the year.

____3. Accruals represent the primary component of spontaneous financing.

____4. Banks are more likely to make working capital loans to small businesses than to make general, unsecured loans to small businesses.

____5. Bank loans represent the primary source of short-term financing for most companies.

____6. Investing in marketable securities will usually satisfy a firm's precautionary and speculative demands for holding cash.

____7. Pledging receivables and factoring receivables both involve a firm selling its accounts receivables.

____8. A line of credit is a binding agreement where the bank guarantees that a specific amount of money will be available to a business.

____9. Because companies typically have some level of working capital that is permanent, working capital requires some permanent investment of funds.

____10. A firm's need for cash varies inversely with its sales level.

____11. A tighter credit policy tends to reduce sales.

____12. JIT works best when the manufacturer is large and has power over its suppliers.

____13. A firm cannot do business without working capital.

____14. It is easier and cheaper to run a business with less working capital

____15. If a firm has a large receivables balance, it should expect big interest charges to finance this balance and relatively large bad debt losses.

____16. Overfinancing a project is acceptable if the overfunding is modest.

____17. The primary reason why most firms seek short-term loans is for working capital.

____18. Accruals are short-term, high interest loans from whomever provides the service.

____19. Trade credit is secured and backed by elaborate contractual support.

____20. Customers who excessively abuse trade credit may find they can no longer obtain it.

____21. Both lines of credit and revolving credit agreements are generally secured by specific assets.

____22. A compensating balance compensates the bank for its services.

____23. The biggest drawback for the issuers of commercial paper is the lack of flexibility for repayment terms.

____24. Inventory financing is popular, cheap, and easy to administer.

____25. Specialized inventories and perishables have high collateral value.

MULTIPLE CHOICE QUESTIONS

1. Banks may make a working capital loan to small businesses but not a general loan because:
    a. the working capital loan is short term.
    b. the working capital loan is self-liquidating.
    c. the working capital loan can be secured by inventory or receivables.
    d. all of the above.

200   Chapter 15

2. Using short-term funds to support all temporary, and a large part of permanent, working capital needs:
   a. is an example of the maturity matching concept.
   b. represents an aggressive working capital policy.
   c. represents a conservative working capital policy.
   d. none of the above.

3. Commercial paper:
   a. tends to be purchased by insurance companies, banks, money market mutual funds, and pension funds.
   b. is a debt security of the issuing company.
   c. is unsecured.
   d. all of the above.

4. Large inventories:
   a. minimize production delays.
   b. cost more to finance.
   c. require more storage space.
   d. all of the above.

5. When a firm pledges its receivables:
   a. customers are always notified that their receivables have been sold.
   b. customers now pay their bills to the new lender.
   c. customers are usually not aware that their account has been pledged.
   d. both a and b.

6. Holding cash to use for emergencies is an example of:
   a. the transaction demand.
   b. the precautionary demand.
   c. a compensating balance requirement.
   d. the speculative demand.

7. A borrower using inventory financing would probably prefer:
   a. a blanket lien.
   b. a warehousing agreement.
   c. a trust receipt agreement.
   d. any of the above; it would make no difference to the borrower.

8. A revolving credit agreement:
   a. is a non-binding line of credit.
   b. usually specifies a fixed interest rate.
   c. is a binding line of credit that requires the borrower to pay a commitment fee.
   d. is always secured by the assets of the firm.

9. A large accounts receivables balance:
   a. tends to increase sales but means more bad debt and interest charges.
   b. tends to decrease sales but means less bad debt and interest charges.
   c. means tighter credit policies and more unhappy customers.
   d. both b and c.

10. When the vendor's terms of sale are 3/12, net 60:
    a. the net amount is due within 60 days.
    b. a 12% discount is given if payment occurs within 3 days.
    c. a 3% discount may be taken if payment is made within 12 days.
    d. both a and c.

11. All companies are both payers and payees, so:
    a. they want to speed up their collection of cash.
    b. they want to slow down their disbursement of cash.
    c. both a and b.
    d. none of the above.

12. The EOQ model:
    a. is concerned only with the ordering costs of inventory.
    b. minimizes total inventory costs.
    c. is concerned only with the carrying costs of inventory.
    d. is useless for many firms because it cannot be modified to include safety stock.

13. Options for financing working capital include:
    a. long-term sources.
    b. short-term sources.
    c. both a and b.
    d. neither a nor b.

14. When a firm arranges a line of credit with a bank:
    a. it pays interest only on the amounts actually borrowed.
    b. the agreement is binding.
    c. it pays interest on the entire line of credit, even if no money is borrowed.
    d. the minimum amount that must be borrowed is always specified.

15. Compensating balances:
    a. decrease the effective interest rate on a loan.
    b. increase the effective interest rate on a loan.
    c. have no impact on the effective interest rate.
    d. increases the amount of money the borrower can use.

16. A firm receives the same interest rate from two financial institutions, but Institution A requires a compensating balance and Institution B requires an average balance. Which of the following statements is true?
    a. The entire loan from Institution B can be used but not all the time.
    b. A certain percentage of the loan from Bank A is unavailable for use.
    c. Bank B's requirement will not present as much of a problem as Bank A's.
    d. all of the above.

17. For the appropriate fee, a factor will:
    a. finance a firm's inventory.
    b. provide a blanket lien against inventory.
    c. collect cash from customers.
    d. all of the above.

202   Chapter 15

18.   Good cash management:
      a. can make a weak business strong.
      b. can make a strong business weak.
      c. has no impact on the business.
      d. can improve financial results.

19.   Remote disbursing:
      a. keeps checks in the clearing system longer.
      b. speeds checks through the clearing system.
      c. decreases transit float.
      d. benefits the payee.

20.   Spontaneous financing:
      a. is the most stable way to fund working capital
      b. uses accruals and accounts payable to fund working capital
      c. can be used for long term as well as short-term financing
      d. all of the above

FILL-IN THE BLANK QUESTIONS

1.   Matching the _____ of financing to the duration of an asset or project is known as the maturity matching concept.

2.   Requiring that borrowers periodically pay off all unsecured short-term debt and remain out of debt for a specified number of days is known as a _____ requirement.

3.   _____ receivables involves using their cash value as collateral for a loan.

4.   Using long-term funding predominantly to support all working capital needs except for temporary peaks is considered to be a _____ working capital policy.

5.   Gross working capital minus spontaneous financing equals _____.

6.   A _____ gives the lender a lien against all inventories held by the borrower.

7.   _____ a receivable means selling it at a discount to a financing organization.

8.   _____ is unsecured debt issued by a limited number of the nation's largest and strongest companies.

9.   Paying a vendor late is known as _____ payables.

10.   _____ includes cash, accounts receivables, and inventory.

The Management of Working Capital   203

11. A firm's _____ policy is the most important decision variable influencing the level of receivables.

12. Labor that has been received but not yet paid for is reflected in an _____.

13. A large receivables balance tends to make customers happy and to _____ sales.

14. _____ is the elapsed time from the disbursement of cash for raw materials to the receipt of cash for the sale of a product.

15. When using a revolving credit agreement, the borrower pays a _____ on the unborrowed balance.

16. A _____ warehouse provides maximum security for the lender.

17. ZBA stands for _____.

PROBLEMS

1. What is the borrowing rate for a firm that is offered terms of sale of 3/12, net 60 that does not take advantage of the discount?

2. Miller Corporation has an $18 million revolving credit agreement with its bank at prime plus 3%, based on a calendar year. It borrowed $3 million on June 1, when it accessed the agreement for the first time. Prime is 8.75% and the bank's commitment fee is 1/4% annually. What bank charges will Miller incur for the month of June?

3. A business borrows $250,000 subject to a 10% compensating balance. The interest rate is 14%. How much money can the business draw out and use? What is the effective interest rate?

4. Docking Yogurt, Inc. has average receivables of $80,000, which turns over once every 60 days. It pledges 80% of its receivables to a bank that advances 80% of the total pledged at 4% over prime and also charges a 2% administrative fee on total receivables pledged. If prime is 10.5%, what total interest rate is Docking paying for its receivables financing?

5. Chalgren, Inc. operates primarily in the Southeast but has a number of customers in Phoenix who remit about 8,000 checks a year with an average amount of $2,400. It currently takes the Phoenix checks an average of seven days after mailing to clear into Chalgren's account. A Phoenix bank has offered Chalgren a lock box system for $2,400 a year plus $.22 per check. This will reduce the clearing time for the checks to four days. Is the bank's proposal a good deal for Chalgren if it borrows at 11%? How much will the lock box system save?

6. What would a three-month, $500,000 commercial paper note paying an annual rate of 8%, sell for?

Chapter 15

7. Below are the account balances for Robbins Sports:

Accounts Payable	179,000
Accounts Receivable	644,000
Accruals	235,000
Cash	315,000
Inventory	837,000

Calculate Robbins' net working capital. What percentage of Robbins' gross working capital is financed spontaneously?

8. Hilton Industries is reviewing its credit policy. Their bad debt expense is currently 2.7% of revenues. They believe that a tighter credit policy would reduce that number to 1.2% of revenues. However marketing has indicated that this would probably cause a loss in total revenues of about 5.0%, and Hilton averages about 12% operating income for every dollar of sales, before bad debt expense. Assume that Hilton's revenues are currently $10 million annually. Should the tighter credit policy be implemented?

9. Graebner Corp. orders 500,000 microchips per year at an average cost of $130. The carrying cost of each chip is $25, and each order costs $150. Compute Graebner's EOQ.

10. Use the information from the previous problem. Calculate separately the (1) ordering costs and (2) carrying costs if Graebner uses the EOQ model. Do your answers support your understanding of the EOQ model?

ANSWERS TO QUESTIONS

TRUE-FALSE

1. t
2. f
3. f
4. t
5. t
6. t
7. f
8. f
9. t
10. f
11. t
12. t
13. t
14. f
15. t
16. t
17. t
18. f
19. f
20. t
21. f
22. t
23. t
24. f
25. f

MULTIPLE CHOICE

1. d
2. b
3. d
4. d
5. c
6. b
7. a
8. c
9. a
10. d
11. c
12. b
13. c
14. a
15. b
16. d
17. c
18. d
19. a
20. b

FILL IN THE BLANKS

1. maturity date
2. clean up
3. Pledging
4. conservative
5. net working capital
6. blanket lien
7. Factoring
8. Commercial paper
9. stretching
10. Gross working capital/Current assets
11. credit
12. accrual
13. increase
14. Cash conversion cycle
15. commitment fee
16. public
17. zero balance accounts

ANSWERS TO PROBLEMS

1. $\dfrac{365}{48} \times .03 = 22.81\%$

2. $(8.75\% + 3\%) / 12 = .97917\%$

    $.25\% / 12 = .0208\%$

    $\$3,000,000 \times .97917\% = \$29,375$

    $\$15,000,000 \times .0208\% = \$3,120$

    $\$29,375 + \$3,120 = \$32,495$

3. $\$250,000 \times .10 = \$25,000$

    $\$250,000 - \$25,000 = \$225,000$ available

    $\$250,000 \times .14 = \$35,000$ interest

    $\dfrac{\$35,000}{\$225,000} = 15.56\%$ effective interest rate

4. $\$80,000 \times .8 = \$64,000 \times .8 = \$51,200$ average loan outstanding

    $360 / 60 = 6$ times a year

    $\$64,000 \times 6 = \$384,000$ in new receivables pledged each year

    $\$384,000 \times .02 = \$7,680$ administrative fee

    $\dfrac{\$7680}{\$51,200} = 15\%$ administrative fee

    $15\% + (10.5\% + 4\%) = 29.5\%$ total financing cost

5. $8,000$ checks $\times \$2,400 = \$19,200,000$ total billing

    $\dfrac{7}{365} \times \$19,200,000 = \$368,219$ current float

    $\dfrac{4}{365} \times \$19,200,000 = \$210,411$ projected float

    $\$368,219 - \$210,411 = \$157,808$ reduction in float with the lock box

    $\$157,808 \times .11 = \$17,359$ interest savings

2,400 + .22(8000) = $4,160 cost of operating the lock box

$17,359 – $4,160 = $13,199 total savings

6. 500,000 / 1.02 = $490,196

7. Net Working Capital = 315,000 + 644,000 + 837,000 – 179,000 – 235,000 = $1,382,000

% Spontaneously Funded = (179,000 + 235,000)/(315,000 + 644,000 + 837,000)
= .2305 or 23.05%

8. Current operating income after bad debt expense:

$10,000,000 x (.12 - .027) = $930,000

Operating income after bad debt expense if the tighter credit policy is implemented:

$10,000,000 x .95 x (.12 - .012) = $1,026,000

Based on this information, the tighter credit policy should be implemented.

9. EOQ = $[2FD/C]^{1/2}$ = $[2 \times 150 \times 500,000/25]^{1/2}$ = 2449.49 or 2,450

10. Number of orders = 500,000/2450 = about 204 orders

Ordering Costs = 204 x $150 = $30,600

Average inventory = 2,450/2 = 1,225

Carrying Costs = 1,225 x $25 = $30,625

EOQ theory says that costs will be minimized when carrying costs = ordering costs. Considering that fact that we rounded the number of orders, the two costs are essentially equal which means that the EOQ is correct.

CHAPTER SIXTEEN

FINANCIAL PLANNING

LEARNING OBJECTIVES

After studying this chapter you should understand the following terms and concepts:

1. the nature and purpose of business planning and the role that financial planning plays as part of business planning;
2. the parts of a business plan, its purpose, and the types of information it provides;
3. the four variations of the basic business plan;
4. how financial projections are estimated and the problems that arise in forecasting debt and interest expense;
5. the percentage of sales method to forecast financial statements for an existing business;
6. estimating external funding requirements and the sustainable growth rate for a business;
7. incorporating detailed assumptions into the forecasting process;
8. direct and indirect planning assumptions;
9. management issues in financial planning;
10. risks in financial planning, and the scenario analysis.

CHAPTER SUMMARY

This chapter begins by addressing the importance of business planning in general, and financial planning in particular. Before financial planning can be discussed, it is essential to understand the broader topic of business plans, so that the relationship between the two can be understood. The components of a business plan are introduced and their purposes discussed. The four kinds of business plans are examined, and then the discussion of the financial plan itself begins. The planning assumptions associated with financial forecasts are illustrated, including the development of a problem using the percentage of sales method. A comprehensive example of a financial plan for an existing business is presented in detail. The development of a cash budget is also shown through a detailed example. In addition, the potential problems that can be introduced into the planning process as a result of both aggressive optimism and underforecasting are discussed.

CHAPTER REVIEW

BUSINESS PLANNING

1. Planning involves anticipating and preparing for the future. The higher a manager's position in the firm, the more time he or she should spend in planning. A **business plan** is a combination of words and numbers that describe what the business will become in the future. Because the plan deals with the future, the numbers are **projections** or **estimates** of what is expected to occur if the assumptions in the plan prove to be accurate. Financial statements based on assumptions are called **pro forma** financial statements.

   The business plan includes information about a firm's products, markets, employees, capital, sales, revenue, profitability, etc. It also includes information about the firm's mission and strategy. Small firms prepare the business plan for the benefit of their own management and also outside investors. Large firms usually share selected portions of their business plans with security analysts who, in turn, share that information with their clients (who are current or potential investors). The section of the business plan that deals with financial projections is the firm's **financial plan**.

2. Business planning presents several benefits to a firm's management. The first is that it helps bring managers together into a cohesive team working toward common goals. The second benefit is that it gives managers a detailed recipe for helping the organization achieve those goals, and provides standards against which to measure results. The financial plan provides firms with projected financial statements as well as estimates of when and how much financing will be needed by the firm if its goals are to be achieved. For firms that are decentralized, the divisional business plans allow divisions to communicate with corporate managers. For business plans to be credible and not just to reflect the dreams of overly optimistic mangers, they must include supporting details to illustrate that this plan is based on reasonable assumptions.

3. There are four types of business planning that produce four variations of planning documents.

   a.) The first type of planning is called **strategic planning**, which has a long planning horizon and is a broad, conceptual picture of the business and where it will be in five years. It is expressed more in words than in numbers and conveys ideas and concepts.
   b.) The second type of planning is called **operation planning** and involves translating the ideas and concepts of the strategic plan into a shorter term, more detailed projection with a focus of approximately one year. It includes details about how much product the company will sell, to whom, for what price, and where the inputs and equipment will come from.
   c.) **Budgets** are the third type of planning and are short term updates of operating plans that include supporting detail about how much money, material, and labor will be used, and which departments and/or individuals are responsible for specific results. Budgets include lots of numbers and very few words.
   d.) The fourth type of planning is **forecasting**. Forecasts are quick estimates of short-term financial results. They usually involve estimating cash flow or profits over a one to three month planning horizon.

   Most large companies practice all four kinds of planning, while small companies often use only the business plan that includes all the other types of plans.

MAKING FINANCIAL PROJECTIONS

4. The **financial plan** is the part of a business plan that includes a set of pro forma financial statements. Projecting financial statements involves translating activities into dollars, starting with a sales forecast. After revenues are estimated, all of the additional requirements for the planning period have to be estimated, including expenses, capital investments and sources of external funding. Both new and existing businesses prepare financial plans, but it is much easier for an existing business to prepare one because they have historical information to use as a starting point.

    Planning assumptions for an existing business are primarily changes to what has happened previously, such as changes in levels of sales growth, product price changes, labor cost improvements, etc. The financial planning process begins by using the results from the previous period (e.g. last year) to forecast the results for the next period. The income statement and balance sheet must be forecasted, and from these the statement of cash flows is developed. The projected income statement will be developed based on any planning assumptions that affect revenue or expenses. Work on the income statement forecast is stopped just before the interest expense section, which is when the balance sheet projections begin. All assets and liabilities are then forecasted, except for long-term debt and equity. Estimating interest expense and the capital components of the balance sheet requires an iterative process to makes sure that interest expense is reflective of the average debt for the planning period.

5. The **percentage of sales method** is a simple approach to use in forecasting financial statements for an existing business. This method assumes that all income statement and balance sheet items will change by the same percentage as sales. This is rarely the case, but it does provide a simple method for making rough approximations for the planning period. Modifying the method to recognize that expenses, assets and liabilities may grow at different rates for different reasons can produce more accurate results.

    One of the major purposes for financial projections is to forecast a firm's needs for external financing. An increase in the requirement for debt means that the firm needs more cash and will have to borrow more. A decrease in the requirement for debt means that excess cash is available to pay down the existing debt levels.

    If the percentage of sales method is used (assuming that all income statement and balance sheet items grow at the same rate as revenues), then the following formula, called the **external funding requirement (EFR),** can be used to calculate the need for additional external funding.

    EFR = (GROWTH RATE × THIS YEAR'S ASSSETS) – (GROWTH RATE × THIS YEAR'S CURRENT LIABILITIES) – CURRENT EARNINGS RETAINED

    Or

    EFR = g(assets $_{this\ year}$) – g(current liabilities $_{this\ year}$) – [(1 – d) ROS][(1 + g) sales $_{this\ year}$)

    where **g** is the growth rate and **d** is the dividend payout ratio.
    Both the unmodified percentage of sales method and the EFR are of limited practical use because they imply that everything varies directly with sales, which is not usually the case.

212   Chapter 16

6. A firm's **sustainable growth rate** is the rate at which a firm can grow if none of its financial ratios change and if it does not raise any new equity by selling stock. The sustainable growth rate is:

SUSTAINABLE GROWTH RATE = (1 – DIVIDEND PAYOUT RATIO) ROE

Or

$$g_s = (1 - d) \times \frac{EAT}{sales} \times \frac{sales}{assets} \times \frac{assets}{equity}$$

This last formula uses the DuPont model to break ROE into its component parts. This is a largely theoretical concept that gives an indication of the factors that determine a firm's inherent growth capability. The firm's ability to grow depends upon its ability to earn profits on sales, its ability to use assets to generate sales, its use of leverage (the equity multiplier), and the percent of earnings it retains. These ideas can then be analyzed to compare a firm's growth to other firms in its industry. A firm can then look at why its growth rate is different from the norm and can take corrective action, if necessary.

7. The modified and unmodified percentage of sales methods are useful for quick estimates, but are not generally used for formal plans because they include too many unreasonable assumptions. More typically, each component of a financial plan is estimated individually, and these separate pieces of information are incorporated into the formal financial projections.

A financial planning assumption can be made directly about the financial item to which it is related, or it can be made indirectly through a derivative of the item, usually a ratio. Direct assumptions can be made about items such as capital expenditures, while indirect assumptions can be made about items such as receivables using the average collection period ratio.

8. A business plan for an existing business can be developed using the results from the current year and then incorporating any and all changes into the projections. Relevant changes to be included would be items such as any projected sales increases due to new products or new marketing campaigns, any cost reduction efforts, any new collection efforts or initiatives, and any new production efficiencies. The impact of such changes would be considered when the pro forma balance sheet and income statement are developed.

9. The financial plan is completed by constructing a projected statement of cash flows, which comes entirely from the forecasted balance sheet and income statement. The statement of cash flows provides beginning and ending cash balances for the planning period, but firms usually need more detail regarding the timing of cash flows during the period. As a result, most businesses will prepare a **cash budget**, which will estimate the timing of cash receipts and disbursements during the planning period. This is typically done on a monthly basis so that forecasts for short term financing can be made with more accuracy.

MANAGEMENT ISSUES IN FINANCIAL PLANNING

10. Financial plans may create a number of managerial problems. The plan is often used to help manage the company and to motivate employees to achieve the established targets. When the plan approved by top management is seen as a **stretch goal** that is beyond the ability of the firm

to deliver, and when bonuses and evaluation of managers are dependent upon its achievement, management may quickly give up on the goal because they consider it almost impossible.

The opposite of a stretch goal occurs when lower level managers, knowing they will be evaluated on how well they achieve the goals, set up goals that are easy to meet and require little effort but do not maximize the capabilities of the company. This is called **underforecasting**. If the plan is not a very good scenario of what is likely to happen and is used for specific requirements such as short- or long-term cash needs, real problems can occur. Only when the planners have used realistic assumptions to develop the plan will it be safe to use the plan for these other purposes. This is an important function of financial planners: to strike a balance between unrealistic stretch goals and underforecasting.

The commitment of resources and the decisions made that are based on the plan require that it be an accurate projection of what is likely to happen. The plan should encourage goals that require effort, but not so much effort that the goals are unattainable.

11. Some companies use **scenario analysis** to produce a number of different plans based on variations of the assumptions that underlie the plan. These scenarios give planners a feel for what will happen if some or all of their assumptions are not realized.

12. Almost all financial planning is done with computers. Computers make repetitive calculations easy and help in the creation of plans, but they are not used to make decisions about the assumptions that are used in plan development. Computers make the job faster and allow changes to be more easily incorporated, but they do not improve the quality of the plan.

TESTING YOUR UNDERSTANDING

TRUE-FALSE QUESTIONS

____1. Computers have replaced the need for planners' judgments in the planning process.

____2. Projecting financial statements begins with a sales forecast.

____3. The two primary audiences for a firm's business plan are the firm's own management and outside investors.

____4. The cash flow statement is developed from forecasted balance sheet and income statements without additional projections.

____5. The higher a person's position in the managerial hierarchy, the less time he or she should devote to planning.

____6. Bottom-up plans tend to understate achievable performance.

____7. Financial plans are entirely accurate and 100% believable.

____8. By law, companies are required to engage in all four kinds of planning and to submit the resulting documents to all managers.

____9. A direct forecast of debt and interest expense is impossible.

____10. Comparing actual operating performance to the business plan should reveal problem areas that need to be investigated.

____11. A business plan normally consists of a combination of text, graphs and numbers.

____12. A business plan could be viewed as a set of goals for the organization and its departments.

____13. Planning for many large firms is an almost continuous process.

____14. Large firms tend to combine variations of all four types of planning into one plan.

____15. Strategic plans are expressed with precise and detailed figures.

____16. Financial projections are of primary importance in the strategic plan and central to its presentation.

____17. Forecasting for an established business is easier than forecasting for an entirely new business.

____18. If top management is using a stretch goal internally, the CFO should take a modified plan to the bank to arrange next year's borrowing.

MULTIPLE CHOICE QUESTIONS

1. When developing bottom-up plans, lower level management tends to:
    a. put in stretch goals.
    b. use aggressive optimism.
    c. under-forecast if their evaluation depends upon meeting the plan.
    d. all of the above.

2. If the debt balance increases on a firm's projected balance sheet:
    a. the firm will have to arrange for additional borrowing or sell more shares of stock.
    b. the firm will have excess funds to pay debt down.
    c. the firm will have lower interest expenses if interest rates remain the same.
    d. none of the above.

3. The cash flow statement:
    a. requires extensive new projections.
    b. comes entirely from information on the balance sheet.
    c. comes entirely from information on the income statement.
    d. comes from information on both the balance sheet and income statement.

4. When top management puts unrealistic stretch goals in its plan:
   a. it tends to encourage all managers to put forth 100% effort to reach these goals.
   b. it tends to discourage managers from trying because the goals are considered to be unreachable.
   c. it tends to result in very accurate estimates of borrowing requirements.
   d. none of the above.

5. Which of the following statements is most likely to be inaccurate?
   a. If sales increase by 15%, COGS should also increase by 15%.
   b. If sales increase by 15%, current assets should also increase by 15%.
   c. If sales increase by 15%, fixed assets should also increase by 15%.
   d. If sales increase by 15%, current liabilities should also increase by 15%.

6. A firm's business plan can:
   a. communicate to outside investors what the firm is going to be.
   b. predict when additional outside financing will be needed.
   c. assist divisions in communicating with corporate headquarters.
   d. all of the above.

7. The four kinds of planning are:
   a. strategic, long term, overall, and short term.
   b. strategic, operational, budgeting, and forecasting.
   c. hourly, daily, monthly, and yearly.
   d. first line, supervisory, middle management, and executive.

8. The strategic plan typically covers five years and is revised:
   a. annually.
   b. monthly.
   c. every five years.
   d. never.

9. The EFR:
   a. says that growing firms need no new funds to purchase assets but should make better use of existing funds.
   b. is equal to the growth in assets minus the growth in current liabilities and current earnings retained.
   c. says that growing firms must have enough money to purchase new assets to support growth.
   d. both b and c.

10. The ideal financial planning process:
    a. consists of stretch goals and aggressive optimism.
    b. is a combination of top down and bottom up elements.
    c. consists only of bottom up elements.
    d. none of the above.

11. The following components are typically part of a business plan:
    a. executive summary, market analysis, and contingencies.
    b. table of contents, mission and strategy statement, and operations of the firm.
    c. management, staffing, and financial projections.
    d. all of the above.

12. Operational planning involves:
    a. a five year horizon.
    b. detailed projections that usually encompass a one-year period.
    c. simple and approximate numbers.
    d. primarily concepts and text.

13. A firm's EFR is reduced by:
    a. spontaneous growth of current assets.
    b. spontaneous growth of current liabilities.
    c. current earnings retained.
    d. b and c only.

14. Computers:
    a. have resulted in faster and better planning.
    b. have resulted in faster but not necessarily better planning.
    c. have taken the assumptions out of planning.
    d. have replaced humans in the planning process.

15. Which of the following lists the various planning processes in order from most conceptual to most detailed?
    a. operating, strategic, budget, forecast
    b. strategic, operating, forecast, budget
    c. strategic, operating, budget, forecast
    d. operating, strategic, forecast, budget

16. The small business "business plan" would typically include which types of planning?
    a. strategic planning only
    b. strategic and operating planning only
    c. strategic, operating and budget planning only
    d. all planning types would be included in the business plan

17. Which of the following would be possible planning assumptions for a financial plan?
    a. a 7% increase in unit sales
    b. a 5% decrease in unit pricing
    c. a decrease in interest rates from 6.5% to 5.5%
    d. all of the above
    e. only a. and c. above

18. The percentage of sales method of preparing financial forecasts:
    a. is the primary tool used by most companies for making financial forecasts
    b. applies the growth in unit sales to all of the income statement and balance sheet items
    c. can be used to make a rough estimate of external funding requirements (EFR)
    d. both b and c.

19. The calculation for the sustainable growth rate:
    a. assumes that no equity is generated through the sale of new stock
    b. is independent of the dividend payout ratio
    c. assumes that no new debt will be issued
    d. all of the above are true

20. Based on history, a firm expects to collect 70% of its credit sales in the month of sale, 25% in the first month following sale, 3% in the second month following sale and 2% will be uncollectible. Which of the following correctly computes cash received from credit sales for March based on this information.
   a. 70% of March sales, 25% of April sales, 3% of May sales and 2% of June sales
   b. 70% of March sales, 25% of April sales and 3% of May sales
   c. 70% of January sales, 25% of February sales and 3% of March sales
   d. 70% of March sales, 25% of February sales and 3% of January sales

FILL-IN THE BLANK QUESTIONS

1. _____ planning involves broad conceptual thinking about the nature of a business.

2. A _____ is some physical or economic condition that is expected to exist during the planning period.

3. A document that is a picture or model of what a business unit is expected to become in the future is called a _____.

4. The rate at which a firm can grow if none of its financial ratios change and no new shares of stock are sold is called the _____ _____.

5. In _____ analysis, a number of different plans are produced with assumptions varying singularly or in combination.

6. Financial statements based on hypothetical circumstances are called _____.

7. The _____ method forecasts financial statements for an existing business by estimating sales and then assuming that all balance sheet and income statement items grow at the same rate.

8. _____ planning specifies how much the company will sell, to whom, and at what prices.

9. When top executives force a plan on the rest of the organization, it is called _____ planning.

10. Forecasting related ratios instead of a particular item is known as a(n) _____ planning assumption.

11. Financial planning is part of a broader activity known as _____ planning.

12. A _____ horizon is the most common period for strategic planning.

13. If a person questions why a firm exists and what it does, he or she is engaged in _____ planning.

218   Chapter 16

14. _____ are short term updates of annual plans that typically cover three-month periods.

15. _____ sets up a goal that is easy to meet but doesn't necessarily use the full capacity of the firm's resources.

PROBLEMS

1. This year Bauman's Sausages sold one million sausages per month to wholesalers for $2.50 each. The firm had year end receivables equal to 1 1/2 months of sales. Next year Bauman's will increase its price by 10% and expects to sell 5% fewer sausages. Collections efforts will be relaxed, and year-end receivables are expected to increase to 2 months of sales. What are this year's revenue and year-end receivables? Forecast next year's revenue and year-end receivables.

2. What will a company's EFR be if sales are expected to grow by 20%, and sales this year are $30,000, assets are $14,000, current liabilities are $420, and its dividend payout ratio is 30% with EAT of $6,000? Assume that Net Fixed Assets and EAT will grow at the same 20% rate as sales.

3. What is a firm's sustainable growth rate if it retains 40% of earnings, has a ROS of 9%, sales of $5 million, total assets of $4 million, and equity of $2 million?

4. Forecast the following firm's Net Fixed Assets account for the next year:
   Ending Balance Sheet
   Fixed Assets
      (Gross) $9,000,000
      Accumulated
       Depreciation   6,000,000
           Net $3,000,000

   New assets totaling $2 million will be acquired next year with an average life of 4 years. Assume 9 months of depreciation. Next year's depreciation on existing assets is $625,000 with no assets being disposed of.

5. What will a firm's ACP be with receivables of $2 million on revenue of $14 million? In order to help increase sales by 10% this firm will increase its ACP to 60 days. What Balance Sheet figure for receivables should be included to reflect the additional assets?

6. This year, Monroe, Inc. had $600 in sales, a 25% gross margin percentage, $60 in other expenses, $10 in interest expense and a 40% tax rate. If sales are forecast to increase by 10% next year with no other changes, calculate Monroe's estimated EAT for next year.

7. Use the information from the previous problem. Monroe had inventory turns of 6.0 (based on cost of goods sold) this year, and they expect to improve that to 8.0 next year. Calculate Monroe's average inventory level for next year.

8. Brookfield Industries has made the following projections for next year:
   Return on sales   8.5%
   Total asset turnover   1.3
   Equity multiplier   1.7
   Sustainable growth rate 8.265%

   What is Brookfield's dividend payout ratio assumption?

9. Lambert, Inc. has historically collected 50% of credit sales in the month of sale, 30% in the first month after sale, and 18% in the second month after sale. If Lambert projects credit sales of $100,000 in January, $110,000 in February and $135,000 in March, calculate Lambert's cash receipts from credit sales in March.

10. If the sales figures from the previous problem are total (both cash and credit sales), and Lambert typically has 30% cash sales, calculate cash receipts from all sales for March.

ANSWERS TO QUESTIONS

TRUE-FALSE

1. f
2. t
3. t
4. t
5. f
6. t
7. f
8. f
9. t
10. t
11. t
12. t
13. t
14. f
15. f
16. f
17. t
18. t

FILL IN THE BLANKS

1. Strategic
2. planning assumption
3. business plan
4. sustainable growth rate
5. scenario
6. pro forma
7. percentage of Sales
8. Operational
9. top down
10. indirect/derivative
11. business
12. five-year
13. strategic
14. Budgets
15. Underforecasting

MULTIPLE CHOICE

1. c
2. a
3. d
4. b
5. c
6. d
7. b
8. a
9. d
10. b
11. d
12. b
13. d
14. b
15. c
16. c
17. d
18. c
19. a
20. d

ANSWERS TO PROBLEMS

1. $1{,}000{,}000 \times \$2.50 \times 12 = \$30{,}000{,}000$ this year's revenue

    $1{,}000{,}000 \times \$2.50 \times 1.5 = \$3{,}750{,}000$ this year's AR

    $1{,}000{,}000 \times \$2.75 \times .95 \times 12 = \$31{,}350{,}000$ next year's revenue

    $950{,}000 \times \$2.75 \times 2 = \$5{,}225{,}000$ next year's AR

2. EFR $= g(\text{Assets}_{\text{this yr.}}) - g(\text{Liabilities}_{\text{this yr.}}) - [(1-d)\text{ROS}][(1+g)\text{Sales}_{\text{this yr.}}]$

    $= 0.20(\$14{,}000) - 0.20(\$420) - (1-0.30)\left(\dfrac{\$6{,}000}{\$30{,}000}\right)(1.2)(\$30{,}000)$

    $= \$2{,}800 - \$84 - 0.7(0.2)(1.2)\$30{,}000$
    $= \$2{,}800 - \$84 - \$5{,}040$
    $= -\$2{,}324$

    The firm will generate cash, rather than need it from external sources.

3. $g_s = (1-d) \times \dfrac{\text{EAT}}{\text{SALES}} \times \dfrac{\text{SALES}}{\text{ASSETS}} \times \dfrac{\text{ASSETS}}{\text{EQUITY}}$

    $= (1-0.6) \times 0.09 \times \dfrac{\$5M}{\$4M} \times \dfrac{\$4M}{\$2M}$

    $= 0.4\,(0.09)(1.25)(2)$
    $= 0.09 = 9\%$

4.
    ```
    $ 9,000,000           $2,000,000 × 3 = 375,000
    + 2,000,000                    4    4   625,000
    $11,000,000 Ending Gross Assets      1,000,000
    ```

	Actual Beginning	Planned Additions	Planned Ending
Gross	$ 9,000,000	$ 2,000,000	$11,000,000
Acc Dep.	(6,000,000)	(1,000,000)	(7,000,000)
Net	$ 3,000,000	$ 1,000,000	$ 4,000,000

5. $\text{ACP} = \dfrac{2}{14} \times 365 = 52.14$ days

    $\text{ACP} = \dfrac{?}{15.4} \times 365 = 60$ days

    A/R = $2,531,507

6.

	This Year	Nest Year
Revenues	$600	$660
Cost of Goods Sold	450	495
Gross Margin	150	165
Other Expenses	60	60
EBIT	90	105
Interest	10	10
EBT	80	95
Tax	32	38
EAT	48	57

7. This year's inventory   450/6.0 = 75

   Next year's inventory   495/8.0 = 61.875

8. 8.265 = (1-d) x 8.5 x 1.3 x 1.7
   8.265 = (1-d) x 18.785
   .44 = (1-d)
   d = .56, so the dividend payout ratio is 56%

9. $135,000 x .5 + $110,000 x .3 + $100,000 x .18 = $113,500

10. Credit sales have to be recalculated at 70% of the previous levels and then added to 30% of March's sales to compute the total cash receipts.

    $135,000 x .7 x .5 + $110,000 x .7 x .3 + $100,000 x .7 x .18 + $135,000 x .3 = $119,950

CHAPTER SEVENTEEN
CORPORATE RESTRUCTURING

LEARNING OBJECTIVES

After studying this chapter you should understand the following terms and concepts:

1. basic definitions, terminology, and procedures for corporate restructuring;
2. friendly and unfriendly mergers;
3. economic classification of business combinations;
4. antitrust laws and mergers;
5. the reasons behind mergers and their history in the U.S.;
6. merger analysis and the price premium;
7. paying for the merger with junk bonds;
8. the capital structure argument to justify high premiums;
9. defensive tactics against mergers;
10. leveraged buyouts (LBOs) and proxy fights;
11. the definition of a divestiture, the reasons behind it, and the methods of divesting;
12. bankruptcy and the reorganization or liquidation of failed businesses.

CHAPTER SUMMARY

This chapter begins with a discussion of the importance of mergers in modern business and a definition of the terms and procedures associated with the process. The difference between friendly and unfriendly mergers is explained, as are the various economic classifications of business combinations. United States antitrust laws and their impact on business mergers are discussed, along with the underlying reasons behind mergers. The four periods of merger activity in the U.S. are examined, followed by an analysis of the price an acquiring business should be willing to pay for a merger target. The effects of paying too much for a target and the use of junk bonds to fund the acquisition are presented. The defensive tactics that can be utilized to prevent a merger are defined. Lastly, the chapter looks at LBOs, proxy fights, divestitures, and the reorganization of businesses after bankruptcy.

CHAPTER REVIEW

MERGERS AND ACQUISITIONS

1. **Corporate restructuring** is a general term that refers to changes in capital structure, company ownership, merging or divesting organizations, modifying asset structures, and changes in methods of doing business.

2. **Mergers, acquisitions, and consolidations** all mean the combination of two or more business units under a single controlling ownership. A **merger** is a combination of two or more businesses in which only one business legally continues to exist, and the combined firm continues under the original name of the surviving organization. A merger is also called an **acquisition,** and the acquired business is called the **target**. A **consolidation** occurs when all of the combining legal entities dissolve, and a new entity with a new name is formed.

3. All mergers and acquisitions represent a change in ownership, and no one can force the shareholders of a corporation as a group into a merger or an acquisition. They must be willing to give up their shares for the price offered in the deal.

    a.) A **friendly merger** occurs when the management and board of directors of the target company agree that the combination would be a good idea and cooperate with the takeover. Negotiations between the two groups result in a price to be paid for the target's stock, and the proposal is then submitted to the target's stockholders for approval. If the stockholders approve the merger, the deal is then accomplished.
    b.) An **unfriendly merger** occurs when the target firm's management and board of directors are opposed to the merger and will not take it to the shareholders for approval. The acquiring firm then makes a **tender offer** directly to the target's stockholders, a special proposal to pay stockholders a fixed price for shares. The price that is offered for the stock is binding on the acquiring firm only if they are able to purchase enough shares to consummate the takeover. If stockholders offer enough shares for sale, the acquiring firm purchases them and takes over. A target firm's management may resist a merger because they do not feel that stockholders are being offered enough for their shares, or because they fear the loss of their own jobs after the merger.

4. Business combinations are classified according to the relationship between the businesses of the merging firms.
    a.) A **vertical merger** occurs when a firm acquires one of its suppliers or customers, in the same sense that this new firm is now **vertically integrated**.
    b.) A **horizontal merger** occurs when the merging firms are in the same kind of business, which has the effect of reducing competition in the industry.
    c.) A **conglomerate merger** occurs when the lines of business of the merging firms are unrelated.

5. **Antitrust laws** in the United States are designed to maintain a fair and competitive economy and to prevent certain activities that can reduce such competition. When mergers reduce competition in an industry, they come under the review of antitrust laws that can be used to limit companies' freedom to merge. Most antitrust laws were enacted between 1890 and 1940.

6. There are several primary reasons that mergers occur:
   a.) The most persuasive reason for firms to merge is that the combined firms will perform better than the sum of the performance of the individual companies. This is called **synergy**.
   b.) Another reason for mergers is for firms to achieve rapid growth, which is most easily accomplished by acquiring a rival firm in the same business.
   c.) A third reason for mergers is to reduce risk by acquiring firms that are in different industries.

   Horizontal mergers can lead to economies of scale that allow lower costs, while vertical mergers can lock in a firm's sources of supplies or can create captive markets for products. Sometimes mergers can allow firms to save on taxes by offsetting the losses of one firm against the gains of another. However, the IRS will disallow this tax savings if it is the primary reason for the merger.

7. There have been four merger waves of activity in this country over the past 100 years.

   a.) The **first wave** occurred during the early 1900's and transformed our country from a nation of small companies to a nation of industrial giants, which in many cases were almost monopolies.
   b.) The **second wave** started near the close of World War I and ended with the stock market crash of 1929. Mergers during this period tended to be horizontal and resulted in industries that were dominated by a few powerful firms.
   c.) The **third wave** occurred in the late 1960's and was the era of the conglomerate merger where firms acquired other firms in totally diverse industries.
   d.) The **fourth wave** of merger activity started during the 1980's and continues today. These mergers tend to involve firms that are leaders in their industries, with more hostile takeovers occurring, leading to more defensive tactics to prevent such takeovers.

   The creation of large and powerful organizations may lead to an increased ability to take advantage of worldwide opportunities, but may also change the openly competitive nature of our economy.

8. A **merger analysis** attempts to determine what an acquisition is worth to an acquiring firm. It utilizes a capital budgeting exercise that projects cash flows the target is expected to generate, and analyzes the inflows to determine if the acquisition has a positive NPV. Accurately estimating these cash flows can be difficult, because the acquiring company does not usually have access to detailed financial information about the target. Even when the merger is friendly, the target company may provide overly optimistic financial information to the acquiring firm. Another part of the analysis is determining how far into the future to consider cash flows. A conservative approach will only look a few years into the future, while an aggressive approach may consider cash flows into perpetuity, using techniques such as the Gordon Model.

9. The price offered to the target company's stockholders must always be higher than the stock's market price. Otherwise, the stockholders of the target company won't be interested in selling. The difference between the market price of the target's stock and the amount offered is called the **premium**. The price chosen should be just high enough to attract the majority of shares needed for the merger, but no higher because a higher price reflects a waste of the acquiring company's funds. When an investor buys the stock of a firm that is acquired shortly afterward, he or she is assured of a quick profit because of the premium. As soon as a firm becomes

publicly acknowledged as an acquisition target, its stock price tends to increase rapidly and is said to be **in play**. It is illegal **insider trading** for persons associated in any way with the merger to make a short-term profit from the price increases associated with the merger.

10. Stockholders of an acquired firm can receive a combination of any of three valuable items in return for their shares: cash, stock in the acquiring firm, or debt of the acquiring firm. When acquisitions are well structured, all of these assets are valuable. However, in acquisitions where a large proportion of the capital needed to complete the acquisition is raised through the issuance of bonds, significant additional risk is introduced to the transaction. Bonds issued in these circumstances are often called **junk bonds**—low quality bonds that pay very high yields because the firms that issue them are so risky. The use of junk bonds was popular during the fourth wave of mergers, but they fell into disfavor in the late 1980's because of the economic downturn. Risky firms fail only slightly more often than stable firms in good economic times, but they fail much more often in bad economic times.

11. **Defensive tactics** are ways that managers can prevent their companies from being acquired.

   a.) Once a takeover is underway, management can try to convince stockholders that the acquiring firm's price is too low.
   b.) Management can also approach the Justice Department and claim that the merger is anti-competitive.
   c.) Issuing additional debt and repurchasing shares can drive up the stock's price, making the acquirer's price less attractive, and making the firm less desirable because of the additional debt.
   d.) If the acquiring firm is unattractive, the target firm's management can seek a **white knight**, an alternative firm that is seen as more desirable.
   e.) A final tactic that is sometimes used is **greenmail:** buying the stock of a powerful group of stockholders that is threatening to takeover the company at a premium price.

   Defensive tactics that can be used to prevent being acquired *without* the cooperation of management include
   a.) Using a **staggered election** of boards of directors to prevent an acquirer from being able to immediately take over the firm by replacing the entire board at the same time.
   b.) Requiring a large majority (up to 80%, called a **supermajority**) of stockholders to approve any merger can make it very difficult for the firm to be taken over.
   c.) **Poison pills** are legal devices in the corporation's bylaws that make it very expensive for outsiders to take control without the help of management. These include **golden parachutes,** which are contracts that guarantee top management exorbitant severance packages if they are fired after a merger. Other examples of a poison pill are requirements that principal amounts of debt become due immediately upon a takeover, and a **share rights plan** that gives current stockholders rights that enable them to buy shares in the merged company at a reduced price.

OTHER KINDS OF TAKEOVERS – LBOs AND PROXY FIGHTS

12. Another kind of takeover is known as an **LBO - leveraged buyout**. This is a transaction where a publicly traded company's stock is bought out by a group of investors who then take the firm private and usually become its top managers. The group finances the buyout primarily with borrowed funds that are secured by the firm's assets. LBOs are risky because of the high amount

of debt that the firm assumes. In order to reduce the risk, the debt load is reduced as quickly as possible after the deal is completed, often by selling assets of the corporation.

13. A **proxy** is a legal document that gives one person the right to act for another on a certain issue. Stockholders often give their proxies to management to enable them to vote for management's recommended board members in board of directors elections. A **proxy fight** occurs when more than one group tries to obtain shareholders' proxies for the election of differing groups of directors.

DIVESTITURES

14. A **divestiture** occurs when a business gets rid of one or more of its business operations. There are various reasons for divestitures, including a firm's need for cash, a change in a firm's strategic thinking that no longer includes a certain business, or the poor performance of a business division or operation.

    a.) The first way to divest a business unit is to **sell it** to another company in a friendly acquisition or to sell it to an investor group as an LBO.
    b.) The second way to divest a business unit is to **spin it off** as a separate corporation. The shareholders of the original corporation are given new shares in the new firm, and they are then free to keep them or to trade them.
    c.) The last way to divest a business unit is to simply close it down and sell off its assets. This is known as **liquidation** and is usually a last resort for business operations that have been very unsuccessful.

15. Over 50,000 businesses fail each year.
    a.) A business fails **economically** if it does not provide an adequate return to its stockholders.
    b.) A business fails **commercially** when it cannot pay its debts and is said to be **insolvent**. A firm is **technically insolvent** when it cannot meet its short-term obligations and is said to be **legally insolvent** when its liabilities exceed its assets.

16. In most cases it is better for creditors if the firm remains in business and slowly pays off its debts, rather than have the firm shut down and sell off its assets to pay off only part of its debts. **Bankruptcy** is a legal proceeding designed to protect all creditors and to determine if the firm should continue to operate or to shut down. If an insolvent company appears to be worth more as a going concern, it goes through a court-supervised **reorganization** and a **restructuring** of its debt with a plan that will pay off the creditors as soon as possible.

    If the court decides the company is worth more closed down than as a going concern, it orders a **liquidation**, with a sale of its assets and the proceeds distributed to pay creditors. A firm is insolvent until an action is filed in court, at which time it becomes **bankrupt**. A **bankruptcy petition** can be initiated by the insolvent firm or by its creditors.
    a.) When the firm files the petition, the **bankruptcy is voluntary**.
    b.) When creditors file the petition, the **bankruptcy is involuntary**. As few as three unsecured creditors owed as little as $5,000 in total can force an involuntary bankruptcy.

    A **reorganization** is a business plan that allows the firm to continue to operate and to pay off its debts. All reorganization plans must be **fair and feasible** and must be approved by the bankruptcy court and the firm's creditors and stockholders. Firms become insolvent because they cannot pay their debts, so any reorganization plan must involve a **restructuring of debt**. An **extension** is when creditors give the firm a longer time to repay its debts. A **composition** is when creditors agree to settle for less than the full amount they are owed.

When a liquidation is ordered, the distribution of funds follows an order of priority established by the bankruptcy code. Because the funds available from a liquidation typically represent a small fraction of the creditors' claims, thus priority of repayment is critical. **Secured creditors** are paid from the proceeds of the sale of the related assets. After all secured creditors are paid, the claims of unsecured creditors are paid out of the remaining pool of funds, with common stockholders being the last claimants. There is often nothing left for these stockholders.

TESTING YOUR UNDERSTANDING

TRUE-FALSE QUESTIONS

____1. The first wave of merger activity in this country resulted in a greater number of small businesses.

____2. Liquidation is usually a last resort for an unsuccessful business.

____3. A composition is when creditors give a firm a longer time to repay its debts.

____4. Bankruptcy is a legal action that follows insolvency.

____5. When the creditors of a firm file a bankruptcy petition, the bankruptcy is said to be involuntary.

____6. The stock of a firm that is an acquisition target tends to rapidly increase after the intended acquisition is announced.

____7. All mergers must be approved by at least a simple majority of a corporation's stockholders, although the required percent for approval varies.

____8. Bankruptcy is a legal proceeding designed to protect the employees of the company.

____9. Corporate restructuring refers only to changes in an organization's capital structure.

____10. Insolvency always leads to liquidation.

____11. The size of combining companies determines the nature of the combination.

____12. A two-thirds approval from stockholders is required for all mergers.

____13. An unfriendly merger is created by hostility between the stockholders of the two companies.

____14. The managers of a corporation are supposed to make decisions for the sole benefit of the stockholders.

____15. Conglomerate mergers tend to be the most anticompetitive.

____16. Synergies sound like a good reason for mergers, but have been difficult in practice to find and implement.

____17. Internal growth is usually more rapid than external growth.

____18. The IRS will not allow a tax offset from a merger if that was the primary purpose for the merger.

____19. A holding company controls a subsidiary by controlling all of its stock.

____20. The long-term political and economic implications of mega-mergers are unclear.

____21. An LBO results in a publicly held corporation becoming a privately held corporation.

MULTIPLE CHOICE QUESTIONS

1. Spin-offs, LBOs, and shutting down a business are examples of:
    a. mergers.
    b. acquisitions.
    c. divestitures.
    d. all of the above.

2. If Dairy Queen, Inc. acquires the dairy that provides its ice cream, this would constitute a:
    a. horizontal merger.
    b. vertical merger.
    c. conglomerate merger.
    d. none of the above.

3. Risky firms tend to fail slightly:
    a. more often in bad economic times than less risky firms.
    b. more often in good economic times than less risky firms.
    c. less often in good economic times than less risky firms.
    d. less often in bad economic times than less risky firms.

4. When a liquidation is ordered, the order of the distribution of funds:
    a. requires that secured creditors be paid first out of the proceeds of the sale of the related assets.
    b. requires that common stockholders be paid at least 50% of their original investment.
    c. requires that all creditors receive the same percentage of their investment.
    d. requires that common stockholders be paid before preferred stockholders.

5. A firm that cannot pay its short-term obligations:
    a. is a commercial failure.
    b. is technically insolvent.
    c. is legally insolvent.
    d. a and b only.

6. Reasons for mergers include all of the following except:
   a. synergy.
   b. rapid growth.
   c. economies of scale.
   d. the creation of more top management positions.

7. Capital restructuring includes:
   a. only changes in capital structure.
   b. changes in capital structure, company ownership, and changes in methods of doing business.
   c. modifying asset structures, mergers, and divestitures.
   d. both b and c.

8. In most cases, creditors:
   a. prefer liquidation to bankruptcy.
   b. prefer that the firm continue to operate as a going concern and slowly pay off its debts as opposed to liquidation.
   c. have no preference between liquidation and the firm continuing to operate.
   d. none of the above.

9. When a takeover is underway, defensive tactics can include:
   a. attempts to convince the stockholders that the price being offered is too low.
   b. issuing additional debt and repurchasing shares of stock.
   c. seeking a white knight.
   d. all of the above.

10. The reasons for divestiture include:
    a. a firm's need for cash.
    b. the poor performance of a business unit.
    c. a change in a firm's strategic thinking.
    d. all of the above.

11. The term that means "the combination of two or more business units under a single controlling ownership" is:
    a. merger.
    b. acquisition.
    c. consolidation.
    d. all of the above.

12. A merger can be blocked by:
    a. the Justice Department
    b. a firm's customers.
    c. a firm's suppliers.
    d. all of the above.

13. Which of the following is typically not a reason for the management of a target company to try to block a takeover?
    a. the premium offered is too small
    b. the existence of golden parachutes
    c. the concern for loss of jobs after the takeover
    d. none of the above

14. When Keller Foods purchased Keystone Carpets, it was considered a:
    a. horizontal merger
    b. vertical merger
    c. conglomerate merger
    d. none of the above

15. Antitrust laws:
    a. were primarily enacted early in the 20th century
    b. are designed to maintain a competitive economy
    c. are employed when an industry is becoming too concentrated
    d. all of the above

16. Diversification to reduce risk is:
    a. equally valuable to a company's management and its stockholders
    b. is more valuable to a company's management than to its stockholders
    c. is more valuable to a company's stockholders than to its management
    d. is not valuable to either a company's management or its stockholders

17. Hostile takeovers became an accepted business technique:
    a. before Wave 1 of merger activity
    b. between Wave 1 and Wave 2 of merger activity
    c. between Wave 2 and Wave 3 of merger activity
    d. between Wave 3 and Wave 4 of merger activity

18. The appropriate discount rate to be used when calculating the NPV of a target company is:
    a. the WACC of the target company
    b. the cost of equity of the target company
    c. the WACC of the acquiring company
    d. the cost of equity of the acquiring company

19. If the constant growth model is used to calculate the value of a target company, the:
    a. terminal value becomes a significant cash flow in the analysis
    b. terminal value is an insignificant part of the cash flow analysis
    c. cash flows more than five years into the future will not be considered
    d. none of the above

20. Which of the following defensive tactics would not be used in anticipation of a takeover?
    a. poison pills
    b. approval by a supermajority
    c. issue debt and repurchase shares
    d. staggered election of directors

FILL IN THE BLANKS

1. A _____ merger occurs when the businesses of the merging firms have nothing to do with each other.

2. A _____ merger is when a firm acquires one of its customers or suppliers.

3. _____ bonds are low quality bonds that pay very high yields because the issuing firm is so risky.

4. A _____ is getting rid of a particular business operation.

5. A _____ is a combination of two or more firms where only one legally continues to exist under the original name of the surviving organization.

6. _____ are legal devices in the corporation's bylaws which make it expensive for outsiders to take control of the firm without management's help.

7. A _____ is when all the combining legal entities dissolve and a new entity with a new name is formed.

8. A _____ is a legal document that gives one person the right to act for another on a certain issue.

9. The difference between a stock's market price and the price offered by the acquiring firm is called the _____.

10. _____ are actions taken by the management of companies to prevent the firm from being acquired.

11. In an unfriendly merger, the acquiring firm makes a _____ to the target's stockholders for their stock.

12. _____ laws were enacted to prohibit certain activities that reduce the competitive character of the U.S. economy.

13. A _____ industry has fewer firms that are more powerful.

14. _____ in a corporate merger means that the whole is greater than the sum of its parts.

15. A corporation that owns other corporations called subsidiaries is known as a _____ company.

16. A _____ is a financier who maker his or her living by mounting hostile takeovers.

PROBLEMS

1. Calculate the EAT of the following two companies, first operating independently, then merged. Both companies have a tax rate of 35%.

	A	B	Merged
EBT	$4,000,000	($1,500,000)	

2. What is the capital structure of a firm before and after an LBO if the firm had $225M in equity and $10M in debt with the stock selling at book value? The management team purchased the stock at book value, contributed $10M of its own money, and borrowed the remainder.

3. Firm A, whose stock is selling for $20 a share, agrees to acquire Firm B for $30 a share. What possible combinations might be offered for 100 shares of Firm B's stock, using cash and/or shares of Firm A's stock.

4. TNT, Inc. is considering making a tender offer for Blasting Caps Corp. (BCC), one of their primary suppliers. The equity section of BCC's balance sheet totals $4.95 million, and BCC stock is currently selling 20% above book value. TNT is planning to offer a 15% premium in an effort to make the offer attractive to current BCC stockholders. If BCC currently has 200,000 shares outstanding, calculate the per share price of the tender offer.

5. PFM Corp. is considering making a tender offer for WRL Corp's stock. PFM wants the investment to breakeven (NPV =0) within five years. They have estimated WRL's cash flows for the next five years as follows: $3.4 million, $3.7 million, $4.0 million, $4.0 million, $4.2 million. PFM has determined that the appropriate discount rate is 9.0%. If WRL has 400,000 shares outstanding, what is the maximum PFM should be willing to offer per share for WRL stock?

6. Use the information from the previous problem. PFM has decided that they would be willing to consider cash flows beyond five years but want to include a conservative estimate into perpetuity. They have decided to assume that WRL will generate $3.0 million in cash every year beginning in Year 6. What would PFM's maximum offer be based on these additional cash flows?

7. Use the information from the previous two problems. PFM has now decided that the conservative $3.0 million estimate is OK for Year 6, but that they expect cash flows to grow by at least 5% each year beyond Year 6. What would PFM's maximum offer be based on these revised cash flows?

ANSWERS TO QUESTIONS

TRUE-FALSE

1. f
2. t
3. f
4. t
5. t
6. t
7. t
8. f
9. f
10. f
11. f
12. f
13. f
14. t
15. f
16. t
17. f
18. t
19. f
20. t
21. t

FILL IN THE BLANKS

1. conglomerate
2. vertical
3. Junk
4. divestiture
5. merger
6. Poison pills
7. consolidation
8. proxy
9. premium
10. Defensive tactics
11. tender offer
12. Antitrust
13. concentrated
14. Synergy
15. holding/parent
16. corporate raider

MULTIPLE CHOICE

1. c
2. b
3. b
4. a
5. d
6. d
7. d
8. b
9. d
10. d
11. d
12. a
13. b
14. c
15. d
16. b
17. d
18. b
19. a
20. c

ANSWERS TO PROBLEMS

1.
	A	B	Merged
EBT	$4,000,000	($1,500,000)	$2,500,000
TAXES	1,400,000	0	875,000
EAT	$2,600,000	($1,500,000)	$1,625,000

2.
	BEFORE LBO	AFTER LBO
DEBT	$10M	$225M
EQUITY	$225M	$ 10M
CAPITAL	$235M	$235M

3.
CASH	FIRM A STOCK
$3,000	0
0	150 SHARES
$1,000	100 SHARES
$2,000	50 SHARES

   Other combinations are possible.

4. Book value per share: $4.95 million/200,000 shares = $24.75

    Market value: $24.75 x 1.2 = $29.70

    Tender offer: $29.70 x 1.15 = $34.16

5. C01 = $3.4 million
    C02 = $3.7 million
    C03 = $4.0 million
    C04 = $4.0 million
    C05 = $4.2 million
    I = 9.0%
    PV = $14,885,629 / 400,000 shares = $37.21 per share

6. The present value of a perpetuity beginning five years in the future would be:
    $3.0 million/.09 = $33,333,333 discounted five years @ 9% = $21,664,380
    $21,664,380/400,000 shares = $54.16 + $37.21 = $91.37

7. The present value of an infinite stream of cash flows growing at a constant rate would be:
    ($3.0 million) x (1.05)/(.09 - .05) = $78,750,000 discounted @ 9.0% = $51,182,097
    $51,182,097/400,000 shares = $127.96 + $37.21 = $165.17

    Problems 6 and 7 highlight the importance of the terminal value in making the correct valuation when a merger is being considered.

18

CHAPTER EIGHTEEN

INTERNATIONAL FINANCE

LEARNING OBJECTIVES

After studying this chapter you should understand the following concepts:

1. how international business has changed and grown in the last 40 years;
2. currency exchange rates, why exchange rates change, and why these changes introduce exchange rate risk to businesses;
3. the international monetary system;
4. international capital markets, the unique role of the dollar in these markets, and the Eurodollar and international bond market;
5. transaction and translation risks.

CHAPTER SUMMARY

The chapter introduction stresses the magnitude of the changes in international business over the past forty years and the way the changes have occurred. The purchase of currency in the foreign exchange market is explained, and the effect of exchange rates on the domestic price of imported goods is illustrated. The impact of moving exchange rates and how that impacts exchange rate risk is discussed, as is the terminology associated with such exchange rate movements. Factors that affect changes in the demand for products of other countries are examined within the context of how these changes influence movements in the exchange rate. The importance of keeping the exchange rate in balance is presented as the reason why governments intervene in the foreign exchange market. The chapter then looks at international markets and explains the functioning of these markets and how political risks affect international investments. Lastly, transaction and translation risks are defined and examined.

CHAPTER REVIEW

CURRENCY EXCHANGE

1. During the past forty years, the importance of international business has been growing. The U.S. does more business with other countries than ever before as evidenced by the increase of imports and exports as a percentage of Gross Domestic Product (GDP). A shift has occurred in the nature of international business as well. It now includes (1) **significant direct investment in facilities and equipment in other countries** by U.S. businesses, and (2) **portfolio investments in foreign stocks and bonds** by individual investors.

2. Companies operate and expect to be paid in the currency of the country in which they are located. If a business wants to buy from a firm in another country, it must first acquire some of that country's currency. This purchase takes place in the **foreign exchange market**, a network of brokers and banks based in financial centers around the world.
   - a.) The **direct quote** shows the number of U.S. dollars required to buy one unit of a foreign currency (e.g. $1.42/British Pound).
   - b.) **Indirect quotes** represent how many units of a foreign currency it takes to purchase one U.S. dollar (e.g. .70 British Pounds/U.S. Dollar).

3. The exchange rate is part of the cost of a product to a firm that imports foreign goods. If the exchange rate changes so that a dollar will purchase **less** foreign currency, then the price of the product will increase in terms of dollars. If the exchange rate becomes more favorable so that a dollar will purchase **more** foreign currency, the price of the imported product will decrease. As the price increases, demand for the product tends to decrease and as the price decreases, demand for the product tends to increase.

4. **Cross rates** allow exchange rates for two currencies to be developed without using dollars. Using the direct quotes for two currencies quoted in table 18.1, or from an exchange rate table on the Internet, the formula is:

$$\frac{\text{DIRECT QUOTE FOR CURRENCY A}}{\text{DIRECT QUOTE FOR CURRENCY B}} = \text{CURRENCY B PER CURRENCY A}$$

5. The movement in exchange rates causes **exchange rate risk**, the chance that a firm can make or lose money on an international transaction due to exchange rates, typically if the movement takes place between the time a business contract is entered into and when it is settled in the foreign currency. Transactions subject to exchange rate risk and the companies involved in such transactions are said to have **exchange rate exposure**. **Spot rates** are good for immediate transactions, and **forward rates** are quotes on the delivery of the currency in an indicated number of days in the future.

When a currency becomes more valuable in terms of dollars, it is said to be **stronger, or rising against the dollar**. Likewise, when a currency becomes less valuable in terms of dollars, it is said to be **weaker, or falling against the dollar**. When a firm knows that it will need foreign currency in the future, it can **hedge** against exchange rate risk by locking in the exchange rate for future delivery at the appropriate forward rate. By using hedging, companies can eliminate exchange rate risk.

6. Movement in exchange rates comes from shifts in the supply and demand curves for foreign currencies. Following is a list of actions and preferences that can affect the supply of and demand for a specific currency:

   a.) **Preferences in consumption:** anything that makes products from one country more or less desirable to another country's population.
   b.) **Government policy** can affect supply and demand by encouraging or discouraging importing and foreign investment.
   c.) Prosperous and growing economies demand more products and have more investment opportunities than do stagnant or depressed economies. Therefore, **the state of a country's economy** can affect the demand for a specific currency
   d.) When a significant number of people engage in **speculation** (investing in foreign currencies) caused by exchange rate changes, this too can affect the demand for a specific currency.
   e.) Lastly, **direct government intervention**—when governments buy or sell their own currencies to keep exchange rates within a certain range—will affect the supply of that currency.

7. When any currency strengthens relative to the currencies of other countries, there are advantages and disadvantages. **Imported goods become cheaper, consumers are happy, but demand for domestically-produced products declines. Exports from that country become more expensive, so fewer are sold.** If a currency weakens, **imported products become more expensive, but exports will increase because their prices decline**.

8. It is not good for the economy if exchange rates move too far in either direction. Governments sometimes intervene to prevent this from happening by buying and selling their own currencies in the foreign exchange market. Even though some intervention by governments occurs, free market forces essentially determine exchange rates. This is known as a **floating exchange rate** system.

9. In order for a country's currency to be **convertible**, the country must allow it to be traded on the foreign exchange markets and to accept the resulting value. When a country's currency is not convertible—which is the case for Russia and China—it is a serious barrier to doing business internationally.

10. The net money flow between two countries from trade is known as the **balance of trade**. A **trade deficit** exists when a country imports more from another country than it exports to that country. A **trade surplus** exists when a country exports more to another country than it imports from that country.

INTERNATIONAL CAPITAL MARKETS

11. The dollar functions as international currency, because most international business people are willing to take dollars in trade. A **Eurodollar** is an American dollar deposited in a bank outside of the U.S. They are loaned to international companies and to foreign governments that need American currency. Bonds that are sold outside the home country of the borrower are called **international bonds**. A **foreign bond** is issued by a foreign borrower but denominated in the currency of the country in which it is sold. A bond denominated in a currency other than that of the country in which it is sold is called a **Eurobond.** In most countries, Eurobonds require a

much lower disclosure level than that required for domestic or foreign bonds, which lowers the cost of issuing them. They are issued as **bearer bonds**—bonds that protect the identity of their owners—and the government does not withhold income tax on the interest payments, which could help investors avoid paying their own countries' income taxes.

POLITICAL RISK

12. **Political risk** is the probability that the value of a firm's investment in another country will be reduced by actions taken by that country's government. The worst-case scenario involves **expropriation**, when a government seizes property owned by foreign investors. Other actions which are not as extreme, but which still negatively impact investors include: limiting the amount of profit that can be taken out of the country; raising taxes; requiring that key inputs be purchased only from local suppliers; requiring partial ownership by citizens of the host country; and limiting the prices that can by charged for the products sold within that country. Political risk is almost nonexistent in highly industrialized nations that are friendly with the U.S., but it can be significant in newly developing nations with unstable governments.

TRANSACTION AND TRANSLATION RISK

13. Exchange rate risk is also known as **transaction risk**. Exchange rates also generate the potential gain or loss that arises from translating the financial statements of a foreign subsidiary from the local currency into dollars for consolidation with the parent company's financial statements. This is known as **translation risk**.

If the foreign currency weakens against the dollar, the value of the foreign investment can decrease, which will result in a translation loss. If the foreign currency strengthens against the dollar, the value of the investment can increase, which will result in a translation gain. These are "paper" gains or losses that will mean nothing unless the company sells the investment and attempts to repatriate the proceeds back to the U.S. These types of gains and losses are not included in consolidated income statements, but are shown cumulatively in an account that adds to or offsets stockholders' equity.

TESTING YOUR UNDERSTANDING

TRUE-FALSE QUESTIONS

____1. The worst-case scenario involving political risk is expropriation.

____2. When the British pound becomes less expensive in terms of U.S. dollars, British products get more expensive in the U.S.

____3. Since 1960, U.S. imports have decreased but exports have increased.

____4. When a government imposes additional quotas, tariffs, and duties on imports, this will raise the price of imports and lower demand.

____5. When a currency becomes or is expected to become more valuable in terms of dollars, it is said to be rising against the dollar.

_____6. Japan encourages imports and discourages exports.

_____7. Countries with very high inflation rates tend to make poor investment targets.

_____8. Investors today make portfolio investments in the stocks of foreign companies all the time.

_____9. Governments may intervene in foreign exchange rates to keep those rates within reasonable ranges.

_____10. The foreign exchange market is located exclusively in the capital city of a nation.

_____11. The currency of all nations is convertible.

_____12. Exchange rate risk comes from moving exchange rates.

_____13. Nonconvertible currencies do not have foreign exchange rates.

_____14. When the host country raises taxes on a foreign venture in its country, it is increasing that business's political risk.

_____15. Translation gains are abstractions unless the gain is repatriated to the U.S.

_____16. Forward rates and spot rates are always identical.

_____17. A strengthening dollar produces only positive results.

_____18. Countries with inconvertible currencies face serious difficulties in doing business internationally.

_____19. Expropriation is very common.

MULTIPLE CHOICE QUESTIONS

1. Exchange rate movement can be due to:
   a. government policy.
   b. economic conditions.
   c. preferences in consumption.
   d. all of the above.

2. The U.S. dollar:
   a. is the world's leading currency.
   b. functions as international money.
   c. enjoys the confidence that people have in its continuing value.
   d. all of the above.

3. Between 1950 and the early 1970's:
   a. a floating exchange rate was in effect.
   b. exchange rates were determined by free market forces.
   c. a fixed exchange rate system was in place.
   d. none of the above.

4. Governments intervene in foreign exchange markets by:
   a. selling their currency if it is getting too weak.
   b. buying their currency if it is getting too weak.
   c. refusing to intervene because that is not their job.
   d. none of the above.

5. Eurodollars:
   a. are used for payment for U.S. exports, portfolio investment in U.S. stocks and bonds, and as a medium of exchange between parties that do not want to deal in their own currency.
   b. may be deposited only in European banks.
   c. are usually small deposits of no more than $1,000.
   d. are deposited because international rates on dollars are lower than domestic rates.

6. Dominance in the international arena:
   a. is clearly in the hands of the U.S. as both an exporter and net investor.
   b. has shifted away from the U.S..
   c. has the sum of direct and portfolio investment in the U.S. by foreigners exceeding the amount the U.S. invests elsewhere.
   d. b and c only.

7. Which of the following countries' currencies are not convertible?
   a. Britain and France
   b. Mexico and Brazil
   c. Russia and China
   d. Japan and Korea

8. When a nation's currency strengthens relative to the U.S. dollar:
   a. U.S. exports become less expensive in that country.
   b. U.S. exports become more expensive in that country.
   c. that nation's exports become cheaper in the U.S..
   d. demand for U.S. exports decreases.

9. If the U.S. imports more than it exports from one country:
   a. it has a trade deficit with that country.
   b. it has a trade surplus with that country.
   c. it could strengthen the value of the U.S. dollar in relation to that country's currency.
   d. both b and c.

10. Economic conditions that influence the foreign exchange market include:
    a. low interest rates in a particular country discourage investment in that country.
    b. depressed economies attract fewer investors.
    c. slowly growing economies provide more investment opportunities.
    d. a and b only.

11. Eurobonds:
    a. are denominated in a currency other than that of the country in which they are sold.
    b. are most often denominated in U.S. dollars and sold in other countries.
    c. have lower flotation costs than foreign or domestic bonds.
    d. all of the above.

12. The foreign exchange market:
    a. is headquartered on Wall Street.
    b. is based in financial centers around the world.
    c. can be accessed only by U.S. banks.
    d. none of the above.

13. Changes is the U.S. involvement in international business in the last 40 years includes all of the following except:
    a. an increase in imports as a percent of GDP
    b. an increase in exports as a percent of GDP
    c. a decrease in investments in foreign stocks and bonds by individual investors
    d. an increase in direct investments in foreign countries by U.S. corporations

14. Rates that are quotes for the delivery of currency at some time in the future are called:
    a. spot rates
    b. forward rates
    c. exchange rates
    d. hedge rates

15. The following rate -- $1.45/British pound – could be:
    a. a direct rate
    b. an indirect rate
    c. a cross rate
    d. all of the above

16. If the U.S. dollar weakens against the Euro,:
    a. U.S. products will be less expensive in Europe
    b. European products will be less expensive in the U.S.
    c. investors will be able to purchase more Euros per U.S. dollar
    d. all of the above

17. One of the primary benefits of hedging is to:
    a. purchase foreign made products less expensively
    b. sell U.S. products at a higher price
    c. eliminate exchange rate risk
    d. take advantage of a currency that is weakening against the U.S. dollar

18. All of the following economic conditions influence foreign exchange markets except:
    a. more prosperous economies demand more imports than less prosperous ones
    b. rapidly growing economies have more investment opportunities than slower growing ones
    c. countries with high inflation rates make poor investment targets
    d. countries with low interest rates attract foreign investment

244   Chapter 18

19. Political risk in international finance includes all of the following except:
    a. expropriation
    b. raising taxes
    c. limiting the removal of profits
    d. requiring purchase from local suppliers
    e. all of the above a re part of political risk

20. Translation gains and losses
    a. are recorded on the consolidated income statement
    b. arise from translating financial statements of a foreign subsidiary
    c. don't significantly impact a business unless foreign assets are sold
    d. both b. and c. are true

FILL-IN THE BLANK QUESTIONS

1. The _____ quote shows how many units of a foreign currency are required to buy one U.S. dollar.

2. When the U.S. dollar is getting too _____, the U.S. treasury will buy dollars.

3. When a nation allows its currency to be traded on foreign exchange markets, its currency is said to be _____.

4. A _____ is an American dollar deposited in a bank outside the U.S.

5. Any bond sold outside its home country is called a(an) _____ bond.

6. The net flow between two countries from trade is known as the _____.

7. The _____ quote shows the number of U.S. dollars required to buy one unit of a foreign currency.

8. A _____ exchange rate system means that exchange rates are determined by free market forces.

9. _____ rates are good for immediate transactions in the foreign exchange market.

10. Companies that have divisions and branches in other countries are known as _____ corporations.

11. A bond that is issued by a foreign borrower but denominated in the currency of the country in which it is sold is called a(an) _____ bond.

12. Exchange rate risk is also known as _____ risk.

13. The _____ market is organized for the purpose of exchanging currencies.

14. Direct and indirect quotes are _____ of each other.

15. _____ means that a firm can make or lose money because of rate movements.

16. The process that eliminates foreign exchange risk is called _____.

PROBLEMS

USE EXCHANGE RATES IN TABLE 18-1 FOR PROBLEMS 1 - 3.

1. How many U.S. dollars are required to purchase the following?
   a. 26£ (pounds)
   b. 116 krone
   c. 9,000¥ (yen)

2. How many British pounds are required to purchase the following?
   a. $1,462
   b. $379
   c. $46,791

3. Calculate the cross rate between:
   a. yen and pounds
   b. krone and real
   c. Canadian dollars and pounds

4. Assume it is the mid-1980s when there were 250 ¥ (yen) to the dollar. A car cost 1.5 million ¥ to produce and was marked up 30% for sale in the U.S. Assume everything stays the same except the exchange rate is 100¥ to the dollar.
   a. What did the car sell for in dollars in the U.S. in the mid-80s?
   b. What will it sell for after the exchange rate change?

5. You have just signed a contract to purchase a machine from a British manufacturer for 400,000 £(pounds) three months from today. You have decided to hedge against exchange rate risk with a forward contract. Use the information from Table 18.1 to determine how much better/worse off you are with the forward contract if the direct rate in three months is:
   a. $1.67
   b. $1.62

6. Use the information from the previous problem. Suppose you decide to purchase the pounds today and forgo the use of a forward contract. How much better/worse off are you if the direct rate in three months is:
   a. $1.67
   b. $1.62

ANSWERS TO QUESTIONS

TRUE-FALSE

1. t
2. f
3. f
4. t
5. t
6. f
7. t
8. t
9. t
10. f
11. f
12. t
13. f
14. t
15. t
16. f
17. f
18. t
19. f

FILL IN THE BLANKS

1. indirect
2. weak
3. convertible
4. Eurodollar
5. international
6. balance of trade
7. direct
8. floating
9. Spot
10. multinational
11. foreign
12. transaction
13. foreign exchange
14. reciprocals
15. Exchange rate risk
16. hedging

MULTIPLE CHOICE

1. d
2. d
3. c
4. b
5. a
6. d
7. c
8. a
9. a
10. d
11. d
12. b
13. c
14. b
15. a
16. a
17. c
18. d
19. e
20. d

ANSWERS TO PROBLEMS

1.   a. $26 \times 1.6521 = \$42.95$

      b. $116 \times .1601 = \$18.57$

      c. $9,000 \times .008455 = \$76.10$

2.   a. $1462 \times .6053 = 884.9$ pounds

      b. $379 \times .6053 = 229.4$ pounds

      c. $46,791 \times .6053 = 28,322.6$ pounds

3.   a. $\dfrac{.008455}{1.6521} = .005118$

      b. $\dfrac{.1601}{.3402} = .4706$

      c. $\dfrac{.7299}{1.6521} = .4418$

4. $1,500,000 \times 1.3 / 250 = \$7,800$

      $1,500,000 \times 1.3 / 100 = \$19,500$

5.   a. If the exchange rate goes to $1.67, the cost without the forward contract would be $1.67 x 400,000 = $668,000. With the forward contract the cost is $1.6426 x 400,000 = $657,040. Therefore, you would save $668,000 - $657,040 = $10,960.

      b. If the exchange rate goes to $1.62, the cost without the forward contract would be $1.62 x 400,000 = $648,000. With the forward contract the cost is $1.6426 x 400,000 = $657,040. Therefore, you would lose $648,000 - $657,040 = ($9,040).

6.   a. If the exchange rate goes to $1.67, the cost would be $1.67 x 400,000 = $668,000. Your cost was $1.6521 x 400,000 = $660,840. Therefore, you would save $668,000 - $660,840 = $7,160.

      b. If the exchange rate goes to $1.62, the cost would be $1.62 x 400,000 = $648,000. Your cost was $1.6521 x 400,000 = $660,840. Therefore, you would lose $648,000 - $660,840 = ($12,840).